BEHIND

THE DESERT STORM

Published by Price World Publishing, LLC
1300 W. Belmont Ave, Suite 20G
Chicago, IL 60657
Book cover design by Raja Sekar R
Book layout Ramesh Kumar P.
Printing by Sheridan Books
First Edition, August 2011
ISBN: 978-1-932549-67-6
Library of Congress Control Number: 2010932718
Printed in the United States of America
10 9 8 7 6 5 4 3 2 1

BEHIND

THE DESERT STORM

A *Secret Archive* STOLEN FROM THE KREMLIN THAT SHEDS NEW

LIGHT ON THE ARAB REVOLUTIONS IN THE MIDDLE EAST

by
Pavel Stroilov

CONTENTS

Introduction

This book, I am proud to say, proceeds from a grand theft aggravated by high treason.

To be more precise, it concludes a whole series of crimes—and puts a stop to it.

I have stolen these secrets from Mikhail Gorbachev, the last Soviet dictator, a Nobel Peace Prize winner. I covertly copied thousands of secret Politburo documents from the Gorbachev Foundation Archive, and then smuggled them out of Russia.

Gorby himself, however, had also acquired them illegally. In the final weeks and days of the Soviet regime, when boundless crowds went to the streets of countless cities to demand, "down with Gorbachev!," and the Evil Empire had already collapsed into independent republics, the dictator, with a handful of remaining loyalists, took refuge in the last stronghold they still controlled—the Kremlin. It was from there that he advanced his desperate, doomed designs to raise a new Soviet Union from the ashes of the old. However, his game was up; the few loyal aides who accompanied him in the Kremlin knew that. They knew some sort of bailiffs from the new Russian government would eventually come and evict them from the property.

It was during these final weeks that Gorbachev's aides took home top-secret archives of their better days: their notes from Politburo meetings, transcripts of Gorbachev's talks with foreign leaders, and countless confidential memos of all sorts. A few years before, or a few years later, this would have been seen as a great crime. In revolutionary Moscow of 1991, nobody cared.

The documents were then scanned and kept in the computers of the Gorbachev Foundation. The new masters of the Kremlin knew nothing about that archive. As years passed, and the events receded into the past, Gorby wanted to tell his version of the history of his rule to the world. To this end, some Gorbachev-friendly researchers were granted very limited access to parts of the archive. This is how I came in—in the capacity of a friendly researcher.

Draconian measures were taken to keep the research tightly under control. To copy a document, one needed special permission, often from Gorbachev personally, which he would never give unless he understood exactly how the copy would be used. All hardware that could be used to copy files, like CD and floppy drives, were removed from the computers. The dark holes gaping in their place reminded the researchers how very serious it all was. The Internet could only be accessed by using the administrator's password. Otherwise, it was a one-way system—the administrators could access our computers, but we had no access to the local or global networks. Even so, the most interesting documents—notes from Politburo discussions—were not shown to anyone at all. Instead, we were told some selected papers would later be published in a volume edited by the Gorbachev Foundation itself.

I played the role of a naïve, shy, and respectful student. Hardly did Gorbachev or the keepers of his archive suspect that I was acting as a spy. With my unassuming demeanor, I was able to exploit their carelessness. They did not notice that, with some modest manipulations in the computer system, I had turned my limited access to the archive into unlimited one. Their secrets were rapidly leaking out, one-thousand pages after another, as quickly as I could send e-mails.

Meanwhile, other copies of the very same documents remained top secret in the official Kremlin archives. The present regime regards itself as a legal heir of the Soviet Union, and guards the Soviet secrets as zealously as its own. It was not until 2003 that the KGB junta in the Kremlin learned of the existence of the private Gorbachev Archive. Gorbachev was summoned to Putin's Presidential Administration for a difficult conversation about divulging Russia's state secrets. Within hours, the Gorbachev Foundation closed the more sensitive parts of the archive to any outside researchers. However, it was too late.

In this way, Gorbachev's sloppiness helped me to commit my crime against the State Security of Russian Federation. Putinist jurisprudence defines my actions as high treason, which they define as "divulging state secrets, or giving assistance, to a foreign state, a foreign organization, or their representatives."[i] People in Putin's Russia are imprisoned as "spies" for much less than what I have done, especially considering Putin has expanded this definition to include routine academic research, which often consists of publicly available information.

Thus, scientists such as Valentin Danilov, Igor Reshetin, Sergei Vizir, Ivan Petkov, Yevgeny Afanasyev, and Svyatoslav Bobyshev are now imprisoned for divulging public domain "state secrets." Valentin Danilov, the astrophysicist convicted of high treason for his participation in an official Russian-Chinese research program, is now dying in the Putlag. If Danilov and others are criminals, then I am an arch-criminal—after all, I stole thousands of real, top-secret documents with the intent on divulging them in the West.

History will judge, however, whether it is a crime to divulge state secrets and whether it is a crime to conceal them.

What right does Gorbachev have to claim copyright for the history of his reign? What right does the Putin government have to classify our shared knowledge as a state secret?

It is axiomatic that, unless we can learn lessons from the past, we are bound to make the same mistakes in the future. In such a sensitive area as international relations, our mistakes are more than mere mistakes; mistakes mean crises and genocides, wars and revolutions. It is a crime to conceal the true history from the public and to feed them misleading "official" versions. To steal not a state document but a nation's narrative is, indeed, high treason.

I discovered this stolen treasure in Moscow. By sheer luck, I have managed to steal it back. Now I return it to the public domain where it belongs.

In today's worldwide cold war between the political class and the public, divided by the iron curtains of government secrecy, I have had the honor to be your spy behind the enemy lines.

[i] Criminal Code of Russia, Article 275

Three cheers for Wikileaks

Every day, among other news, we are being informed that the U.S. President received the Saudi foreign minister to discuss peace-making in the region, or that the State Secretary met the Russian dictator to reaffirm their friendship, or that the Chinese leader phoned the Elysee Palace to talk about sustainable development. Our sight passes along indifferently, for such items hardly contain any meaningful information. Leaders emerge from behind the closed doors only to tell the press one or two banalities about their joint commitment to international partnership and global prosperity. We are relieved to conclude that the two people have just wasted a few hours (and an unknown amount of taxpayers' money) telling nonsense to each other. Nothing to worry about. No harm done.

In truth, however, they are doing more behind those doors than spouting feel-good platitudes and reassuring each other of their aspirations of cooperation. They are negotiating and coming to important decisions about the future of this world, yet their secrets remain between themselves—great minds solving great problems. All they tell us in their communiqués is that they are as committed as ever to a world order based on moderate development and sustainable diversity.

So-called "conspiracy theorists" are racking their brains in search for some hypothetical, well-hidden bunker where the masters of this world secretly meet to agree on a common agenda. Meanwhile, the answer lies on the surface. They talk to each other nearly every day in their official capacity, under the cover of diplomatic secrecy. We are so used to the idea that only trivial matters are discussed at diplomatic negotiations that we fail to notice there is no need for secret societies; the whole world conspiracy is being made right under our noses.

Recently, an edge of that curtain of secrecy was lifted in a daring surprise attack from the World Wide Web—thousands of diplomatic documents from the State Department appeared on Wikileaks. Of course, these were just dispatches from US embassies; the talks reported there were held no higher than at Ambassadorial level. These were not summit meetings or even ministerial meetings. The greatest secrets were not there. These were mostly just embarrassing anecdotes. Yet, this was an intrusion into a secret world which simple mortals have no right to enter.

The entire political class, from the Left to the Right, went into grotesque panics. There were absurd claims that the release of diplomatic cables puts people's lives in danger (though nobody ever gave a remotely credible example) and calls, in full seriousness, to declare Wikileaks a terrorist organization. A full-scale global war was declared on the Internet, with the governments coercing web-providers to remove the site from their domains, and the rebels keeping it alive by creating hundreds of mirror websites around the world. A worldwide hunt was announced to round up the perpetrators; pressure was put on banks to block their accounts—so much so that even the famously robust Swiss gave in. The rebels responded by attacking government and banking servers.

A special fatwa was issued to catch Wikileaks founder Julian Assange by using the atrociously oppressive procedure of a "European Arrest Warrant." The EAW obliges EU member-states to arrest and extradite people on the force of a piece of paper, without even examining prima facie evidence in courts. Assange was duly arrested in Britain on the charge of politically incorrect behavior while in bed with a Swedish feminist. Do we really believe he is just paying the price for that melodramatic experience? Is there but one person anywhere in the world who seriously thinks worldwide hunt for Assange was organized for purely romantic reasons? And yet, we are prepared to ignore a crude fabrication of criminal charges and to tolerate the existence of a political prisoner in the middle of the Western world - only to ensure that the details of secret diplomacy are safely kept from the public.

In the old days, when the media secured some sensitive leak, the government would gloomily say, "Fair enough. You have beaten us here. Congratulations." Alas, the days of chivalry are now gone; this has grown to the proportions of an all-out guerrilla war. Being a whistleblower used to be honourable; today, whistleblowers are treated as terrorists.

Dozens of high-ranking people who shared confidential information with the KGB during the Cold War are now in honourable retirement or even in positions of power. But Bradley Manning, the young soldier suspected of aiding Wikileaks, is facing the capital charge of 'aiding the enemy', and President Obama has publicly declared him guilty even before the trial at the military tribunal began.

The global war on Wikileaks was declared just for telling embarrassing anecdotes, merely for looking in the direction where - still far, far away -

the real secrets of wars, revolutions, big money and great powers may be found. However, we cannot say that the Establishment is overreacting. Wikileaks strikes at the very root of their power: the *official versions* of events.

We did not need Wikileaks to know that Russia is run by a KGB Mafia. We all knew that it was its leader, Vladimir Putin, who ordered Russian agents commit an aggression against Britain and its NATO allies by murdering a British citizen on British soil in a 2006 radioactive terrorist attack. Is it really important to learn from Wikileaks that the State Department knows all this as well? Yes it is. The government cannot deny its knowledge of the culprit any longer. It cannot "reset" its relations with the aggressor because there is not enough evidence against him. It cannot offer us an official version to hide the truth we know they know.

Likewise, we knew without Wikileaks that Iran's neighbors eagerly wait for Western forces to come and save them from the Iranian threat. Nevertheless, the official version has always been this: we cannot do that without antagonizing the Muslim world. Here, Wikileaks has not really revealed any new truth, but it has killed a lie.

When politicians tell us that Wikileaks threatens our lives, what they really mean is that it threatens their lies. If the official versions were true, even disclosing the greatest secrets could not have shaken them. Because the official versions are false, any secrets, even the anecdotes from routine ambassadorial negotiations, can disprove them. The very existence of Wikileaks is the sword of Damocles hanging over all official versions, present and future. This is terrifying news for the Establishment, and very good news for us.

Something we should have learned from the 20th century is that the international relations are too important to be left in the hands of diplomats and politicians. If only Wikileaks had existed for the last hundred years! The governments of the day would have been unable to deny their knowledge of Nazi Holocaust in the 1930s and use their *official version* of what was going on in Nazi Germany to make the case for their policy of appeasement. There could have been no Second World War. Likewise, they would have been unable to deny the knowledge of Communist GULAG and make the case for the appeasement of the Soviet Union. The Cold War could have ended much sooner and with much better results. The examples are legion—I have only cited two notorious ones. Many millions of people could have survived, but instead died because the worldwide secrecy protected their hangmen from the power of the free world.

What is the matter with the Middle East?

This is particularly true about the history of the Middle East, which is genuinely the most complicated region in the world. Consequently, the policy-making on the Middle East has been traditionally monopolized by a narrow circle of specialists.

Any narrow circle has its own narrow interests. Almost inevitably, its members will make up official versions for the outsiders and secret versions for insiders. Then they work out some "consensus" based on their secret views, and then decide how to make it look plausible against the background on the official version. Policies constructed at this factory normally lead to disasters - and then the same experts write an official version of history to explain why it was not their fault.

If only our policies in the Middle East were decided by the people and in the interests of the people, many wars and revolutions of the past half century could have been avoided, or at least ended differently.

One example, which later became infamous purely by chance, was the appeasement of Saddam Hussein before his invasion of Kuwait in 1990. That policy was pursued right until the last minute, when the emboldened tyrant, confident of impunity, directed his tank hordes to cross the border and begin the historic blitzkrieg to controlling two-thirds of the world's oil supplies. Till the last moment, the State Department, in its infinite wisdom, had viewed Islamic Fundamentalism as the greatest threat in the Middle East and Saddam's version of Socialism as a lesser evil. So the experts decided that the enemy of our enemy was our friend. It was this policy that enabled Saddam's regime survive until so very recently (if it is really dead), and encouraged Iraq's wars with both Iran in 1981-1988 and the West in 1990-2010 (if it has really ended). None of this would have happened if not for the secret diplomacy.

Of course, it is now too late. Millions of lives have been lost and cannot be returned. But at least, we must not let the architects of that policy make up an official version of history to cover up their faults and follies.

This book reveals the documents from Gorbachev's archive that relate to the Gulf War and, more broadly, to the Middle East at the final stage of the Cold War. One may ask—what had the Soviets to do with the Gulf War? They did not participate in the military action, did they? However, as we shall see in these documents, Moscow was central to all the *secret diplomacy* around that war. Moreover, the war itself was only one round in a long and complicated game between the Socialist World and the Free World, because the Middle East was an important front of the Cold War—second only to Europe.

You will not find this in the official version. If you enquire about the historic causes of the bloodbath (or, if you like, *instability*) in the Middle East, *the consensus* between *the experts* is, roughly, something like this:

Before World War II, the Middle East was under the power of Western colonial empires, mostly the British. Then countries of the region gradually gained independence. Unfortunately, the de-colonization was poorly carried out, mainly because the British were more concerned with preserving their own oil interests than with the welfare of the natives. As a result, the post-colonial Middle East was torn apart by revolutions and wars.

The longest and bloodiest conflict is the Arab-Israeli one, caused mainly by Israel's reluctance to let the Palestinians have their own independent state. All the international peace-making efforts have achieved only limited success. Additionally, the rise of various extremist movements, most notably Radical Islamism, turned the region into a breeding ground for international terrorism. Regional tensions were also intensified by the Cold War rivalry between the two superpowers, both arming and supporting their respective allies and seeking to dominate the strategically-important region. However, after a pro-Western democratic reformer, Mikhail Gorbachev, came to power in the USSR, he ended the Cold War, which made some progress in the region possible. The first example of that was the splendid victory in the 1990-1991 Gulf War.

This is what we learn from an average reference book, political speech, or CNN report. Not a word of it is true.

It was the Soviet Empire - not British Empire - that was responsible for the instability in the Middle East. In fairness, the modern history of a country like Iraq begins not from getting its independence from the British, but from losing its independence to the Soviets.

All major conflicts in the region were caused by the Soviet expansion. The Cold War was not a rivalry between two superpowers, but a ruthless crusade of communist hordes against dwindling oases of freedom, like Israel. The "Palestinian problem" was largely created artificially as a weapon in this war against Israel and, even more so, as a weapon in the global war against the West.

The international terrorism, too, was created by the Soviets as a Cold War weapon. The Islamist version only emerged much later. Furthermore, the Islamist threat is also a by-product of the Cold War. Islamists could have never become a serious global force were they not supported by Socialists.

Gorbachev was *not* a democratic reformer, he was *not* pro-Western, and he did *not* end the Cold War.

And the Gulf War was not all that simple either.

Chapter 1: Red Arabs

One Arab nation with a holy message:

Unity, liberation, and socialism!

The Baath Party motto

History repeats itself.

In the run-up to the Allied military operation against Saddam Hussein in 1991, a question of enormous political and military importance was how far Saddam had advanced in developing weapons of mass destruction.

It was known that Saddam had chemical weapons—he had used them against Iranians - and against Iraqis. However, there were conflicting reports as to whether he had already secured other types of weapons of mass destruction: bacteriological and nuclear. If he such WMDs, it was still unknown how much he had, whether he would use them in the upcoming war, and how.

He had publicly sworn to God to burn half of Israel. He had also sworn to burn the whole Arabian Peninsula, with the exceptions of Mecca and Medina.

Was that a bluff? Was that a real plan? Supposing he did not have enough WMDs for both Israel and the Arabian Peninsula, which of them was in a greater risk? If he could not burn the entire Arabian Peninsula, then which part of it would he target? The camps of the US forces? Oilfields? The palace of Saudi king? On the other hand, perhaps he deceived everyone and actually planned all along to target Mecca and Medina?

Each of these questions provoked different theories in the West, but those who planned the Operation Desert Storm had an obligation to know for sure. A wrong answer to any single one of them could cost hundreds of thousands, if not millions, of lives.

And the Soviets knew all the correct answers. All the Iraqi war plans had been prepared under supervision of Soviet military advisors.

Now the Soviet Union was led by "pro-Western" Mikhail Gorbachev. By the time of the Gulf crisis, he had become a personal friend of President George W. H. Bush and Prime Minister Margaret Thatcher. Gorbachev decisively and unreservedly condemned Saddam for his invasion of Kuwait. Indeed, he became one of the leaders of the worldwide anti-Saddam coalition. Once again, like in the heroic age of the Second World War, the United States, Britain, and the Soviet Union stood side by side in opposing the aggressor. Even though the Soviets could not send troops to the Middle East this time, they gave the US and Britain full political backing and voted with them for the UN resolution that authorized use of force.

Surely, as loyal ally, Gorbachev would now share information about Iraq's WMDs with his Western friends.

Indeed, as they were considering the "military option," his two most trusted advisors proposed exactly this:

Dear Mikhail Sergeevich [Gorbachev],
It would be expedient to share the data we have about Iraq's
military preparations with the US government, in strictly
confidential order. The data includes information about Iraq's
preparations to use chemical and bacteriological weapons in case of
a military attack against it.

On the one hand, sharing this data would be seen in the USA as
an act reasserting our confidential relations. On the other hand,
this might pose some restraining influence on the circles favoring the
military option.
[Signature] Y[evgeny] PRIMAKOV

[Signature] A[natoly] CHERNYAEV

October 23, 1990
On the margins of this memo, there is a note in Gorbachev's handwriting:

C[omrade] Shevard...

Apparently, Gorbachev's first reaction was to forward the memo to his Foreign Minister, so that he would put the wheels in motion and contact the Americans. This half-completed note is crossed out by Gorbachev's hand. Mid-way through spelling the name "Shevardnadze," he changed his mind.

There is also Gorbachev's signature on the document and a note in Chernyaev's handwriting:

M.S. [Gorbachev] disagreed. October 23, 1990.

Уважаемый Михаил Сергеевич,

было бы целесообразным передать в строго конфиденциальном порядке американскому руководству имеющиеся у нас данные о военных приготовлениях Ирака, в том числе о подготовке к использованию химического и бактериологического оружия в случае военного удара по нему. С одной стороны - это было бы расценено США как акт, подтверждающий наши доверительные отношения, с другой - могло бы оказать сдерживающее воздействие на те круги, которые выступают за военную развязку.

Е.ПРИМАКОВ

А.ЧЕРНЯЕВ

"23" октября 1990 г.

One might say: well, in matters of war, alas, it takes many years to overcome the traditional mistrust towards historic enemies - and, after all, they had never asked for this intelligence.

Of course, the Western allies knew perfectly well about the Soviet Union's role in arming Iraq. It was generally assumed that the Soviet information on that issue would be more reliable than the Western one. However, the archival documents reveal only one, very delicate attempt by a Western leader to raise the issue with Gorbachev—one month after he rejected the idea of Chernyaev and Primakov.

That was not a demand to do his duty as an ally; that was not even a request. However, when talking to Gorbachev, Margaret Thatcher was bold enough to indicate her interest. Even if he would not share detailed intelligence, even if Soviet hardliners limited the freedom of his action, she expected that his oral reply could help to resolve some Western doubts. Needless to say, his word would carry much weight.

In response, Gorbachev told her a lie:

20 November 1990

[...]

> **M. THATCHER.** *Of course, [the military action against Iraq] is an equation with many unknowns. One is whether Iraq will use chemical and bacteriological weapons, which we know it has. As for the nuclear weapons, I believe Iraq still has not got them.*
>
> **M. S. GORBACHEV.** *We have no information to suggest that Iraq has nuclear or bacteriological weapons. It does have chemical weapons.*[1]

In fact, Iraq had bacteriological weapons, but no nuclear weapons. Thatcher's information was correct. Gorbachev saw that - and tried to mislead her to doubt it. Furthermore, he knew—as we now know from Primakov and Chernyaev's memo - that Iraq had plans to use bacteriological weapons in some of the possible scenarios of the future war.

Arab Liberation

> *"Has any of you ever seen a Soviet man as a coloniser in the Arab world?"*

Such was the rhetorical question that Hafez Assad, the Baathist dictator of Syria, asked at Islamic summit-meetings to persuade his colleagues that his Soviet patrons were by far not as bad as the West. Of course, they had to agree — The Soviet expansion in general, and in the Arab world in particular, had little in common with Western colonization of past centuries. Western colonizers were interested in profits, so they would try to develop the economy of their colonies. The Soviets were interested in social justice, so they would organize revolutions, establish puppet governments, and nationalize whatever the colonizers had built before. Unlike the colonial empires, the Soviet Empire incurred huge costs but brought no profits; it was more important to keep the satellites economically dependent than make them economically efficient.

Sometimes, the Soviets would follow on the imperialists' footsteps and build some roads, schools, or hospitals for the natives. That was as successful as socialist construction projects can be. One Soviet official in 1982 visited People's Democratic Republic of Yemen and then shared his impressions with comrades:

> *We are building a hospital for them since 1975, and three floors have been completed so far. If you ask someone in the capital 'how are things?' they reply 'like in the hospital'. And the French have built a top-class 9-storey hotel there in just two years.*

> *We have been building a thermal power plant for ten years, but it is still in the ground-work stage. The Japanese have built a more powerful plant in one year and a half.*

> *Seeking oil there, too: just one well has been drilled since 1974.*

> *Our idle specialists are everywhere, walking around and swimming in the ocean.*[2]

That was not the worst impression yet—the worst was the Soviet state visit by Churbanov, a high-ranking official and Brezhnev's son-in-law:

> *The ambassador and his wife are horrified: it is difficult to imagine anything more shameful and discrediting to our country, leadership and all our policy. To begin with, Churbanov went out of the plane absolutely drunk and nearly fell down (they caught him) in front of the 'high receiving party', guard of honour, etc. All 'business meetings' had to*

be cancelled, because he would spend every night getting awfully drunk with his yes-men, and then it was impossible to wake him up before the dinner time. They managed to do it once, and then it was even worse. He was saying such delirium that the interpreter had nothing to interpret. The president had to enquire with the ambassador whether 'the guest should be received at the presidential level'. In the Central Committee, they simply refused to receive him: cancelled the planned meetings.

Of course, the ambassador organised a reception, but the high guest was completely out of his senses and poked his nose in the plate now and then. They had to take him away, because his uniform looked like God knows what after a while.

At times of enlightenment, his clearest phrase would always start from "Galina Leonidovna [i. e. Brezhnev's daughter] and I..." The Eastern people can take a hint: he left loaded with innumerable suitcases and boxes.[3]

No colonizer or viceroy could have ever behaved like that, especially not in Islamic colonies, with their teetotaler traditions. Those reactionary emirs and maharajas, on whom colonial powers relied, would never tolerate such insults. By contrast, the rulers of people's republics treated the Soviet visitors in the spirit of fraternal comradeship.

The Soviets knew perfectly well whom they sent on state visits and where. When they rewarded the Yemeni comrades with a notoriously corrupt drunkard, they knew what they were doing. That was a deliberate humiliation, a sign of Moscow's displeasure, and there was no need for the messenger to come to his senses to deliver the message. Behind his stupid, drunken face and his messy uniform, clever and sober Arab comrades could see the iron fist of the Soviet Empire.

Every working day of the Soviet Foreign Minister began with two hours of sitting in silence and staring at the map of the world. At least, so it was rumoured; and whether the anecdote is factually correct, it is accurate in reflecting the spirit of the Soviets regime. Even if that was not the Foreign Minister, someone in the Kremlin had to do this.

What he thought about during these mornings can only be deduced from the character of subsequent wars, revolutions, and terrorist attacks - so one would imagine his gaze often fell upon the Middle East. What a peculiar world it is, he probably thought, with most its oil, all its best oil, concentrated in one place. If we could just take control of the Middle East, we would have the whole world by the throat.

Soon after Stalin's famous failure to create a People's Republic of Israel, Soviets got another chance to establish their presence in the region. In 1952, a national-socialist military junta deposed the King of Egypt. Moscow would have preferred a communist revolution, but a Nazi one was close enough. After some brief hesitation, the Soviets gave the new dictator, Colonel Nasser, their full support, plenty of weapons, countless military advisors, and the title of Hero of the Soviet Union.

Following the Soviet example, Nasser organized a Comintern-style network of revolutionary terrorists all over the Arab world. The Nasserite Comintern operated out of Cairo, and united its efforts with the real Comintern in Moscow*; together they captured power in one Arab country after another: Syria in 1954, Iraq in 1958, Algeria and North Yemen in 1962, South Yemen in 1967, and Libya in 1969. The 1975 civil war in Lebanon resulted in Syrian occupation. Heroes of the Soviet Union, who desperately hated each other, but still hated the rest of the world even more, now governed more and more Arab states.

Arab Unity

Discipline, admittedly, was a recurrent problem in the camp of Red Arabs. Every new dictator promoted his own version of Arab Socialism and saw himself as the great leader of the pan-Arab and world revolution. Their Cominterns multiplied respectively, as if the two that ran from Moscow and Cairo were not more than enough.

Thus, the Baath ideology asserts that all state borders in the Middle

---

*The Comintern (Communist International) was formally dissolved by Stalin in 1943 on the request of the World War II Allies. In fact, however, the organisation was simply reorganised and continued to exist until 1991 as the International Department of the CPSU Central Committee, which inherited the Comintern's staff, structure, and functions. For simplicity, in this work I refer to the International Department as "Comintern" when discussing its operations in the post-1943 context.

East are illegitimate, because imperialists deliberately drew them in order to divide the Arab nation. Therefore, there could be no such thing as a Syrian Baath Party or an Iraqi Baath Party. Instead, there is the Arab Socialist Baath Party based in Damascus, which has a Regional Department for every present Arab country. The Syrian department governs Syria, while every other department is preparing a revolution elsewhere.

At the same time, there was another Arab Socialist Baath Party based in Baghdad, whose Iraqi department governed Iraq while other departments exported the revolution. Both Baath Parties denounced each other as impostors.

Moscow alone could suppress the endless infighting and make Red Arabs work together—if only temporarily and only to an extent.

In 1986, for example, Soviet leader Mikhail Gorbachev told the visiting Foreign Minister of Syria:

Look at this example: Gaddafi [of Libya] and Bendjedid [of Algeria] had very bad relations between themselves. We told the Algerians and Libyans to talk directly to each other. As a result, the relations more or less improved.

Another example is the relationship between Syria and Iraq. We know everything about Saddam Hussein's biography and his record. But Iraq is a reality. We believe the Syrian leadership has shown a responsible approach by taking steps to improve its relations with Iraq.

Yesterday, I talked to [Foreign Minister of Libya] Djellud. He expressed himself in extremist terms, and said that Libya deems it necessary to overthrow Saddam Hussein. I told him that, after all, some people may also dislike Gaddafi, Assad [of Syria], or Gorbachev. So, what then?[4]

This passage is touching in terms of socialist fraternal solidarity and comradeship it reveals. However, it is also remarkable in terms of their approach to deposing foreign leaders. Many people in the world, including top leaders of great powers, wanted to overthrow Saddam Hussein but had no idea how to do it. Gorbachev and Gaddafi had no questions on whether it was in their power; they only disagreed whether it was necessary at the time. Gaddafi proposed to depose Saddam Hussein. Gorbachev said no. That concluded the business. However, if Gorbachev said yes, Saddam probably would not have lived long enough to invade Kuwait in 1990.

The Soviets themselves, though backing the Arab socialists, still held them in utmost contempt. Just after the Red Arabs were beaten in the Yom-Kippur War in October 1973, Leonid Brezhnev told his Foreign Minister that the USSR would need to restore diplomatic relations with Israel at some point in the future:

> **GROMYKO**: *But the Arabs would be offended... [reads the note in a witness's diary]*

> **BREZHNEV**: *They should go fuck themselves! We've been offering them a reasonable method for many years, but no - they wanted a war. Okay, as you please! We gave them the equipment, the most modern one, unseen even in Vietnam. They had double superiority in tanks and aircraft, triple superiority in artillery, absolute superiority in anti-aircraft and anti-tank defences. So what? They were smashed again. They bunked again. They cried for us to save them again. Sadat twice woke me up in the middle of a night by phone: 'Save us!' He demanded me to send a Soviet landing force there immediately! No! We are not going to fight for them. The people would not understand us. Even more so, we are not going to start a world war because of them. That is it. We shall do what I said.[5]*

> *After every defeat in the Middle East (of which they had plenty), the Soviets blamed the Arabs, the Arabs blamed the Soviets and each other, and each of them started thinking about a separate peace with the enemy. While Brezhnev was cursing war-mongering Sadat, Sadat cursed war-mongering Brezhnev and began negotiations with Israel through the US.*

Three years later, Sadat had second thoughts and sent his Foreign Minister to the Soviets to propose a summit meeting. As a sign of goodwill, Sadat's envoy revealed some fresh Mid-Eastern gossip—war-mongering Assad of Syria was so scared of a possible assassination that he shivered when hearing a camera shutter.

According to the same diary, Gromyko relayed that story to Politburo and suggested that, if Brezhnev held a summit meeting with Sadat, he would need to balance it by meeting Assad. Weary Brezhnev replied:

"I don't believe any of them. The only honest people among them, if any at all, are the Palestinians." Other Politburo members expressed polite

skepticism. Kosygin said that all of them (Arabs) rejoice if any of "their brothers" are beaten or defeated. All of them, he said, lie to us and to each other. [6]

One of the worst vendettas was between formerly Syrian-backed PLO leader Yasser Arafat and the Syrian dictator Hafez Assad, who had deposed Arafat's former patrons in Syria in an internal Baathist coup. For years, Assad lobbied Moscow to let him replace Arafat with his own protégé, but Moscow would not permit that:

> **M. S. GORBACHEV.** *Of course, we could take this approach: tell Arafat to go to hell. You can't tell whether he does more good than harm. But at present, such an approach (correct in principle as it may be) would have only further undermined the Palestine Liberation Organisation and played into the Americans' hands. [...]*

> *[Syrian Foreign Minister] A. H. HADDAM. [...] But we cannot ignore the fact that we rely on the toiling masses to pursue our anti-imperialist policy. [...] We can appeal to our citizens to reduce their consumption of meat to twice per week, consumption of fruits to once per week, we can draft their sons for a war where they can be killed. The people will agree to all this if they know this is necessary for victory over the enemy. But they will not support those who let the Chairman of PLO Executive Committee take the course which serves the interests of the US and Israel. This is why we cannot support Arafat.*

> **M. S. GORBACHEV.** *[...] Let the Palestinians themselves decide about Arafat, we don't need him. [...] He will either support our common agreed course, or unmask himself and have to piss off.*

> **A. H. HADDAM.** *[...] As for Arafat, he lies more often than he breathes. [...]*

> **M. S. GORBACHEV.** *[...] With or without Arafat, we need unity of the PLO, as a detachment of the national liberation movement, on the anti-imperialist and anti-Zionist basis.[7]*

Moscow doled out abuse and insults to Arabs, all the while financing and arming its Middle East satellites. The Arab socialist dictators, however insincere their love to communists may have been, never questioned

Moscow's leadership in their war for the control of the Middle East.

Whenever another Arab comrade captured power in a successful coup, he would first seek an audience with the Supreme Leader of the World Revolution in Moscow. If it was granted, initiation proceeded along these lines:

M. S. GORBACHEV. [...] You should pay more attention to the legacy of Lenin. The experience of our Party and our revolution is useful to everybody. [...] You, I am confident, can lead the country if, firstly, you work out the policies [...] which the people understand and need [...] and if, secondly, you preserve unity in the leadership. [...] You should be decisive and wise, cautious and demanding, firm and flexible...

Detailed instructions followed, with concrete examples from Lenin's experience, on what to do with the divided party (show no mercy to leading dissenters, but spare the others and re-educate); on how to run the economy (spend no more than you can afford); and on foreign affairs (always stick to the Soviet line, and do not invade thy neighbors unless so instructed).

A.S. AL BEID. May I express sincere gratitude for the opportunity to meet you and for such a frank, comradely conversation. We know you are very busy with [...] global problems of the survival of humankind. [...] We are proud that the problems of our revolution in our small country are also within the field of your attention. [...] I would like to assure you that [...] developing Democratic Yemen on the path of socialist orientation is the strategic course of our party, which is firm and unshakable. [...] Whatever difficulties [...] we may face, we shall never deviate from this strategic line, we shall literally 'cling' to it. [...] Thank you for your valuable comradely advice. [...] May I assure you that you will see very soon how firmly we follow your recommendations in our work.[8]

These people glorified themselves as great revolutionary leaders defying the Western Imperialism. In reality, they were just mercenaries serving the Soviet Empire. They may have enjoyed unlimited power in their own countries, but they were never free from the higher power of their Soviet masters. All the intrigues that Arafat, Gaddafi, Bendjedid, Assad, or Saddam initiated against each other and against the rest of the world, all their plots both started and ended in Moscow.

Arab Socialism

Although the difference is hard to spot, the Arab Socialists (Nasserites, Baathists, Islamic Socialists, etc.) are not exactly communists. For that matter, as "national" socialists they are closer politically to the German Nazis, with whom they collaborated when rioting against the British Empire during World War II.

Arab Socialists have dedicated themselves to fighting what they call "the legacy of colonialism," which includes all non-socialist and non-Arab countries in the Middle East. The socialist regimes in Egypt, Syria, Iraq, Algeria, or Libya planned to export their revolution to other countries until the entire Arab world united as one socialist super-state. The immediate priority was to destroy the most pro-Western forces and regimes, like Israel or Gulf monarchies.

What made it different from communism was the element of Arab nationalism. The problem is that the Arab nation is as difficult to define as the Aryan Race or the World Proletariat. The League of Arab States officially defines an Arab as "a person whose language is Arabic, who lives in an Arabic speaking country, and is in sympathy with the aspirations of the Arabic speaking peoples." This could have been perfectly clear criteria, but the Arabic spoken in Iraq, Egypt, and Morocco are three different languages. Arabic was the region's ancient Lingua Franca, which today has about as many versions as the Romanic family of languages in Europe.

The truth is that Arabs are not a nation, simply because the nation-state had not developed in that part of the world. There were tribes, empires, principalities—but no nations. The word *Arab* originally meant just "nomad." During the late Ottoman Empire, some dissident intellectuals in Beirut invented an elegant theory: we are descendants of those Arabic (nomadic) tribes who actually started the Islamic civilization, so these Turks have no right to govern us. This became a popular theme in Mid-Eastern mythology, not unlike the theme of direct descent from Prophet Mohammed. Until the middle of the 20th century, however, only the peoples living between Persia in the East and Egypt in the West would ever call themselves Arabs. Egypt's claim of independence was based on a different mythology that was about the Pharaohs. Lands to the West of Egypt had their own different myths.

Unfortunately, in the 20th century, Arab nationalism was mixed with socialism. The idea of an Arab nation was further jeopardized when the first

Arab socialist revolution succeeded in Egypt, a non-Arab country. What could the new regime do? Nasser boldly proclaimed Egyptians to be Arabs, which started the explosive expansion of the definition in all directions. Somalia became a purely Arab land populated by Arab people (especially because it is located right on the route of Western oil tankers coming from the Gulf). Mauritania? No problem there. By 2006, this went so far that Venezuela joined the League of Arab States as an observer, followed by India the next year. After all, they do sympathize with Arab aspirations, and, on thorough linguistic analysis, there must be something Arabic in the way they speak.

The definition expanded not only in space, but also in time. Saddam Hussein, for example, would often tell the bemused public that ancient Babylonians were Arabs and their kings were great Arab leaders—almost as great as Saddam himself. His favorite was Nebuchadnezzar II, who conquered Jerusalem and destroyed the Jewish Temple in 597 BC.

After an initial brief hesitation, the Kremlin had to accept that Arab Socialism was flexible enough to serve as the local version of Proletarian Internationalism for the time being. Egyptian Communists were instructed to dissolve their party and join Nasser's Arab Socialist Union (but to keep in touch with Soviet comrades). Syrian and Iraqi Communists united with Baathists as junior partners in their ruling "Progressive Front" and "Patriotic Front," respectively. Arab dictators knew, however, that "fronts" with communists normally ended with backstabbing. Therefore, they shot their communists on a considerable scale, just to be sure. Moscow weakly protested.

All these were typical small inconveniences of the socialist comradeship: struggle for power, personal hatred, collective treachery, and ideological discrepancies. However, the deepest divisions were caused by tactical disagreements.

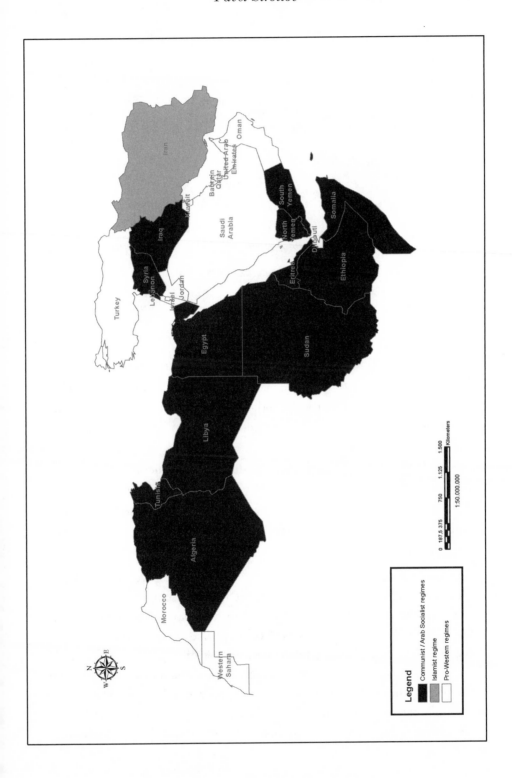

Chapter 2: Jews and Oil

Iraq lost its national independence in the early morning of July 14, 1958. Several Iraqi army units, whose commanders called themselves "the Free Officers" after the Egyptian mutineers of 1952, surrounded the royal palace in Baghdad and opened artillery fire. The inhabitants had to run outside for their lives, only to face the semicircle of armed Free Officers and yield to them. All the captives, including numerous women and children, were immediately shot in the palace courtyard. The young king's body was taken away and buried in a secret location, and the others were handed over to Baghdad mob for desecration and dismemberment.

Thus began the new era of liberation under the government of Free Officers and their thin-voiced leader, General Qassem. However, it soon emerged that the Free Officers lacked unity; they served two different Heroes of the Soviet Union. Some of them had betrayed their king and country to Colonel Nasser and wanted Iraq to join Egypt and Syria in the United Arab Republic ran from Cairo. Others, including Gen. Qassem, owed allegiance to Comrade Khrushchev and wanted Iraq to be a People's Republic ran from Moscow. Respectively, the twin pillars of their regime were the pro-Egyptian Arab Socialist Baath Party and the pro-Soviet Iraqi

Communist Party. Soon, they began killing each other at massive scale.

In 1959, one year after the coup, the Baath Party decided to assassinate Qassem for his pro-communist orientation. Twenty-two-year-old Saddam Hussein and several other comrades were assigned to the hit squad. Unfortunately, an over-excited Saddam prematurely drew a machine-gun from under his cloak and opened fire at Qassem's car. Qassem's body guards realized what was happening and retaliated before the rest of the assassins squad could draw their own guns. In the ensuing shoot-out, Qassem was only wounded, while one of the assassins was killed. The other assassins, including Saddam, fled to Cairo. The slain assassin was identified, his connections traced, the whole plot exposed, and the Baath Party was banned. Qassem recovered, and his regime became purely communist.

In due course, the Baathists finally killed Qassem, captured power, were overthrown, split up, reunited, and captured power again. Saddam returned to Baghdad, served a prison term for yet another failed murder plot, became the dictator, killed many thousands of Communists, Baathists, Jews, Kurds, Shiites, and Sunnis, quarreled with Egypt, and aligned with Moscow. He did everything Qassem dreamt of and many things Qassem never thought about. His first political adventure—the failed assassination attempt, which was nothing to be proud of—was glorified as a jewel of his heroic biography in countless propaganda movies and books. Indeed, Saddam never learnt his lesson. In the main adventure of his life, his Mother of All Battles, he repeated the same mistakes. He opened fire at the wrong moment, jeopardized a carefully laid plan, and let down his accomplices. He achieved nothing, played into the enemy's hands, became an outlaw, and then declared all this a heroic victory.

Qassem's secret police failed to catch and hang Saddam, but they investigated and avenged the plot. In Saddam's confrontation with the West, the opposite happened: he was eventually caught and hanged, but the plot was never investigated.

Indeed, what *was* the original plan that Saddam jeopardized with his sharp move?

Operation SIG

In their battle for the Middle East, comrades had two strategic targets of supreme importance: Israel and the Gulf. The first choice they faced was making one of them the priority.

Control of the Gulf would mean the control of the world's oil supplies. However, this control could only be established through direct military aggression. The typical Soviet tactics of sponsoring well-calculated and well organized revolutions did not work in such countries as Saudi Arabia, Kuwait, or United Arab Emirates. Those countries were incredibly rich and governed by ancient, clever, and ruthless dynasties. In human rights terms, kings and emirs had no problem hanging every communist on identification, and their secret police services were not too bad at identifying them. At the same time, too few of their subjects had 'nothing to lose except their chains', as the infamous Marxist phrase goes. They could not be deposed by a revolution; they could only be conquered in a war.

In 1961, Kuwait received independence from British Empire. Qassem, who had so luckily survived his recent encounter with Saddam, declared Kuwait to be part of Iraq and moved Iraqi troops to its borders. On Kuwait's request, British forces urgently returned to the Emirate, and the Iraqi invasion was thus prevented. Qassem was deposed and killed by Baathists soon after, and Iraq formally recognized the independence of Kuwait.

It became clear that the West would go any length to defend its Gulf allies. The West would swallow many things, but not an invasion of the vital oilfields. An invasion of Kuwait or Saudi Arabia would be taken as an open declaration of war on the non-socialist world. This message was received and understood, so the comrades postponed the conquest of the Gulf—although some of them were sorely disappointed with that decision.

Instead, the subversion and eventual destruction of Israel were declared the primary objective. Though not as good as the Gulf oilfields, Israel would also be a big prize. It was the only democracy in the region, the strongest military power in the pro-Western camp and, indeed, the bridgehead of the Western world. Even more importantly, the very process of crusading (or jihadding) against Israel offered fantastic political opportunities. A besieged Israel effectively meant millions of Jewish hostages in the hands of the comrades, and the threat of genocide could intimidate the West into making great concessions in the Gulf or elsewhere. On the other hand, by making the Israeli-Palestinian conflict the central problem of the

Middle East, the Soviets could exploit Arab nationalism, anti-Semitism, and even Islamic religious feelings to mobilize support for their policies. Indeed, under the banner of Arab solidarity, the socialist influence in the region grew far beyond the socialist regimes and parties.

General Ion Mihai Pacepa, the highest-ranking defector from the Soviet Bloc, recalls a conversation he had in 1972, as the head of Romania's intelligence service, with the KGB chairman Yuri Andropov:

> *We needed to instill a Nazi-style hatred for the Jews throughout the Islamic world [Andropov said], and to turn this weapon of the emotions into a terrorist bloodbath against Israel and its main supporter, the United States. No one within the American/Zionist sphere of influence should any longer feel safe.*

> *According to Andropov, the Islamic world was a waiting petri dish in which we could nurture a virulent strain of America-hatred, grown from the bacterium of Marxist-Leninist thought. Islamic anti-Semitism ran deep. The Muslims had a taste for nationalism, jingoism, and victimology. Their illiterate, oppressed mobs could be whipped up to a fever pitch.*

> *Terrorism and violence against Israel and her master, American Zionism, would flow naturally from the Muslims' religious fervor, Andropov sermonized. We had only to keep repeating our themes — that the United States and Israel were "fascist, imperial-Zionist countries" bankrolled by rich Jews. Islam was obsessed with preventing the infidels' occupation of its territory, and it would be highly receptive to our characterization of the U.S. Congress as a rapacious Zionist body aiming to turn the world into a Jewish fiefdom.*

> *The codename of this operation was "SIG" (Sionistskiye Gosudarstva, or "Zionist Governments"), and was within my Romanian service's "sphere of influence," for it embraced Libya, Lebanon, and Syria. SIG was a large party/state operation. We created joint ventures to build hospitals, houses, and roads in these countries, and there we sent thousands of doctors, engineers, technicians, professors, and even dance instructors. All had the task of portraying the United States as an arrogant and haughty Jewish fiefdom financed by Jewish money and run by Jewish politicians, whose aim was to subordinate the entire Islamic world.*

In the mid 1970s, the KGB ordered my service, the DIE — along with other East European sister services — to scour the country for trusted party activists belonging to various Islamic ethnic groups, train them in disinformation and terrorist operations, and infiltrate them into the countries of our "sphere of influence." Their task was to export a rabid, demented hatred for American Zionism by manipulating the ancestral abhorrence for Jews felt by the people in that part of the world. Before I left Romania for good, in 1978, my DIE had dispatched around 500 such undercover agents to Islamic countries. According to a rough estimate received from Moscow, by 1978 the whole Soviet-bloc intelligence community had sent some 4,000 such agents of influence into the Islamic world.

In the mid-1970s we also started showering the Islamic world with an Arabic translation of the Protocols of the Elders of Zion, a tsarist Russian forgery that had been used by Hitler as the foundation for his anti-Semitic philosophy. We also disseminated a KGB-fabricated "documentary" paper in Arabic alleging that Israel and its main supporter, the United States, were Zionist countries dedicated to converting the Islamic world into a Jewish colony.[9]

For purely geographical reasons, targeting the Gulf would automatically turn Iraq into the flagship of the Soviet advance in the region. Likewise, the choice of Israel as the strategic priority reserved the leading role for Nasser's Egypt.

Red Jihad

In 1964, Nasser founded the Palestine Liberation Organization as his future puppet government for whatever would remain of Israel and Jordan, and began preparing for war. The war began on June 5, 1967. The next day, all Arab Socialist regimes declared an oil embargo on the West, and put pressure on other Arab countries to do the same. However, Israel won the war in just six days, and the oil embargo had to be lifted soon afterwards. It did not last long enough to produce a serious energy crisis or even to affect the oil prices. However, the 1967 embargo was only the beginning of many efforts by Nasser and his successors to keep Jews and oil in the same flask—to interlink genocidal threats with energy blackmail.

Nasser died in 1970, but his successor Anwar Sadat and other Red Arab dictators were eager to try another invasion of Israel. On July 15, 1972, a high-positioned Soviet diarist wrote:

> *Last Sunday, Anwar Sadat publicly demanded an immediate withdrawal of all Soviet specialists and all Soviet militaries from Egypt, in protest, because he did not receive what Brezhnev promised to him at the latest negotiations in Moscow, namely the offensive weapons: SU-17 fighter bombers. This began a turmoil. Egypt's Premier Sidki was persuaded to come to Moscow, and, I think, they have settled it. I mean, they must have given much to him, if not all he wanted.*
>
> *President of Syria Assad, too, was here a week ago. Although he is a moderate, he has forced us to practically approve the 'military solution', and received a lot from us.*[10]

Even though Sadat eventually removed the Soviet military advisors from Egypt, Soviets still played bigger role in the 1973 Yom-Kippur War than is widely believed. The quote above makes it clear that Moscow had approved "the military solution." Brezhnev later confirmed this with the comment, *"They wanted a war. Okay, as you please! We gave them the equipment."* However, the crucial Soviet intervention came at the end of war.

The Yom-Kippur war began when Egypt and Syria invaded Israel on October 6, 1973. They were joined by Iraqi reinforcements within a few days. However, the attack was defeated, and the Israelis advanced into Egyptian and Syrian territories. By October 19, the Israeli tanks had crossed the Suez Channel and headed towards Cairo.

According to Chernyaev:

> *At 4 am on Saturday, Sadat summoned [Soviet] Ambassador Vinogradov. Sadat was absolutely in panic, could not control himself, and literally pleaded with the ambassador to phone Brezhnev immediately (i. e. wake him up) and ask him to demand an immediate ceasefire.*
>
> *In the morning, that was finally agreed with [U.S. State Secretary] Kissinger and passed to the UN in New York. The Security Council immediately passed the resolution by 14 votes (China abstained), both Egypt and Israel agreed with it straightaway. Assad, however, grumbles that no one bothered to ask his opinion.*

The parties were given 12 hours to cease fire.

Kissinger, however, did notice with laughter that the normal term in international practice was 24 hours.

"But why should people be killed for another 12 hours?" was the reply.

"Okay, let it be 12," said Kissinger.[11]

In fact, the difference was significant—the Israeli forces needed time to cut the Suez Canal from the Egyptian capital and encircle the Egyptian forces on the canal's Eastern bank. Thanks to Kissinger's kind concession, the cease-fire formally came into effect several hours before they could do that. The combat troops in the field, however, were unable or unwilling to disengage, and the Israeli offensive continued. It was then that Sadat again woke Brezhnev in the middle of the night on October 23 and asked for a Soviet landing party.

At that point, he would not tell Sadat where to go. Instead, he sent an urgent message to Washington that he was sending a Soviet landing party to the battlefield, and invited the Americans to join the peace-making mission if they wished. Simultaneously, Brezhnev sent a memo to the members of Soviet Politburo with a proposal to "do something" immediately:

Move the Soviet Navy towards Tel Aviv, or let the Egyptians strike at Israel with our medium-range missiles (but not at Tel Aviv or Jerusalem), or do something else.[12]

As far as Chernyaev could figure out, the Politburo then decided to send a Soviet transport ship with nuclear missiles to Alexandria.

The United States raised nuclear alarm (causing natural worldwide panic), and put pressure on Israel to cease-fire. The Israelis obliged. The Soviet transport turned back, and the military action was over.[13]

However, in the course of war, the Red Arabs had started another oil crisis, which was much more successful than their previous attempt. In 1974, the price of oil quadrupled to $12 per barrel, which was terribly high at the time. The embargo was formally lifted in 1974, but the prices did not fall. However humiliating the Arab defeats were, the strategy of targeting Israel began to pay off—in the "oil war" and elsewhere.

Terrorist merry-go-round

Israeli victories in 1967 and 1973 had many consequences, and one of them was the change of the PLO's leadership and tactics.

When Nasser created the PLO in 1964, he made it into more than just a Palestinian section of his Arab Comintern. In the interests of "Arab unity," he invited other Arab-Socialist dictators to pool their Palestinian subversive groups into one umbrella organization (that is why the PLO has always had so many different factions). At first, Nasser's own creatures governed the PLO. However, after the defeat in Six Day War, Nasser's authority declined, and the power in the PLO was captured by a Syrian-sponsored Baathist faction called Fatah, which was led by Yasser Arafat.

As opposed to Nasserites' reliance on old-fashioned conventional war, the Fatah advocated terrorism as the ultimate weapon. In addition, Comrade Arafat recommended not to limit terrorist attacks to Israel, but to develop a wide network of international terrorism. Under Arafat and the Fatah, the PLO operated all over the world, pioneering the novel arts of hijacking airplanes, blowing them up in the air, taking hostages, assassinating diplomats, massacring schoolchildren, and so forth.

Changes in the PLO reflected the broader change of the Soviet Cold War tactics after the Six Day War defeat. General Alexander Sakharovsky, the then head of the KGB's intelligence arm, enthusiastically explained to his East European colleagues:

> *In today's world, when nuclear arms have made military force obsolete, terrorism should become our main weapon.*

In the narrow circle of high-ranking Soviet Bloc spymasters, Sakharovsky boasted that airplane-hijacking was his own invention. His personal office decoration at KGB headquarters was a large world map, covered with countless red flags, each pinned by Sakharovsky to mark a successful hijacking. Another notorious species of a terrorist attacks, mass shootings in airports and other public places, was also invented by the KGB in the wake of the successful campaign to hijack 82 airplanes in 1969 alone.[14]

Thus began the golden age of international terrorism, which continued until the very downfall of the Soviet Union, and is probably remembered in some quarters with much nostalgia. Of all terrorists and terrorist organizations of those times, Arafat and the PLO were the most infamous, as infamous as Osama bin Laden and al-Qaeda today, and much more powerful. It was a great terrorist empire; the PLO itself united dozens of terrorist organizations, and apart from that, there were numerous proxies and splinter groups secretly controlled by Fatah (the most notorious of them was the Black September). Nevertheless, the supreme headquarters of the whole network was, of course, the Kremlin. The complete history of international terrorism is yet to be written, but the evidence accumulated at this point leaves no doubt that the whole system was invented by Moscow as a weapon against the West, and the PLO was a jewel in their crown.[15] In the KGB, the PLO was known under the codename Karusel, which means "merry-go-round"[16] in Russian.

All three major factions of the PLO—Fatah, Popular Front for Liberation of Palestine (PFLP), and Democratic Front for Liberation of Palestine (DFLP)—received weapons, ammunition, and training from the KGB. That secret was guarded very carefully, and was only revealed after the collapse of the Soviet Union. The evidence of KGB support for Palestinian terrorism was smuggled out of Russia, amid a much wider collection of secret documents, by former Soviet dissident and political prisoner Vladimir Bukovsky. Further details became known from the Mitrokhin Archive.

The documents from Bukovsky and Mitrokhin's collections reveal the story of the KGB's relations with one of the largest PLO affiliates, the Popular Front for Liberation of Palestine (PFLP). Notorious terrorist Wadia Haddad, a member of PFLP Politburo and the head of its "External Operations," was a KGB agent since 1970. In 1974, the KGB secretly reported to Brezhnev:

> *The nature of our relations with <u>W. Haddad</u> allows us a degree of control over the activities of the PFLP's <u>external operations section</u>, to exercise an influence favourable to the USSR, and also to reach some of our own aims, through the activities of the PFLP while observing the necessary secrecy.*

In April 1974, Haddad met the KGB station chief in Lebanon and outlined the following "prospective program of sabotage and terrorism by the PFLP":

> *- employing special means to prolong the "oil war" of Arab countries against the imperialist forces supporting Israel,*
>
> *- carrying out operations against American and Israeli personnel in third countries with the aim of securing reliable information about the plans and intentions of the USA and Israel,*
>
> *- carrying out acts of sabotage and terrorism on the territory of Israel,*
>
> *- organizing acts of sabotage against the Diamond Center, whose basic capital derives from Israeli, British, Belgian and West German companies.*

In order to implement the above measures, the PFLP is currently preparing a number of special operations, including strikes against large oil storage installations in various countries (Saudi Arabia, the Persian Gulf, Hong Kong et al), the destruction of oil tankers and super-tankers, actions against American and Israeli representatives in Iran, Greece, Ethiopia, Kenya, an attack on the Diamond center in Tel Aviv, etc.

Haddad asked the Soviets for the supplies of arms and ammunition required for those terrorist attacks, which was duly granted. Covert supplies continued throughout the 1970s.

In 1974, Haddad secretly visited Moscow to discuss "the questions of strictly clandestine collaboration with the Soviet intelligence aimed at obtaining political, strategic, military, and operative information." The Soviets also persuaded Haddad to follow their own Middle Eastern strategy and concentrate on Israel as the primary target:

> *As a result of our political influence on <u>Haddad</u>, he has concluded it is necessary to shift the focus of his operations from the third countries to the territories of Israel and the occupied Arab lands. He has promised to refrain from unreasonable and pointless attacks.*

However, the question of oil and its linkage to the Jewish question was not forgotten. The following year, Haddad ordered his henchman Ilich Ramirez Sanchez, better known as Carlos the Jackal, to kidnap the OPEC oil ministers from their meeting in Vienna. Following Haddad's instructions, Carlos captured the ministers, hijacked a plane, and began flying around the world, releasing hostages one by one in exchange for their governments' declarations of support for the Palestinian cause. However, while Haddad's orders were to keep and shoot the Saudi and Iranian ministers, Carlos released them as well, in exchange for generous ransom. As a result, Haddad dismissed him from the PFLP External Operations squads.[17]

PLO terrorists were widely used against the non-socialist Arab regimes. Reactionary kings and emirs had no respect for freedom of association, so they banned Communist, Nasserite, and Baathist parties in their countries. Nevertheless, the PLO could freely operate there, because the Palestinian refugee camps were scattered all over the Arab world. The PLO could organize revolutions against kings and emirs, or could at least intimidate them into "Arab solidarity." Under the PLO's pressure, those leaders would embrace Arab revolutionaries. Emir of Kuwait, by the way, was particularly well known for that—he had 300,000 Palestinians in his country.

Soviet aid was not limited to the PFLP; it was given to other PLO terrorists as well, from Democratic Front for Liberation of Palestine (DFLP) to Arafat himself. In 1984, Moscow supplied the DFLP with fifteen million roubles worth of arms and ammunition in exchange for a collection of ancient artifacts. Bukovsky later tried to trace that collection in Moscow and discovered that:

> *Most of it is housed, still sealed, in a safe in the Kremlin Armory. Nobody got around to opening it, and at present nobody dares to touch it, even though the Politburo and the KGB no longer exist. So it is still a mystery, what comprises this collection, and where it was stolen. It would also be interesting to learn how many people were killed with the "special equipment" paid for it.*

The KGB's direct supplies to terrorists were merely the tip of the iceberg, and only resorted to in particularly delicate or complicated cases. For deniability reasons, the regular flow of Soviet support for terrorists went through East Germany, Romania, Yugoslavia, Czechoslovakia, Hungary, Egypt, Iraq, Syria, Libya, Algeria, and South Yemen. In 1983 alone, East German Stazi sent $1,877,600 worth of Kalashnikov (AK-47) ammunition to the PLO-controlled areas of Lebanon. According to Pacepa, since 1968 and at least until late 1970s, Romania sent the PLO two full cargo planes of military supplies every week. Czechoslovakia specialized in explosives—according to Czech President Vaclav Havel, it supplied terrorists with 1,000 tons of the odorless explosive Semtex-H, which remains their favorite to the day.[18] Indeed, the international terrorism can now run, on the Czech supplies alone, for centuries after the collapse of the Soviet empire. Pacepa lists examples of KGB-sponsored acts of terrorism:

> *Here are some terrorist actions for which the KGB took credit while I was still in Romania: November 1969, armed attack on the El Al office in Athens, leaving 1 dead and 14 wounded; May 30, 1972, Ben Gurion Airport attack, leaving 22 dead and 76 wounded; December 1974, Tel Aviv movie theater bomb, leaving 2 dead and 66 wounded; March 1975, attack on a Tel Aviv hotel, leaving 25 dead and 6 wounded; May 1975, Jerusalem bomb, leaving 1 dead and 3 wounded; July 4, 1975, bomb in Zion Square, Jerusalem, leaving 15 dead and 62 wounded; April 1978, Brussels airport attack, leaving 12 wounded; May 1978, attack on an El Al plane in Paris, leaving 12 wounded.*[19]

The documents from my own collection suggest that, in their confidential exchanges, Soviet and Syrians also took the credit for blowing up the US marine barracks in Lebanon in 1984 and other terrorist attacks of the Lebanese civil war, which led to the withdrawal of US forces. In 1986, Syrian foreign minister told Gorbachev:

> We can thwart the imperialists' plans in the Middle East. [...] For example, we have managed to throw Americans out of Lebanon, thwart the US-imposed Lebanese-Israeli agreement, organise a patriotic resistance to Israeli occupation in Lebanon.[20]

Struggle for peace

Perhaps crucially, wars and terrorist attacks were accompanied with a diplomatic and propaganda offensive. The Cold War was all about pressure and blackmail, the projection of force rather than the actual use of force. Nobody on the socialist side hoped that the actual damage from the terrorist attacks, numerous and cruel as they were, would lead to a downfall of "capitalism." Terrorists, like nuclear superpowers, win through fear.

The West's *official versions* concerning the Middle East and its problems developed under a pointed gun. Consequently, they are somewhat colored by a reluctance to upset those who held it.

The best illustration of this is the common misinterpretation of the "Palestinian problem" as a plight of a disinherited nation, fighting at times by unacceptable means, for a right to establish their own state, akin to Kurds, Basques, or Chechens. That problem, we are told, is the cause of most other problems in the Middle East—all Arabs naturally support the Palestinians and all Westerners naturally support the Israelis, hence the everlasting antagonism.

Nothing can be further from the truth. Palestinians do not see themselves as a nation and do not want national independence. They consider themselves a part of the Arab nation and, like Nasser or Saddam, advocate a single socialist Arab super-state. Palestinians are Arabs who had lived in what is now Israel, but were driven out of after Israel's War of Independence. Ethnically, they are no different from Arab citizens of Israel and Jordan, and are often members of the same families—being Palestinian is a choice. An Arab who wants to fight against Israel can always become a Palestinian, just like Yasser Arafat, who was born in Egypt and worked in Kuwait. The Palestine Liberation Organization, as its name makes clear, was created for "liberation" of Palestine *as a territory*. The concept of "Palestinians" was then still at its infancy. The PLO was a revolutionary army in the Red Arabs' war against pro-Western regimes in the region, and in the global Cold War between the socialist East and the democratic West. The "Palestinian refugee camps," scattered all over the Arab world, are in fact military camps or terrorist camps. No wonder the kings and emirs were intimidated; their own regimes were as likely as Israel to become a PLO target—Jerusalem was far away from the "refugee camp," while the royal palace was next door. Arafat was off to Moscow again, and no one knew who he would be instructed to target. King of Jordan barely fought off a Palestinian revolt in his country in 1970, and this example was well remembered. During the first Intifada, it was widely feared that it would spread from Israel to Arab countries. At the time, Arafat gloated to Gorbachev:

> *Let us be frank: some Arabs are frightened by the scope of the Intifada. Egypt's President Mubarak, 'in his simplicity', said the Intifada should be urgently stopped, or it will spread to Arab countries. [...] The popular movement in Arab countries is growing as a result of the Intifada on the occupied territories.*[21]

This threat, Arafat boasted, made Saudi Arabia and other Gulf States offer their financial support to the Intifada. Indeed, on this and other occasions, Arab kings duly paid their ransom to comrades, in both petrol dollars and political concessions.

The carefully selected propaganda term "Palestinian people" (as opposed to nation), came to the forefront as a result of Red Arab's failure to capture Israel by direct military force and subsequent decision to concentrate on terrorism, diplomacy, and propaganda. "Palestinians" were a necessary supplement to the PLO, not vice versa. In a sense, "Palestinian people" are still a paramilitary organization. In 1988, the PLO decided that Palestinians living outside of Israel must contribute money for the maintenance of Palestinians fighting in the Intifada: each three families living abroad were to maintain one family in Israel. As Arafat told Gorbachev, this worked.

In the same conversation, Arafat confided:

> *There are 250,000 Palestinians living in the US. 8,000 of them are university lecturers.*
>
> *Palestinians are highly educated people. Our level of education is higher than the Israelis'.*[22]

May I be so bold as to suggest: the high proportion of American university lecturers among the long-suffering Palestinian people is a factor which needs much more attention from analysts of the Middle East. It may explain a lot.

Under the Soviet and Arab pressure, the PLO was internationally recognized as the "sole legitimate representative of the Palestinian people" (imagine al-Qaeda being recognized today as the sole legitimate representative of the world's Muslims). The UN condemned Zionism as a form of racism, which inevitably implied that Israel should have never existed in the first place. Other UN resolutions demanded the reduction of Israel to its pre-1967 borders, the establishment of a Palestinian state under PLO control, and the right of all "Palestinian refugees" (armed, trained, and organized as they were) to come and settle in Israel. Taken together, the UN resolutions on the Arab-Israeli conflict amounted to the roadmap to destruction of Israel. At the very least, if all UN resolutions were implemented, the Red Arabs would have gained a decisive advantage over Israel and could easily finish it off.

That allowed the Soviet Union and its allies to wrap their demands in an ostensibly civilized form; all they wanted was peaceful settlement of Arab-Israeli conflict based on UN resolutions. In the Soviet scenario, that "peaceful settlement," along with proper solutions of other Middle East problems, would be imposed by an international conference under UN auspices, without any right of veto for Israel (something along the lines of the 1938 Munich Conference, which re-drew the border between Czechoslovakia and Nazi Germany). In the periods of East-West détente, Western leaders and diplomats were increasingly tempted to accept the idea of such a conference.

It happened again in the 1970s, after Brezhnev and Kissinger together resolved the Yom-Kippur War so amicably. A decade later, the Soviet leader took an opportunity to reproach ex-President Carter:

M. S. GORBACHEV. *As we recall the time of your Presidency, we are far from saying that everything was negative there. No, there were some positive things. [...] Important agreements in such areas as [...] convening an International Conference on Middle East in 1977 were, so to speak, close at hand. Unfortunately, however, when this matter was almost decided, President Carter chose to push the Soviet Union aside of this process and take the course of separate deals. Nothing good, however, came out of it. [...]*

J. CARTER. *Yes, I agree with you. Indeed, there was development towards convening a Middle East conference in 1977, and we worked with the Soviet Union on that quite harmoniously. I remember, on my birthday in 1977 we had practically prepared a statement on the Middle East conference which would be co-chaired by our two countries.*[23]

That was, in fact, the spectacular turning point in the history of the Cold War in the Middle East. When the final capitulation of the West seemed imminent, Egypt suddenly defected from the socialist camp and aligned itself with the West. On November 20, 1977, President Sadat arrived in Jerusalem and began official negotiations on peace with Israel. It was that very comrade Sadat who initiated the Yom-Kippur War three years before, extracted an approval of his plan from a reluctant Moscow, and was rescued by a Soviet nuclear missiles transport. Now, however, his break with the comrades was made final, and the countdown to assassination began. Next month, the leaders of Syrian intelligence and of the Popular Front for Liberation of Palestine began working on the operation, with Moscow's knowledge and at least tacit approval.[24]

The defection of Sadat was only the first of many difficulties that the Soviets faced in the Middle East in late 1970s. That was the beginning of the global crisis of socialism, and the Middle East was no exception. With growing dismay, Moscow watched its revolutions get out of control, its invasions thwarted, and the whole Red-Arab "empire" crumbling.

Chapter 3:
Comrades and Ayatollahs

...The movement continues in the right direction: the resistance to imperialist forces. Very important roles belong to Syria and even to Iran. In this sense, Iran is our ally, even though we are very different.

Mikhail Gorbachev to Hafez Assad,
28 April 1990

S adat's defection to the West left the leadership of the Red Arabs vacant. His heritage was claimed by both Syria and Iraq, which also reflected two alternative strategies of the regional Cold War. Syrians, if they won, would continue targeting Israel. Iraq would target the Gulf.

At that point, the President of Iraq was Ahmad Hassan al-Bakr, an elderly hero of the revolution. However, almost all the real power was already concentrated in the hands of his young deputy, Saddam Hussein.

Both Assad and Saddam urgently rushed to Moscow to ask for weapons and blessings. Below is a diarist's account of the Politburo meeting that followed:

[DEFENSE MINISTER] Ustinov agreed that, in general, Iraqis were not as insolent as the Syrians. But then he told about the details, which was very revealing.

'Give us your newest T-72 tanks,' they'd say, 'not just a few ones, but 500! We don't need old ones, you see. And give us the missile like the American Pershing' (that is, 800 km range, ground to ground).

'We don't have any such missile,' Ustinov told Saddam, 'except the nuke.'

'So you have it,' the Iraqis replied. 'We can adopt it for the conventional warhead ourselves.'

And so we would wrangle on and on, Ustinov said.

'Give us your newest 8-inch howitzer.' (And how do they know about it? - Ustinov wondered.)

'We don't have any such howitzer,' I said.

'Yes you have.'

And so on.

Ustinov's story caused indignation. There were voices saying we should be tougher than that with them.

However, [Foreign Minister] Gromyko and [KGB Chief] Andropov said we should bear in mind that if we refuse to give them anything, they would break with us, especially the Syrians. And they really would not take the old stuff.

Brezhnev then noticed: we should give them something, but we must emphasize 'it is not for any aggression'. I said that to Saddam, he added.[25]

By the end of 1978, rivals Bakr and Assad reached a compromise on the leadership issue: Iraq and Syria would unite in a single Baathist state, with Bakr as President, Assad as number two, and Saddam as number three. That solution, apparently approved by Moscow, was good for Bakr (Assad would be a check to Saddam's lust for power), good for Assad (who would rise above Saddam, Bakr counting for little), and very bad for Saddam.

Therefore, one day in 1979, Saddam and several other tough comrades entered Bakr's office for a serious conversation. They were very concerned about Comrade President's state of health. He really seemed to be overworked; it was time to retire, take care of himself, and let others take care of the country. Bakr tried to argue, but comrades were adamant: your health, Comrade President, must come first. The arguments were strengthened with pointed guns and shots fired into the ceiling.

On July 17, Saddam was sworn in as new president. Five days later, a thousand or so of the best sons of Iraq gathered in Baghdad for the Baath Party Conference. Saddam was sitting modestly on the far end of the platform, smoking a huge Cuban cigar and listening to the speech of the new Vice President. Comrade Ramadan seemed very depressed, and then explained why: there were traitors in the Baathist ranks, "A painful and atrocious plot" had been discovered, some very prominent comrades were involved, and all of them were now in this audience.

Then the floor was given to Prisoner Muhie Abdul Hussein Mashhadi who, until two weeks ago, had been the General Secretary of the Revolutionary Command Council. Now, after two weeks of torture, he gave a classical confession in the style of communist show trials. He told how, since 1975, he had been a part of a Syrian plot to take over Iraq, personally masterminded by President Assad. The conspirators successfully hoodwinked President Bakr, but as soon as Saddam took over, they knew all was lost.

When Mashhadi finished, Saddam resumed the floor to express how depressed he was to be among treachery:

After the arrest of the criminals, I visited them in an attempt to understand the motive for their behavior. 'What political differences are there between you and me?' I asked, 'did you lack any power or money? If you had a different opinion, why did you not submit it to the Party, since you are its leaders?' They had nothing to say to defend themselves, so they just admitted their guilt.

The people whose names I am going to read out should repeat the Party motto and leave the hall.

With these words, Saddam produced the list of 66 names. As he called each name, each person declared, "One Arab nation with a holy message: unity, liberation, and socialism!" Then they left one by one, each accompanied by some young, square-built, well-armed comrades who emerged as if from nowhere.

As the ritual proceeded, something new was arising in the hearts of surviving delegates—a passionate feeling of love and loyalty to Saddam Hussein. Repeatedly, they jumped to their feet and chanted, "Long live Saddam! Long live Saddam!" Some of them sobbed. Saddam himself wiped tears with one hand while holding his cigar with the other.

When the hall was free from the enemies, Saddam invited comrades to start a discussion. Comrades said what they witnessed today was certainly not enough. There were more traitors among them, and it was necessary to expose and kill them as soon as possible. Then Saddam invited everyone to volunteer for the firing squads so there would be a "democratic execution" of the traitors. Later, each party cell across the country was obliged to send an armed delegate for the "democratic execution." Thus began the purge to cleanse the Iraqi leadership from anyone directly, indirectly, actually, or potentially linked with the fraternal Baathist regime in Syria.

Saddam's coup was probably the last straw that persuaded Moscow to award the vacant mantle of socialist Saladin to Assad. Moscow did not approve of unauthorized coups.

Enter Ayatollahs

To complicate matters, a new force rapidly gained ground in the region in that period, to rival both Reds and Whites: radical Islamic Fundamentalism. The Iranian Revolution, so carefully prepared for many years, suddenly went out of control, hijacked by Shiite fanatics.

The 1979 revolution in Iran had a long pre-history. After the Second World War, Soviet forces withdrew from Iran under Western pressure, but left behind a bigger espionage network than anywhere in the world: nearly forty KGB residencies (stations) and sub-residencies. The standard ratio is one per country. For the next thirty-three years, all of them worked against the Shah, with the emphasis on active (subversive) measures. Since late 1960s, the network was reinforced even further; the KGB began training numerous illegals from the Soviet republics of Azerbaijan, Kazakhstan, and Kyrgyzstan "who could pass as members of one of Iran's ethnic groups and help in setting up illegal residencies on Iranian territory."

Of the numerous attempts on Shah's life, at least one was organized by the KGB and another one by the Iranian Communist Party (Tudeh). Simultaneously, the KGB ran more or less successful disinformation campaigns to persuade the Shah that the US and Britain were plotting against him, and to discredit the more pro-Western figures in his entourage.[26]

In the KGB Tehran residency, the man in charge of the secret army of illegal agents as well as financing the Tudeh Party was Major Vladimir Kuzichkin, working under the cover out of the Soviet embassy.

In July 1978, KGB Chief Yuri Andropov summoned his Tehran

Resident, or KGB station chief, Ivan Fadeykin, to Moscow, and personally instructed him "to step up active measures designed to destabilize the Shah's regime and to damage its relations with the United States and its allies." Simultaneously, the banned Communist Party of Iran resumed its operations through various proxies and "fronts."[27]

In September, as the protests in Iran were steadily elevating into riots, British Prime Minister James Callaghan told his Cabinet:

We must continue to support the Shah against the mad mullahs and the Soviet agents who are opposing him.

His left wing Energy Secretary Tony Benn commented in his diary:

The American and British establishments are fully behind the Shah at this moment: the primary reason is defense—to keep the Russians out of Iran. [28]

There was hardly any doubt in British government that the whole revolution was Soviet-sponsored and socialist; the mad mullahs were seen as ordinary fellow travellers. The Soviets had always used all sorts of "useful idiots," to recall Lenin's term, to organize revolutions for them.

The British were right. The whole dynamics of the revolution was calculated in Moscow well in advance. The mad mullahs were to clear the communists' road to power and then perish in one of the first revolutionary purges. Any other scenario would be a miracle—and neither communists nor mad mullahs believe in miracles.

However, the world of cloaks and daggers has its own extraordinary twists.

Something Callaghan did not tell his Cabinet was that Vladimir Kuzichkin, the most important KGB spymaster in Tehran, was secretly working for the MI6. Full information about the KGB's illegal network in Iran, full information about the underground Communist Party, all the threads were in his hands—and were leaked to the British.

The British then shared it with SAVAK, the Shah's secret police, but by then it was too late to stop the revolution. The SAVAK was quickly thereafter dissolved and the mad mullahs captured its records.

The formidable Soviet fifth column in Iran, carefully constructed for decades, was lost overnight. With Kuzichkin's intelligence, the Guardians of the Islamic Revolution easily rounded up them all.

In a surprise twist of history, the roles changed. Iranian communists became martyrs, which they never wanted to be, and Ayatollahs lost the paradise they aspired. Instead, their ironic destiny was to do the job meant for their victims: govern Iran and export the revolution.

The Ayatollahs killed the Reds and the Whites with equal zeal. They were newcomers, unexpected either in Moscow or Western capitals. They were something that could jeopardize the most excellent plan for a war: a rapidly emerging third force.

Now the comrades faced another strategic choice: either a war on Islamists or a tactical alliance against the West. Saddam chose war; Assad, backed by Moscow, chose a tactical alliance:

> **M. S. GORBACHEV.** *[…] We appreciate your approach to Iran, which combines consistency with flexibility, and our coordination with Syria on this issue. We should be cautious with Iran, we should manoeuvre. We want good and friendly relations with Iran. Our fundamental interests coincide with theirs.*
>
> *Americans say that Islamic Fundamentalists should be removed. We say this is an internal matter for the Iranians.*
>
> *We are also concerned that they might shift towards America: there are different trends in Iran. We shall handle this in a cold-blooded, balanced way. We shall also show firmness from time to time. […]*
>
> **H. ASSAD.** *[…] When [the Americans] talk about Iran, they use the terms 'moderates' and 'extremists'. Those whom they call 'moderates' are linked with the US.*
>
> **M. S. GORBACHEV.** *Certainly.*
>
> **H. ASSAD.** *'Extremists' in Iran are against America.*
>
> *I have a friend, one Iranian politician. He is very sympathetic to Syria, but his views are pro-Western. He hates the clerics and says he will do anything to remove them. However, even he openly admits that the [only] revolutionaries in Iran are the Sheiks.*

M. S. GORBACHEV. *Yes; and the reforms they have carried out are anti-imperialist in nature.*

H. ASSAD. *Not only are their reforms anti-imperialist, they also educate the people in the anti-imperialist spirit. [...]*

We do not question the anti-American, anti-imperialist nature of the Iranian regime. I am talking about the regime, not about individual people or forces in that country.

The Iran-Iraq war is a very painful factor which causes serious problems. But all responsibility for it rests with Saddam Hussein. I have said so both to the Soviet comrades and to Saddam himself during a summit conference of Arab states in Amman. [...] He was prepared to improve relations with us on one condition: we had to make a statement condemning Iran.

That would mean pushing Iran towards rapprochement with the US and Israel. That certainly would be against the interests of the progressive forces. The fanatical nationalists in Iran would use this to say that all Arabs are against them, even though Iran supports Palestinians, supports Arabs against Israel; so it is better to cooperate with Tel Aviv. That would be against the Soviet interests, too.

M. S. GORBACHEV. *You were right [to reject Saddam's demand...]*

H. ASSAD. *I offered Saddam to make a treaty obliging Syria to support Iraq with all her forces, and vice versa. If we were talking about a union between the two countries before, now I offered to work on political cooperation. If Iran sees that Iraq and Syria have a single position, that we can do much against America and Israel, this would cause positive response in Iran.*

Saddam refused. The only thing he wants is for Syria to take an anti-Iranian stance.

The decision on Iraq's war with Iran is an American decision. The decision to break relations with Syria is also American.

Saddam and I had a secret meeting in Amman. Of course, such a meeting should have taken place in Moscow, and that was what we proposed. But he refused, on security grounds. I think that was just an excuse and the real reason is different.

Our first conversation in Amman airport took 14 hours. Saddam wanted just one thing: our condemnation of Iran. He did not want to talk about anything else, neither about political cooperation nor about economic one.

We have no fear that Iran may swallow Iraq. Iranians don't want that. All they want is the head of Saddam Hussein, because the Iranian nation cannot co-exist with Saddam.[29]

The lesser evil

The loss of Egypt was no coincidence. As we remember, Sadat had been flirting with the West ever since his defeat in the Yom-Kippur War. To a high extent, that was a personal triumph of Henry Kissinger, who (with some modest contribution from Comrade Brezhnev) practically saved Sadat's regime by stopping the war just before the Israeli tanks reached Cairo. Kissinger spent the next few years grooming Sadat and secretly brokering his peace deal with Israel. Therefore, even though the actual peace treaty was made without Kissinger - it was a different Administration by then - it was seen as very much a result of his efforts, and even more so a triumph of his ideas.

Kissinger's strategy for the Cold War survived in the State Department long after Kissinger himself was gone. The idea was simple enough: play on internal divisions in the socialist camp and drag peripheral socialist dictators away from the Soviet sphere of influence. After all, in economic terms, the West could offer them much more than the East, so they would get addicted to Western aid. He tried that even on communist China, since it was quite hostile to the Soviets. The same strategy was adopted for Eastern Europe and the Red Arabs.

Later on, we shall see how Kissinger's theory turned out to be a monumental mistake. In case of Egypt, however, it led to a spectacular success. As an Israeli radio reporter gasped over the air, "President Sadat is now inspecting a guard of honor of the Israeli Defense Force. I'm seeing it, but I don't believe it!" What followed was a grand show played in Jerusalem, Camp David (where Sadat and Begin signed the peace treaty), and Oslo (where they got their Nobel Peace prize). The final act was the equally spectacular assassination of Sadat during a military parade in Cairo. The assassination was organized by the Egyptian Islamic Jihad who, by pure coincidence, unwittingly fulfilled a secret plan of Syrian KGB.

Nevertheless, Egypt was now on the Western side, or so it seemed, and the question of who should be next arose in Washington. At the time, Iraq seemed a natural choice. Saddam come out second best after the fight for Egyptian succession. Saddam certainly thought that Moscow was not giving him enough. Saddam defiantly condemned the Soviet invasion of Afghanistan in December 1979. Saddam hung a lot of communists those days. He suspected they were plotting to overthrow him, and might have been right in his suspicions. Saddam was an enemy of Syria and, even more importantly, an enemy of Iran.

Although the rumor persists, there is no evidence that Saddam decided to invade Iran in 1980 under American influence. However, his initiative soon won broad Western support, including America. In 1982, the State Department removed Iraq from its list of countries suspected of aiding international terrorism, opening the way for American aid to Baghdad. That was a rather bold move, bearing in mind that Saddam, like any respectable Arab dictator, ran his own international terrorist network under the leadership of notorious Abu Nidal, who organized a number of terrorist attacks in those very months. Every new attack provoked rumors that the removal of Iraq from the blacklist was a bit premature. Finally, in 1983, the United States confidentially asked Saddam to get rid of Abu Nidal. Saddam said OK, and a few weeks later, Iraqi press solemnly announced that Comrade Abu Nidal had tragically died of a heart attack. His noble heart could no longer sustain the hardship of the struggle for the liberation of humankind. Celebrations in Washington went on for half a year, until Abu Nidal suddenly re-emerged, alive and well, in Libya.

On examination, the elegant Kissingerian geopolitical strategy had many flaws. For example, Kissinger and others thoroughly discussed his "genius" in the media, so every reader of *Foreign Affairs* knew every detail of his grand design. Saddam, Caeusescu, and their patrons in the Kremlin were fully aware that the State Department was giving out money and weapons to such comrades who openly and loudly quarreled between themselves. The advantages of this system were instantly appreciated. Before long, the socialist world was boiling and bubbling with spectacular feuds, while the State Department paid generously for the performance. When the dust settled, it became apparent that a performance was all it ever was.

This is an old socialist "lesser evil" game. Stalin and Hitler, in their own time, both realized they would gain much more from being mortal enemies than they could ever gain from being friends. Half of the world, out of the very best motives, supported Hitler against Stalin; the other half likewise supported Stalin against Hitler. Therefore, they defended Europe from each other, and liberated it from each other, with the massive support from genuine democrats in the West. Their mutual enmity was partly real and partly artificial, but they both were careful to ensure that the common enemy would not benefit from it at any rate.

Tricks of this kind always remained in the socialists' arsenals, but two latter-day dictators were especially enthusiastic about them: Caeusescu in Europe and Saddam in the Middle East. Saddam idolized Stalin, and liked to think of himself as his Iraqi incarnation, a street-wise gangster who joined the revolution and fought his way to the top, ruthlessly pushing aside all those windbags and intellectuals. He filled his palaces with Stalinist memorabilia and often quoted Stalin's charming maxims like "no man–no problem," and once arranged with the KGB for a secret pilgrimage to several of Stalin's villas on the Black Sea coast. This Stalinist obsession often dominated his decisions; the exposure of a "Syrian conspiracy" at the party conference with the subsequent "democratic execution" was undoubtedly a deliberate imitation of a Stalinist purge.

Saddam also tried to imitate Stalin in foreign policy, and saw himself as an expert on the "lesser evil" game with the West. In this respect, he could calculate his moves and Western reactions very precisely, at least so he believed.

In 1978, he uttered an amazing prophesy about his own downfall. As the Syrians were pushing for Baathist unity, and for sharing oil revenues fraternally, Saddam allegedly told one mediator:

> *Iraq must not get closer to Syria because, if it did, one of the two regimes would inevitably fall. The imperialists would overturn it.*[30]

There were myriad factors that made "the imperialists" spare both regimes for the next quarter of a century, only to depose Saddam—but not Assad—in 2003. How did Saddam know that only one of their regimes would fall, but not both?

There is, of course, a huge element of coincidence in that, but there is certain logic, too. True to the dubious rule that "the enemy of my enemy is my friend," the West confronted Syria but supported Iraq. After Saddam's invasion of Kuwait, the scales turned and he became the greater evil, so the West now confronted Iraq and supported Syria. Either way, the "lesser evil" regime would have sufficient influence within the alliance to restrain the imperialists from doing their worst. However, once both evils were in bed with each other, the game was over. Whoever was considered the greater evil at that point would be doomed.

In a similar game, Saddam started his war with Iran, making the Ayatollah his own little Hitler. Just as Stalin "liberated" half of Europe to defend it against Nazis, Saddam would "liberate" the Gulf to defend it against Islamists. This way, he hoped to avoid a serious confrontation with the West. The West would go along with anything he does if he is seen as "the lesser evil."

Totalitarian leaders may play such games quite successfully because it is simply unthinkable for democratic policy-makers that one can start a terrible war and sacrifice many thousands of lives just to win sympathies in the world. All their instincts tell them that one may resort to war only if driven into a corner, and only to achieve some specific, limited objectives.

In reality, war for the sake of war, and confrontation for the sake of confrontation, is quite natural to those who see themselves as revolutionaries. As Lenin used to say, quoting Napoleon, "it is important to engage in the fight, and then we'll see." War means polarization, divides the world between "them" and "us," and mobilizes widespread support from numerous enemies of your enemies. Saddam disturbingly and vividly dreamt of long and dramatic conflicts that would impress crowds and give him an aura of a heroic warrior:

> *We envision a war... that goes on for many months, not days and weeks [...and] widespread cheering from the masses that will accompany each step we take forward from every corner of the Arab world. This is more important than the metres and kilometres we gain. [...] Each meter of land [would be] bleeding with rivers of blood; we have no vision for a war that is any less than this. [...]*
>
> *What is required is a patient war, one where we fight for twelve continuous months and after twelve months we take stock and figure out how much we have lost and how much has been gained; and plan for*

losses amounting to thousands, thousands [...] fifty thousand martyrs and injured [in one year].[31]

In this particular case, Saddam pictured a future war against Israel and the West. However, that also reflected his general idea of a sensible war, and his war against Iran was exactly like that.

The problem was that Saddam knew nothing about military strategy. In his youth, he failed his entry exams in the Royal Military College of Iraq; that was why he became a professional revolutionary in the first place. After coming to power, Saddam made himself a field marshal, but that did not add anything to his knowledge. He certainly could not entrust the command of war to any real military; he himself had to be the victorious Arab Commander-in-Chief, riding a white horse. On the other hand, a real field marshal would not know much about the specifics of a revolutionary war, nor would he plan military operations aimed at producing "rivers of blood" to impress the masses—Royal Military College never taught that.

Saddam started a war for the liberation of newly founded Arab lands from the Persian yoke. After some thorough ethnographic analysis, Iran's Khuzestan Province, the oil-rich region along the Gulf coast, was renamed Arabistan and declared to be an integral part of the Arab motherland.

The Iraqi army of 1980 was definitely not strong enough for a military victory over Iran. Moreover, an invasion of Iran practically guaranteed an opening a second front, considering Saddam's regime had already been engaged in a prolonged internal conflict with Iraqis who wanted no socialism. The attack on Iran was planned as a "full-scale invasion," but only six out of twelve Iraqi divisions formed the invading force.[32] While half of the army fought Iranians, the other half had to stay home and contain the Iraqis. It is of little wonder that, after the initial advance into Iran, the invasion was soon fought off, and the frontline was pushed into Iraqi territory. The conflict then transformed into trench warfare in the style of World War I, with rivers of blood but no territorial gains for either side.

Saddam and his regime would have never survived that war if not for the massive support from the United States and its allies, the Soviet Union and its allies, all Arab monarchs, and many Arab revolutionaries.

The chain of Saddam's defeats in battle went almost uninterrupted. When he began war with Iran, he had about 2700 tanks, 332 fighter aircraft, 40 helicopters, and 1000 units of artillery. By 1987, Saddam had about 4500 tanks, over 500 fighter aircraft, about 150 helicopters, and over 4000 units of artillery.[33] Supporters provided Saddam with chemical and biological weapons, enabling him to build the fourth-strongest army in the world (the first three were the superpowers: US, USSR, and China). The war consolidated his regime; contrary to the opinion of Ayatollah Khomeini and some Western analysts, most Iraqi Shiites found the idea of an Islamic Republic of Iraq even less attractive than Saddam's regime. Most importantly, Iraq's international isolation gave way to widespread international support.

It is not that the West was so charmed by Saddam, but even in those times, radical Islam was perceived as a greater threat than radical Socialism. Therefore, Saddam successfully became "the lesser evil." This sentiment was best expressed in a famous comment by Henry Kissinger: "What a pity both sides can't lose." Assessing the policy of Kissinger's followers in retrospect, we must conclude that they ensured that neither side would lose. Both Iran and Iraq emerged from the war much stronger than they were before it. From two petty dictatorships on the edge of the world, the State Department created two powerful enemies for the West. It took almost two decades to destroy one of them, and we still dare not counter the other.

Ayatollah Gorbachev?

In a sense, the Iran-Iraq war ended just like nearly all Red-Arab invasions before it. The Red Arabs were beaten, but then rescued by the united efforts of the State Department, Kremlin, United Nations, and the rest of this metaphysical entity known in some Masonic lodges under the solemn and conspiratorial name of the "international community." An Iranian victory would have been a disaster for everyone, and few really believed that the establishment of an Islamic Republic of Iraq would be the end of the Ayatollahs' conquests. Everybody was terrified by the idea of the Gulf under Iran's control.

The Soviets, for their part, began to fear fundamentalist Islam as an ideological rival in the Middle East. In 1986-1987, new instructions were issued to Syrian comrades: Do not go too far in your romance with Iran, and try to come to terms with Saddam. Gorbachev told the Syrian foreign minister:

> *Everything is not so simple with the Iran-Iraq conflict...In Tehran, they follow clerical reactionary ideas which are no good for the Arabs. Iranian leaders are trying to spread those ideas, even in Soviet Central Asia. They pursue the same Shiite course in Lebanon, as you probably know only too well.*[34]

Gorbachev stressed the same point in his subsequent talks with the Syrian dictator. As he then reported to the Politburo, Assad was somewhat taken aback by this sharp turn:

> *GORBACHEV. [...] We restrained Assad a bit. He was particularly amazed by our position towards Iran. He insisted Iran does not want an inch of Iraq's territory. I expressed doubt. Then he said that if we take measures against Iran, he, Assad, is not going to stand up for them.*[35]

In a memo to Gorbachev dated 8 August 1987, Anatoly Chernyaev suggested Assad could be valuable to advance the Soviet influence in 'Iran after Khomeini' (it is not clear whether he meant Khomeini's natural death or a removal of his regime):

> *Of course, Assad is playing his own game with us, although he believes he is right. The reason we need him now is not even the Middle East [...] but Iran after Khomeini (the Syrians have strongly penetrated the various strata of the Iranian society).*[36]

As for Iran's subversion of Soviet Central Asia, that was, of course, a wild fantasy. The advance to Lebanon was more real. However, Moscow was not worried about the Iranian threat as much as the West's response. They did not like the picture of US military ships protecting the Persian Gulf. At his meetings with US State Secretary Schulz, Gorbachev would insist on reducing the American presence in the Gulf and leaving the whole problem to the UN.[37] To the UN Secretary General, in turn, he complained that Schulz and the US Administration in general secretly intended to use their warships to defend the Gulf against the Soviet threat, not just Iran.[38]

In a way, these last stages of the Iran-Iraq war, with Iran becoming a grave threat to the Gulf, were a rehearsal of Kuwait crisis a few years later. The West showed that it was prepared to defend the Gulf by force, so the Soviets urgently eliminated the problem before it backfired. Moscow mobilized all forces, from the Red Arabs like Assad or Arafat (in April 1988, Arafat told Gorbachev: "I mediate in the Iran-Iraq conflict more than anybody else"[39]) to the UN Secretary-General and Security Council. In the documents of this period, we also note the vague dreams about the UN solving the crisis, scoring many points of authority, and thus moving forward along the road towards a world government—a theme that would become very prominent in the next Gulf crisis.

The West had hoped the two sides would paralyze each other, but the war only made things worse. Now the peace made things worse still. Not only were both Iran and Iraq well-armed, but also their hands were now untied. Furthermore, the peace opened the way for closer and easier collaboration between Socialism and Islamism in their struggle against the Western world.

In the final months of the war and the first months of peace, Soviets persistently sought secret contact with Tehran through Assad and Arafat. In response, Imam Khomeini suddenly made a wide gesture, without worrying much about secrecy. In early January 1989, he sent one Ayatollah to Gorbachev to deliver a personal, handwritten epistle—an honor never afforded to any other foreign leader. The text, alas, is still unknown to historians, but the whole Politburo is on record laughing their heads off when reading it.[40] The contents of the message can be easily deduced from the transcripts of the Politburo discussion[41] and of Gorbachev's meeting with Khomeini's envoy, Ayatollah Abdullah Javadi Amoli, on January 4, 1989. Khomeini learned from the Western press that Gorbachev was a great reformer, so he suggested that Gorbachev should forget Marxism and convert to Islam.

> **GORBACHEV** (*laughed at length before speaking*): *He suggested I should destroy communism!...*[42]

This was hardly much sillier than the attitude of most Western opinion-makers, who hoped that Gorbachev would miraculously transform from a communist to a democrat.

When talking to Khomeini's messenger, Gorbachev politely declined to convert to Islam, and then reminded he was the leader, not a destroyer, of the Soviet Union and its Communist Party:

I am not going to try and persuade Imam to join the Communist Party [...]

I must disappoint Imam: my associates and I see our goal as fully restoring the values of Socialism, the Marxist doctrine. That doctrine has absorbed all the best achievements of human thought.[43]

After that discussion, Islam and Marxism were put aside, and the discussion focused on the more practical matter of joint struggle against the American Satan. "Without diplomatic niceties," as Gorbachev said, he told Ayatollahs how Americans and Pakistanis were undermining the well-known Soviet efforts to achieve peace in Afghanistan[44], and hinted that, détente and disarmament notwithstanding, he disbelieved all the US assurances of friendship. This he contrasted with the sincerity of the Soviet-Iranian relations.[45] Soon, Comrades and Ayatollahs would note they were in complete agreement, not only about the situation in the Middle East, but also about South Africa, Latin America, East-West disarmament, and especially about "turning the Indian Ocean into a peace zone," which meant ousting the Americans. Soviet-Iranian joint committees working on these issues mushroomed in 1989[46], while Foreign Ministers Shevardnadze and Velayati had four meeting in six months.[47]

Gorbachev sided with the Ayatollahs in their fatwa to kill British writer Salman Rushdie for his book *Satanic Verses*, which caused the break-up of diplomatic relations between Iran and Britain:

M. S. GORBACHEV. *[...] We share the Muslims' feelings of outrage with this publication. We also believe that some solution of the situation should be found, and the West is beginning to understand this.*

E. A. SHEVARDNADZE. *Many Western countries are already returning their ambassadors to Tehran.*[48]

Discussing the issue with Gorbachev a few days later, Margaret Thatcher commented, "The book is impossible to read, but why incite a murder of its author?"[49]

Khomeini, apparently, was disappointed by Gorbachev's reluctance to have a proper philosophical debate about Islam, so Gorbachev promised to have it at a personal meeting[50]—one that never happened.

Then the discussion topic rapidly moved from heavens to earth, and soon reached the question of weapons:

Politburo, 3 March 1989

Military supplies to Iran

GORBACHEV: *We should talk to Czechs and Hungarians, tell them: Tehran has been knocking at the USSR's doors about this for quite a long while, so, how about organising this through you?*

We need this because this supports our military industry, provides hard currency, and creates military links which guarantee the general relations.

KATUSHEV: *And for many years, too.*[51]

The same month, Gorbachev confirmed to the Iranian Foreign Minister that Moscow was "interested in greater economic cooperation in various fields, including the military one, which the Iranian side shows interest in developing."[52]

Khomeini's death in June 1989, if anything, only accelerated the development of Soviet-Iranian alliance. In the same month, a large Iranian delegation, led by powerful Ayatollah Rafsanjani, then the acting Commander-in-Chief of Iranian armed forces and the future President of Iran, made a pre-arranged visit to Moscow. After the first day of talks, Gorbachev enthusiastically remarked that the visit, "acquired a much broader character than it was originally planned." Rafsanjani replied, "I have only spent 24 hours in the Soviet Union, but I already feel almost at home."

Wide-ranging negotiations were held at all levels during the visit, including detailed talks on military cooperation between the appropriate specialists. The possibility of Soviet involvement in the Iranian nuclear program was also discussed from the outset:

A.A. HASHEMI RAFSANJANI. *[...] Nuclear energy is very important to Iran. Under the old regime, there were plans for construction of 20 nuclear power plants, involving Western companies. After the revolution in Iran all the contracts, with just two exceptions, were cancelled. The West German firms have now completed 80 per cent of work. But in this area,* *we give preference to cooperation with Soviet organisations to construct one nuclear power plant. Please arrange for this issue to be looked into.*

M.S. GORBACHEV. *Fine.*

Nuclear energy was listed as one of fifteen principal areas of cooperation in a long-term agreement signed by Gorbachev and Rafsanjani. Other areas mentioned at negotiations were also mostly military-oriented:

- Space exploration (Rafsanjani even proposed to send his son to the space on a Soviet shuttle, *'as a symbol of Soviet-Iranian friendship'*; Gorbachev thought that was possible and promised to look into it. Sharing Soviet satellite data was also envisaged, ostensibly for exploration of natural resources.)

- Scientific research

- Maritime navigation

- The construction of the Tejen-Mashhad railway, linking the Soviet Union with Bandar-Abbas, the Iranian strategic port on the Straits of Hormuz. The port is the main base of the Iranian navy, conveniently positioned there to threaten the oil supplies from the Gulf. Rafsanjani confirmed Soviet trains would be allowed to reach the utmost South of Iran.

- Construction of the underground in Tehran;

- Metallurgy and other heavy industry (thus, the Soviets agreed to upgrade Isfahan metal plant, tripling its steel production to 4 million tons p.a.);

Overall, joint projects worth $5 billion in total were planned. Iranians were to pay for everything with natural gas supplies (up to 3 million cubic meters p.a.). Another idea was the transit of Iranian gas, up to 2 million cubic meters p.a., through the Soviet territory. A huge apparatus of specialized joint committees were established to make it all work.[53]

Gorbachev and Rafsanjani still remain the darlings of Western public opinion, two rays of light in the dark history of their countries. However, they were the ones who established the alliance between Moscow and Tehran against the West, which continues to the day, stubbornly ignored by the Western policy-makers.

Money in the Nile

The Kissingerian experiment with Egypt also turned out to be less successful than it may have seemed at the time.

After the assassination of Sadat, he was succeeded by his Vice President, Air Chief Marshal Hosni Mubarak, who commanded Egypt's Air Force in the Yom-Kippur War.

Perhaps in protest against the assassination of Sadat, the West readily accepted Mubarak as a trusted ally, kind of Sadat's reincarnation. In those thirty years that Mubarak remained the dictator of Egypt, generation after generation of Western leaders described him as their personal friend, and Egypt as one of the most reliable allies of the West.

The Soviet documents, however, reveal a different Mubarak—a genuine Nasserite whose true loyalty lies with socialism, keen to dissociate himself from his treacherous predecessor. A graduate of a Soviet military academy, Mubarak privately described his continuing relations with the West as a cynical game of extracting loans he had no intention to repay, all the while waiting for a convenient moment to stab the imperialists in the back. "Life is changing," Mubarak told Gorbachev philosophically, "if Nasser was still alive, he would also act differently."[54]

However, he explained, the Egyptian regime still remained as essentially socialist and anti-Western as it was under Nasser:

> **H. MUBARAK.** *[…] Since I came to power, I have been doing my best to return our relations with the Soviet Union to the state of solid and well-developed friendship, once characteristic of these relations. When I became president, the Soviet-Egyptian relations were frozen.*
>
> *[…]*
>
> *I won't conceal it, certain forces tried to veto the development of relations with the USSR. […] After I came to power, the Americans told me they had arranged with Sadat that a military base on Egypt's territory would be given to them. I answered them clearly this was not true. […] Nasser, in his time, eliminated foreign bases on the Egyptian soil. I am not the*

man who would return them back. With all the importance of the US aid for us, I said, if you want to keep good relations with us, stop any talks about the bases.

[…]

We, Egyptians, and Arabs, and Africans, want the Soviet Union to remain a great power and continue to play its role in the world.

M.S. GORBACHEV. *Europeans are of the same mind. Only Americans think differently.*

[…]

H. MUBARAK. *As I said, Arab, African and European countries don't want a decline of the USSR. Is such a case only America would remain in heavens and command everyone as it pleases.*

M. S. GORBACHEV. *[…] Americans are trying […] to tear Eastern Europe away from the USSR and 'attach' the whole region to the West. We are telling our friends in Eastern Europe to be careful. […] At first, they thought they would get a horn of plenty from the West, full of dollars.*

H. MUBARAK. *That is what Sadat thought.*[55]

Mubarak, however, did not mind Western-money-stuffed horns himself. He spoke at length about Egypt's debt-ridden socialist economy. It was some relief that 98 percent of agricultural land was still privately owned. That, Mubarak confided, was because Khrushchev had advised Nasser back in 1964, in strict secrecy, not to create collective farms. Nevertheless, the economy was over-regulated, the black market blossomed, and the only solution Mubarak could find was keeping the regime afloat with Western money:

When I came to power, the economy was in a dreadful state. The infrastructure had practically collapsed. That was the case with roads, railroads, water supply, electric supply, telephone network and so on.

Then Mubarak described how he introduced a five-year plan and everything improved dramatically:

M. S. GORBACHEV. *But where did you get money from? Is it flowing in the Nile?*

H. MUBARAK. We had to borrow a lot. [...] Everyone has debts in today's world. [...] Americans owe money to the Japanese, but Bush does not pay. So what, will Japan declare war to the US? [...] I told Reagan that the Soviet Union had never charged any interest for its loans to us. We no longer borrow money from the US. We only accept non-repayable aid, when they are prepared to give it. [...]

M. S. GORBACHEV. How much is your total debt?

H. MUBARAK. 50 billion dollars. [...] But we can always negotiate on the debts and get postponement of payments again and again. Nowadays, almost nobody repays debts. I'm talking to you absolutely frankly.[56]

At the end of the closed-doors meeting, when, as usual, both sides assured each other that they were determined to develop Soviet-Egyptian cooperation in various fields, Mubarak suddenly said:

I would like to tell you that we continue military cooperation with the USA. They give us $1,3 bn. aid. We still cannot do without it: we need spare parts for military equipment, and so on. But time will come when things turn in different direction. I am telling this to you absolutely frankly.[57]

When the two leaders were joined by their delegations, Gorbachev briefly recounted the golden age of Soviet-Egyptian relations under Nasser, "a different period, which also cannot be crossed out of our history," and concluded:

In this connection, I feel it necessary to give credit personally to President Mubarak for the role he played in restoring all those good things which we once had in our relations.[58]

As for the question of weapons, Gorby and Mubarak returned to it next year:

M. S. GORBACHEV. [...] The need to take measures to limit the arms race in the Middle East is becoming an increasingly prominent issue nowadays. A number if initiatives have been proposed, including by the USA. It is quite clear that we should move in that direction. However, at the same time, there are also legitimate interests of strengthening one's defences. I can say directly that we are prepared to restore an active military cooperation with Egypt, and can instruct our departments to discuss all the related issues, if the Egyptian side has similar wishes.

H. MUBARAK. *Egypt favours a development of our cooperation along these lines. There is cooperation between us concerning the supplies of spare parts, aircraft. I support your proposal. Probably, we would be interested in offers concerning artillery weapons, tanks, and other equipment.[59]*

Gorbachev and Mubarak probably understood each other exceptionally well, because Gorbachev himself was playing exactly the same game on the global scale. He, like Mubarak, had inherited the impossible mission to rescue a bankrupt socialist empire. He had to reform the grossly inefficient and wasteful Soviet economy and make the unworkable work. He had to charm the West, carefully playing on its fears, hopes, academic misconceptions, and official versions, and solicit money and favors in exchange for empty promises. On the top of that, he had a mission to maintain and enlarge his vast and wasteful global empire, to increase its influence in the world, and to work tirelessly on the World Revolution. He had to do everything Mubarak did in the Middle East, only at a much greater scale. In this sense, Mubarak was right to call him "brother-President."[60]

Of course, neither of them could ever make socialism work. Both, however, were extremely successful in fooling the West. The West spent countless billions, and did everything possible, to save the both regimes. With Egypt, it worked - until very recently.

However, nobody could bail out the Soviet Empire—it was simply too big. That reality did not stop Gorbachev from trying until the very end.

Chapter 4:
Gorby the Terrorist

I like Mr. Gorbachev. We can do business together.
Margaret Thatcher, BBC, 17 December 1984

We have never learnt to do anything but socialism.
Mikhail Gorbachev to Hafez Assad, 15 April 1988

The first Western leader who proclaimed Gorbachev to be a democratic reformer was Margaret Thatcher. For some reason, after his visit to Britain in 1984, she imagined it was possible to "do business" with him. Her sensational statement to this effect sparked the global epidemic of "Gorbymania," which determined the Western policy towards the USSR at the critical final stage of the Cold War. In the ensuing collapse of the Soviet Empire, the West stood by Gorbachev up to the very last day of his reign, and did everything possible to save his regime. Fortunately the West was not successful, but their attempt had many disastrous side effects.

Thatcher herself, however, soon realized her enthusiasm was premature. In March 1987, she went to the Kremlin, and as soon as she was alone with Gorbachev behind closed doors, she told him everything she thought about his World Revolution, from Nicaragua to Afghanistan. Among other accusations, she said:

> You supply weapons to Libya, wherefrom they get to Iran. You supply weapons to Syria, who supports terrorism all over the world.[61]

If other Western Gorbymaniacs had taken the trouble to look carefully at the words and deeds of their idol, they too would have noticed one interesting nuance. Gorbachev might have changed Soviet policies in many domestic and foreign areas, but the Middle East was not one of them. Soviet training, financing, and arms supplies to terrorists went on as usual. Baathists, the PLO, and Gaddafi remained the best allies of the USSR in the region while Israel remained the main enemy. The strategic and tactical objectives were the same as under Brezhnev—reduce Israel to its pre-1967 borders and then to nothing, oust the US from the region, and target the oil supplies.

Gorbachev stated this lack of policy change quite emphatically in numerous talks with his Arab allies, much to their pleasure.[62] Page after page, transcript after transcript, he goes on and on about "our common struggle against imperialism and Zionism,"[63] and other "problems we should solve in the Middle East in the interests of Arab people, including the Palestinians."[64] Conversely, at his meetings with US politicians, Gorbachev would swear that, "We are not trying to oust the US from the Middle East."[65]

But at the meetings of his own Politburo, Gorbachev was straightforward about Moscow's goals in the Middle East:

"America is losing positions in this region. We got an opportunity to take advantage of that. And so we did." (April 30, 1987)[66]

"Our objective is to oust America out, at least politically (we just cannot do that economically). The USA has become remarkably active in this region. We must press them harder." (June 11, 1987)[67]

He repeatedly assured the Syrian comrades that, contrary to the "Western propaganda," his reforms would only strengthen Socialism in the USSR and the world.[68] Perestroika would restore and exonerate the discredited socialist ideology, so that "the whole world will be socialist in 50 to 100 years."[69]

When attacked by Thatcher, Gorbachev assured her the Soviet Union had no intention to export socialism, especially not by force. In less than a month, however, he had this conversation with Assad:

M. S. GORBACHEV. *[...] If we successfully implement our plans of social and economic acceleration, the Perestroika, there will be new opportunities to strengthen our relations in various fields - economic, military, ideological, etc.*

H. ASSAD. *[...] Friendship with the Soviet Union is the cornerstone of Syria's policies. [...] Consultations between us help [...] to work out a common approach to our enemies. [...] During my previous visit to the USSR in 1985 you said that imperialists and Zionists would try to use any our mistake to implement their far-reaching plans. [...] Today the imperialist forces, not counting on our mistakes, try to use any pretext in their interests. A proof of this is the campaign of struggle against terrorism, which is unleashed against us in the West. [...]*

M. S. GORBACHEV. *We had a detailed discussion of these issues, including Britain's position on the US actions against Libya and the campaign against Syria waged by London, during the talks with British Prime Minister M. Thatcher. We told the British to think thoroughly about their behavior.*

Unfortunately, the USA don't want to abandon the role of global gendarme, and their British allies don't want to abandon their imperial manners. If a bomb explodes anywhere, Americans and Englishmen immediately send ships, marines, and aircraft there. This is exactly the policy of state terrorism.

Mrs. Thatcher tried to persuade us that Britain has hard evidence of Syria's complicity in terrorist attacks. But we know that Syrians have nothing to do with that. [...] I told the Prime Minister directly: [...] the British Empire is no more, it has exploded like a soap bubble, and you are still possessed by imperial ambitions.

Here it is worth noting that the transcripts of the Gorbachev-Thatcher talks in March 1987 contain no denial by Gorbachev that Syria was involved in terrorism, nor his mentioning the British Empire.

The problem with the politicians of the West [Gorbachev continued] is that they don't want to see the changes in the world and the urgency of problems facing the humankind. They want to undertake a social revenge and restore the positions they've lost. They are not concerned with the questions of peace, development, resolution of conflicts. [...] Any concessions can be dragged out of imperialists only by united efforts of all the states, by pressure of broad people's masses. [...]

H. ASSAD. *[...] The character of the terrorist attack in London attributed to Syria shows that the US and Britain are behind it. Syria was by no* *means interested in such an action. What happened in London was not in our interest and contradicted our methods. If we wanted to organize such a terrorist attack, we would have employed the method of guerrilla warfare used by Palestinians in Israel. This is to say, the man who executed the attack would not surrender to the British, but commit suicide [...] We told King Hussein [of Jordan], an old friend of Britain, that London must understand this: the times of the empire have gone and they cannot operate on the basis of the old ideas.*

M. S. GORBACHEV. *You expressed yourself in the same spirit as we did during the negotiations with Thatcher, even though we had no prior agreement about this.*

H. ASSAD. *This is a perfect illustration of how similar our views are.*

If the English seriously want to tackle terrorism, they should look at Israel. Israeli secret services are responsible for the terrorist attacks that occurred in Britain in recent years. [...]

M. S. GORBACHEV. *The West has attacked Libya, and then Syria, i.e. the two countries which are most consistent in their opposition to the imperialist dictate. Gaddafi is our friend, we support him, even though there are frequent zigzags in his policies. However, the most important thing is Libya's and Syria's irreconcilable attitude to American imperialism...*[70]

Gaddafi and World Revolution

In fact, that imperialist attack on Libya is a story worth explaining.

It all began when Libyan agents in Germany reported to Comrade Gaddafi that the American servicemen frequented a particular disco in West Berlin. Without much hesitation, Comrade Gaddafi ordered it to be blown up. That order was executed on the night April 5, 1986. Two US sergeants and one Turkish lady were killed, and another 230 people were injured, over 50 of them being American servicemen. Gaddafi sent his congratulations for a successful operation by telex. The message was intercepted by Americans, and that was not the first time this terrorist leader was caught with a smoking gun.

This time, however, President Reagan decided enough was enough. The United States retaliated with a bombing raid on Libya. Gaddafi himself survived, only thanks to the treachery of Italian Prime Minister Bettino Craxi, who secretly warned him of the forthcoming attack and its exact date.[71]

Publicly and diplomatically, Gorbachev expressed solidarity with Libya, vociferously condemned the "U.S. imperialist aggression" and all those who failed to condemn it as well. He cancelled his Foreign Minister's visit to Washington and urgently received the Libyan Foreign Minister. The secret documents, however, now make it clear that Gorbachev was under no illusion that his liege was innocent. A memo to Gorbachev from his aide Anatoly Chernyaev, dated April 14, states "Hardly anybody in the world has any doubt that [Gaddafi] is the culprit of the West Berlin explosion and other such things." Chernyaev proposed to send to Libya another notorious terrorist, Comrade Hawi, the leader of the Lebanese Communist Party, who would deliver a collective rebuke to Gaddafi "not only from us, but from all sorts of Arabs." A later note by Chernyaev on the margins states that "I was superseded by the Politburo decision of 13 April," though the substance of that decision is not clear, and a record is not available.[72]

This is not the only document about that crisis strangely missing from the archive. Another one is the transcript of Gorbachev's meeting with Libyan Foreign Minister Duelled on May 27, 1986. In general, the collection contains transcripts of all foreign meetings that Gorbachev had during his term in office, and the rare exceptions may suggest that the document contains something very sensitive.

The record of the subsequent Politburo meeting, however, reveals that the talks with Gadhafi's envoy made Gorbachev rather annoyed:

GORBACHEV. [...] Gaddafi has a very high opinion of his role in the World Revolution. He behaves as if he was dealing with members of kindergartens. One might think, the louder his shouts, the more successful the revolution. This is revolutionary primitivism. Gaddafi went so far that he provoked the United States to whack him seriously. And then he panicked, although we shielded him morally. [...] Gaddafi behaves with more cheek than any other country. He blackmails us. So we had to answer in a way which looks like a rebuff. We told him clearly: we are not going to start the Third World War because of you, nor for any other reasons. They must know this, or they would drag us into it. We said the same to Syrians, too. [...]

All of them want us to work for them, and now they want us to fight for them. Adventurers. We should not make concessions.

[...] All of them - Saddam, Arafat, Iranians - assert the policy of destruction. So primitive. But there is nothing we can do. All our proposals are designed to calm them down, to prevent panics, to discourage them from adventures.[73]

It is unclear what Gaddafi actually wanted him to do - what kind of request would make Gorbachev talk about blackmail and the danger of a Third World War. Be that as it may, this document again confirms Gorbachev had no doubt that the United States was genuinely "provoked" by Gaddafi.

At the same time, Gorbachev kept abusing Reagan Administration, privately and publicly. "We won't get anywhere with these gangsters," he told his Politburo on April 15, and then accused Western Europe of "taking refuge in silence" and "turning a blind eye on criminal actions." He concluded that, "We must show, in our propaganda, where this may lead."[74] Likewise, he urged the Syrians and other Red Arabs to organize more widespread protests against the US "gangsters' raid" in the Arab world.[75]

The Soviets worked with "Libyan friends" to draw lessons from the military defeat. The summary of the analysis that Gorbachev shared with the Syrians (promising to share the detailed conclusions later), appears rather bloodthirsty:

Our attention is drawn to the fact that, during the second and third US aircraft raids, as the Libyans began to act more actively, they managed to shoot 5 to 7 US planes and mounted an effective resistance to the Americans. And the Americans, as we know, are very sensitive to losses. Remember, after several marines were killed in Lebanon, the Congress withdrew the US troops from there. Before their raid on Libya, the Americans did a lot of preparation in order to avoid casualties, using a widespread espionage network. The Libyans made the same mistake which you [Syrians] once made: they used their entire air defense system against the unmanned spy planes. As a result, the Americans learnt combat frequencies of the Libyan air defense systems.[76]

Apart from that, Soviets and Arabs played the same old blame game: Gaddafi told Gorbachev he needed more weapons, and Gorbachev pointed out that any "special supplies" would become a "heap of junk metal" because the Libyan army was not properly manned or trained.[77] Gorbachev, however, did not clearly tell the Libyans no. As he told the Politburo, "We don't need a treaty with them, but tactically, we should drag our feet." Therefore, he ordered to take this line with the Libyans:

> *Let's take care of the mutual interests, and so on. Then we shall pull them towards Warsaw Treaty countries.*[78]

Assad's two homelands

Assad, in turn, sent his Foreign Minister and Chief of General Staff to Moscow to try and convince Gorbachev that the US raid on Libya was a "dress rehearsal" of the upcoming attack on Syria by Americans or Israelis. They asked for more powerful air defense missiles and more powerful radars. The Soviet Chief of General Staff replied:

> *[MARSHAL] S[ERGEI] F. AKHROMEYEV. We have gone a long way in military cooperation. At present, the Syrian armed forces are an effective modern army which has modern weapons. The past five years have been particularly productive. Syria's air defense system is capable of countering an aggression. Obviously, there is always a room for improvement. However, if some radar systems can be suppressed by the enemy, some others would still work. We can think about accelerating supplies of radars.*

> *As for the [Soviet-supplied] ZRK "Tochka" [air defense missiles], they are good missiles. We are working to increase the power of their warheads. After these works are completed, we can think about complying with the request of the Syrian friends.*

> *[The Syrian Chief of General Staff Gen.] H. SHEHABI emphasized the urgency of the problems concerning improvement of Syria's air forces and air defense systems.*

> *M. S. GORBACHEV. [...] The very fact of our meeting is important at this moment, in this situation. It will also be important to mention in the announcement that the Chiefs of General Staffs of both countries took part in the meeting.*

[...] The Soviet Union will continue to support Syria politically and economically and help to strengthen its defense capability.[79]

A year later, Assad came to Moscow himself. After he and Gorbachev completed their ritual curses of Thatcher, Jews, and other Imperialists, Assad constructed this syllogism:

H. ASSAD. *Syria's policies are our common cause, pursued in our common interests. However, we are unable to carry the burden of its practical implementation alone. That is why we have to rely on the Soviet friends' help.*

M. S. GORBACHEV. *We always offer you our shoulder. And [Soviet Defense Minister] S. L. Sokolov offers even more than that. He has a lot of friends all over the world.*

S. L. SOKOLOV. *Still can't make friends with [US Defense Secretary Caspar] Weinberger.*

M. S. GORBACHEV. *That is our "dearest friend," we have to spend a lot on him (common laughter).*

H. ASSAD. *We have the same friends and the same enemies. In connection with that, I would like to talk about our difficulties and our needs. I speak on behalf of all members of our delegation. Our delegation includes a representative of Syrian communist party.*

M. S. GORBACHEV *(jokingly). You probably took him aboard to strengthen your arguments.*

H. ASSAD. *No, our delegation includes representatives of all political trends: Baathists, independents, a communist. The whole spectrum of patriotic progressive forces.*

[...]

Today, Israel is capable of defeating Syria within a few hours. But we are hardly able to strike a similar blow on Israel. The reason is that the Israeli army is equipped with ground-to-ground missiles of greater range and higher precision, as well as radio-electronic means to suppress Syrian air defenses. Syria does not have such weapons.[80]

So, he asked for electronics and ground-to-ground missiles. Gorbachev promised to consider this, but pointed out that Syria had more tanks than Israel, and in any case, Israel should be opposed not by Syrian weapons alone, but by its leading the whole Arab world. Of course, the pooled resources of Arab regimes would greatly exceed Israel's.

> **M. S. GORBACHEV.** *[…] There are many rivals for leadership of the Arab world today. But it is Syria who, due to objective circumstances, can and should undertake the responsibility to unite the Arabs. Given the Syrian leadership's way of thinking, your flexibility and political wisdom, you can do that. […] As for the Soviet Union, you can count on our support in this.*

Assad agreed with that, condemning his stupid predecessors who, back in 1960s, quarreled with Arab Emirs and

> *…did not want to accept money from reactionaries.*

> **M. S. GORBACHEV.** *You should have approached that differently. Who created those material values? The people, the Arabs.*

> **H. ASSAD.** *Yes, many of our actions and decisions were mistaken. We wanted to be revolutionaries, but often forgot about realities.*

> **M. S. GORBACHEV.** *A revolutionary who forgets about that becomes just an adventurer.*

> **H. ASSAD.** *A revolutionary should develop himself and influence the development of the world around him.*

> *As for the specific situations, we should involve all forces to solve the burning problems.*

> **M. S. GORBACHEV.** *All patriotic and national forces, at any rate.*

> **H. ASSAD.** *And use the capitalists' money.*

Gorbachev approved that Leninist approach, especially because, he complained, the Soviet economy was not in its best shape now, to give out money and weapons so generously. However, he promised to help with oil production and the construction of a nuclear power plant in Syria.

> **H. ASSAD.** *Whatever your decision, we are grateful to the Soviet Union for the help it gives us. If the Soviet Union is weakened, the effect on Syria would be very negative, and any weapons would become useless. You are our greatest strength.*[81]

Indeed, the Syrian army in those times was more or less run by Soviet military advisors,[82] while its political Commissars "educate[d] the personnel in the spirit of gratitude for the Soviet Union's help and on the basis of the conviction that the Soviet weapons are best in the world"[83]. Syrian Politburo passed solemn resolutions on "unlimited expansion of cooperation with the USSR in all fields"[84]. Assad proudly reported to Gorbachev that, at any official event in Syria, the audience was obliged to burst in applause whenever a speaker mentioned the Soviet Union. "Syria has always pursued policies which are absolutely identical to those of the Soviet Union", he added.[85]

The numerous meetings between Gorbachev and Assad were remarkably warm and friendly, typically beginning with mutual complaints about their health being undermined by hard work to thwart the imperialist schemes:

28 April 1990

M. S. GORBACHEV. Glad to welcome you here, Comrade Assad, and the Syrian representatives accompanying you. We are always delighted to see our old friends.

H. ASSAD. Seeing you, dear Comrade Gorbachev, and other Soviet leaders, is especially significant to us. All the more so because the political situation in the world is not simple, and needs deep and thorough discussion. It is also very important nowadays to have good health.

M. S. GORBACHEV. I agree. Just yesterday, during a meeting in Sverdlovsk, one woman exclaimed: "Look what is happening with Mikhail Sergeyevich! He was still young just three years ago, and now his hair is white!" That is what the political environment does to a man.

In truth, Gorbachev's hair was not white in 1990. He was as bald as a knee, exactly like three years before. However, comrades would not just leave it there:

H. ASSAD. A member of our delegation has also noted that you have hardly become younger in the past five years.

M. S. GORBACHEV. I have an impression that I get three years older every year.

H. ASSAD. I always tell my colleagues that there is a special burden of responsibility on the head of a state. Something that seems natural to others is a very heavy burden on the supreme leader.

M. S. GORBACHEV. Yes. What a cheerful beginning to a meeting have we had.

H. ASSAD. This is a spontaneous beginning. I think, such a frank exchange is normal between us.

M. S. GORBACHEV. Frankness and openness are, indeed, natural between old friends like ourselves.

H. ASSAD. Yes, when we meet with Soviet friends, we are never discreet or reserved.[86]

In his talks with Gorbachev, Assad seemed to be quite frank not only about his health, but also about the objectives of his regime and his idea of the fair terms of peace in the Middle East:

H. ASSAD. [...] There was no Israel at all before, while Syria did exist. In addition, [...] Arabs have always yearned for unification, creation of a single Arab state. [...] Arabs are a single nation, bound by common language, culture and history. Even the name "Syria" covered contemporary Jordan, Palestine and Lebanon as well as contemporary Syria for many centuries. Thus, Hitti, a famous Arab historian, wrote that every man has two homelands: his own place of birth and Syria as the homeland of Jesus Christ. So, Christ's birthplace is called Syria, though today this territory is known as Palestine.

Israel's approach is different, because the Judaic religion itself states: the land of Israel spreads from Nile to Euphrates and its return is a divine predestination.

M. S. GORBACHEV. But this is racism, combined with Messiahnism!

H. ASSAD. This is the most dangerous form of racism.[87]

Gorbachev's Arab Reich

Gorbachev fully subscribed to the idea of unification of all Arabs in a single socialist super state in the long term, and more general Arab solidarity under the leadership of Comrade Assad in the short term. As he told the Syrian foreign minister in 1986:

M. S. GORBACHEV. [...] We should use any opportunity to enforce Arab solidarity, even if it has national rather than class basis. Let it be based on common anti-imperialist interests of various Arab states. We believe - and please convey this view to Comrade Assad - that Syria, more than anyone else, is capable of undertaking the mission of uniting the Arabs, to give a positive impulse to the movement in this direction.

It is well-known that the Arabs' sacred dream is an establishment of a united Arab state. But it would be absurd right now to advance this slogan as a practical goal. We are yet to go through many stages on our way to this goal. Right now, Arab solidarity on a very general basis of common national interests would play a positive role.

[...]

A. H. HADDAM. [...] On the question of the importance of Arab unity, our positions are identical. For many years, Syria's leadership has been working to achieve Arab solidarity, so that all forces and capabilities of Arab countries were used against Israeli aggression and imperialist schemes. [...] We see the difference between the prospects of forming a single Arab state, to which we still have a long way to go, and working to achieve a single Arab position on the basis of opposing the Zionist aggression and the imperialism. [...] At the same time, we are not under any illusion and realize there are common political and class interests between certain Arab regimes and the United States of America.[88]

Literally at every meeting, Gorbachev pushed the Syrian comrades to work harder on this issue, and promised every support:

M. S. GORBACHEV. [...] The Soviet Union, given the capabilities it has, is also prepared to contribute to the unification of the Arab ranks. Of course, our enemies won't miss the opportunity to present our honest efforts as "Moscow's conspiracy", so we should act accurately and carefully. In any case, you can count on our support. [...] A success of this cause would be a great historic victory with tremendous consequences.[89]

In practice, "promoting Arab solidarity" was a code for undermining any attempt of peaceful negotiations with Israel, especially if the Americans were involved. Any Arab leader who made an open or secret move in that direction would immediately come under as much pressure as Moscow and Damask could arrange.

Thus, in 1986 Syrian comrades proudly reported to Gorbachev that they had: successfully destroyed the prospects of peace between Israel and Jordan, "wrecked" the cooperation between Jordan and the Palestinians, and "effectively blocked" the whole peace plan of President Reagan. Gorbachev encouraged them to continue such efforts. He added:

> *We are satisfied with the fact that Syria firmly defends the positions of progressive forces in the Middle East. [...] Washington has had no success in its attempts to push through the American scheme of settlement through separate deals, pressure the Arabs, split the Arab world. The position of Syria, the firm course of its leadership, have played a huge role in that.*[90]

In 1987, again, Assad boasted to Gorbachev how he had "wrecked" a peace treaty between Israel and Lebanon:

> *US State Secretary had done a lot for that treaty and thought it was historic, a great success of American diplomacy.*
>
> *M. S. GORBACHEV. Poor Schulz keeps trying to achieve some success as State Secretary, but never succeeds.*
>
> *H. ASSAD. [...] At his meeting with Lebanon's President Gemayel, I am told, G. Schulz described the Middle East situation in the following way. In his words, Middle East is a road junction, where Assad sits with his machine-gun and stops the traffic. [...] Reagan himself is of the same view.*[91]

Arafat's Intifada

> *Confidentially, [Gorbachev reminded to Syrian comrades,] you and we have come to a common understanding that we should not move things in the Middle East as far as to a new war. It could exceed the framework of the region and grow into an international conflict, a wide confrontation.*
>
> *Naturally, we don't make this approach public. This is absolutely right. Let our enemies think hard on what might be opposed to their activities.*[92]

This bluff was only a part of Gorbachev's intimidation game in the Middle East; for avoiding a war did not mean he would just sit and talk. Although the "struggle for peace" did not include an actual war at that stage, it was not limited simply to threats and diplomatic pressure either. It also involved throwing stones and Molotov cocktails.

Indeed, another major Middle East crisis of those years—the first Intifada—was also created in close coordination with Moscow. At its earliest stage, in April 1988, Yasser Arafat specifically went to Moscow to discuss his plans and get the Soviet approval.

M. S. GORBACHEV. Welcome to the Soviet Union. First of all, I would like to confirm Soviet people's eternal solidarity with the Palestinian people's struggle for their just cause, for their legitimate national rights, to wish you success in this just struggle. The fate of the Palestinian people is hard and dramatic. But the strength of your movement is that it fights for a just, right cause. Soviet Union has never forgotten that the fate of the Palestinian people is the central point of the Middle Eastern settlement.

Y. ARAFAT. This is very important to us.

M.S. GORBACHEV. This does not exclude, but presumes taking account of the other parties" interests. Without that, it is impossible to establish a stable and fair peace. This means a return of all occupied territories. This also means Israel's right to exist, provided that Israel accepts all the basic positions of settlement for the other parties of the conflict.

Y. ARAFAT. On the basis of international law.

M. S. GORBACHEV. Yes, as it should be in our civilized age. However, when I speak of the civilized world, I believe it needs serious improvements.

Y. ARAFAT. On the basis of Perestroika. [...]

M. S. GORBACHEV. [...] We are friends, so our views, our positions are identical.

Y. ARAFAT. Precisely so. We have no differences of opinion.

M. S. GORBACHEV. One more point. We know all the aspects of the positions of Syria, Jordan, Egypt, Saudi Arabia, we know all the nuances. We are also aware of your tactics of using different forms of struggle. So let's think about the politics of the day. [...]

Y. ARAFAT. First of all, I would like to sincerely thank you for your solidarity with the Palestinian people's struggle. What you've said today gives us a new stimulus to continue our struggle. [...]

M.S. GORBACHEV. We know it is you who are orchestrating this struggle. That is why I am asking this question. Is there any weariness from the struggle among the population of occupied territories?

Y. ARAFAT. No, the tensions are as high as before.

Naturally, at this "summit meeting" level, they discussed mostly the political aspects of the Intifada: industrial action, civil disobedience, the fifth column in Israel (*"Arafat: [...] We pay great attention to working with progressive, democratic, peace-loving forces in Israel. Their weight is growing"*), whether to accept the US peace plan (of course not), etc. However, Arafat mentioned he had "been informing Comrade Dobrynin," the head of Comintern, about the Intifada plan "in detail." Gorbachev acknowledged he knew of the PLO's *"tactics of using different forms of struggle,"* and Arafat did mention the bloodier ones:

Y. ARAFAT. We also continue the struggle in other forms, on other fronts. The armed struggle does not stop in the South of Lebanon. Artillery fire, air raids, other actions take place on daily basis.

However, Gorbachev urged Arafat not to use weapons in Israel itself. As they both agreed, Israelis were only waiting for that, as an excuse to drown the whole Intifada in blood. Indeed, Palestinians mostly confined themselves to throwing stones and Molotov cocktails in that Intifada.

M. S. GORBACHEV. I think you have chosen the correct form of struggle. It is essentially a democratic form. It is very difficult to fight against it. The US and Israel are waiting for you to raise weapons. They will be pushing you to do that. [...] But you must hold on.

Y. ARAFAT. [...] We hold our nerve.[93]

Arafat's visit to Moscow was widely reported in propaganda, as the sign of Moscow's political backing for the Intifada. The next week, however, Gorbachev discussed the Intifada with another Red Arab visitor, President Assad, who came to Moscow in utmost secrecy. The narrow circle knew that he was going for a medical examination; the broad toiling masses knew nothing; and very few indeed knew that Gorbachev visited him in the hospital on April 15, 1988.

M. S. GORBACHEV. Hopefully, the treatment will help a speedy recovery of your health from the cold you have received in these cold days. [...]

H. ASSAD. Thank you. But my illness is rather caused by the political climate. I had the previous relapse in 1983 when Israel, US, and other NATO countries tried to implement their plans in Lebanon. Naturally, it was not from fear that I fell ill. However, the general strain played its part.

Gorbachev replied that he was also overwhelmed by work, but:

M. S. GORBACHEV. [...] As soon as I learned about your visit, I instructed [the Health Minister] E. I. Chazov to make sure the doctors do everything possible for President Assad – our friend, brother and comrade. I would like you to remember under any circumstances: there are Moscow, Kremlin, CPSU Central Committee, your friends in the Soviet leadership who are always ready to help you. You can be sure that we shall never allow any damage to be done to friendly Syria. We shall always think together, act together, constantly keep in touch. Are you satisfied with our Ambassador in Damask?

H. ASSAD. Yes, he is a good, highly moral man, a man of honor. [...] I have instructed all our ministries, the Party leadership to keep in touch with the Soviet Ambassador, to share information with him.

Gorbachev then told him about his meeting with Arafat, to which Assad replied:

What he told you is not true. The Intifada has been planned by Palestinians in the occupied territories, not by Arafat. However, they have no disagreements with him. All Palestinians - those on the occupied territories as well as Arafat - now want to act together.[94]

The Arab comrades, as usual, spoke of each other in the spirit of fraternal solidarity.

Nevertheless, a degree of "Arab unity" was now visible, or at least imaginable, if only for a short time. So, Gorbachev now increased pressure on the Western leaders to accept the Soviet scheme of settlement in the Middle East before those crazy united Arabs invent and enforce something worse than that... Of course, here he would not mention that it was he personally who had been encouraging "Arab solidarity" under Syrian leadership.

Thus, at the Malta summit meeting with George W. H. Bush in

December 1989, Gorbachev said this:

> ...*Something else worries me. The process of consolidation between the Arabs is gradually developing. When they feel that unity is strength, they may reject your and our services. They will try and solve the Middle East problems by other means. That would be something dangerous. So, we must hurry, it is important not to miss the unique opportunity.*

In reply, Bush and State Secretary Baker told him about their renewed efforts to square the circle of the Arab-Israeli conflict. The Soviets, however, insisted that Baker and Bush must ask for Moscow's permission before doing anything in the Middle East. Peace could only be achieved on Soviet terms.

> **M. S. GORBACHEV**. *Maybe, Mr. Baker has taken a leaf out of Schulz's book and decided to try acting unilaterally at first? And then, when he realizes this cannot work, he will return to cooperation?*

> **J. BAKER**. *Unlike Schulz, I do not fly to the Middle East all the time.*

> **M. S. GORBACHEV**. *Maybe you will.*

> *[...]*

> **G. BUSH**. *I am sure you've noticed that our Middle East policy has turned towards cooperation with the Soviet Union.*

> **E. A. SHEVARDNADZE**. *However, you've been consulting us recently only after adapting your own plans and decisions. And cooperation means preliminary discussions.*[95]

Peacemaking Soviet-style

All the above is difficult to square with the reputation of a great democratic reformer which Gorbachev still enjoys in the West. The Gorbymaniacs' excuse for their saint patron would probably be this: Rome was not built in a day, Gorbachev could not change all the long-standing Soviet practices overnight. He could only do one thing at a time. He had a huge and powerful communist apparatus to reckon with, and this apparatus would cling to the old Soviet alliances with Comrade Assad and other Red Arabs.

Even Thatcher behind closed doors, while aggressively pushing her protégé to abandon "the doctrine of world domination of communism", offered him the benefit of the doubt and praised his other reforms. While trying to persuade him not to stop there and reform the Soviet foreign policy as well, she seemed to appreciate that this would not be easy, as he would have to break the resistance of "hard-liners".

This popular myth about the struggle of "hawks" and "doves" in the Kremlin had nothing to do with the reality. It resulted partly from deliberate Soviet disinformation, partly from the logical fallacy of picturing the opponent's system as a mirror image of your own: we have hawks and doves here in Washington, so there must be some in Moscow, too.

In the Soviet system, with the supremacy of the paramilitary Communist Party, all considerations were subordinated to the mission of conquering the world; but within these limits, orders were obeyed without question. The word of the General Secretary was law; it was for him to make final decisions on the strategy and tactics of the world revolution. It was his explicit right and duty to invent all sorts of cunning Leninist manoeuvres to deceive the enemy. This was especially true during the final decade of the Soviet regime, after the rise of KGB chief Yuri Andropov and his protégés (like Gorbachev and Shevardnadze), when the Kremlin's policies at home and abroad became increasingly dominated by "Operative Chekist" deception measures.

Thus, when Gorbachev ordered the Communist cohorts to imitate democracy and market economy, the whole apparatus obeyed his command without question. Likewise, to take a hypothetical example, if Gorbachev decided to go a bit further in his game with Iran, accept Khomeini's advice and convert the Soviet Union to Islam - the Party would have obeyed. They would have called a Party Congress, found the appropriate quotations from Marx and Lenin, and unanimously passed the resolution. Ideologists and propagandists would then explain in *Pravda* that Prophet Mohammed, although not yet armed with the progressive Marxist understanding of the human society, began the national-liberation struggle against Western Imperialism. The Party would calculate how many Mullahs were required at every armed unit and every industrial workplace, and those Mullahs would have been trained and dispatched in appropriate numbers. Incidentally, all this is exactly what some Red Arab regimes did at certain points of their own history. Gorbachev deemed that inexpedient; but whether his decision, once taken, no "hard-liner" would dare contradict it.

The Politburo documents reveal no attempts by Gorbachev to adapt a more balanced policy in the Middle East and no resistance from the "hard-liners". On the contrary, at some points Gorbachev would reject the proposals of his own Foreign Ministry on the grounds that they might upset Red Arabs. Thus, in 1986 the Foreign Ministry drafted another Soviet peace plan for publication, which was then discussed at Politburo. Gorbachev put the plan on halt pending consultations with Arab allies:

11 July 1986

(Deputy Foreign Minister) **Vorontsov** *reports* **on the Middle East policy** *[…]*

GORBACHEV. *How can we realise this? Even Libya, Syria and PLO may be against it.*

The position has always been this: the Soviet Union is always on the Arab side. And now?

If we do not take Syria into our confidence on this plan, we will lose the remaining Arabs.

(Vorontsov's) thinking goes in the right direction. The Arabs want the USSR to get involved more deeply. But… we may gain nothing and lose all we have.

Let's accept Vorontsov's ideas only as a basis for consultations right now. Otherwise, we may blow up the old policy and gain nothing. And this is not for a public announcement.

VOROTNIKOV. *I don't think this will shock anybody. After all, the basic idea dates back to 1984.*

GORBACHEV. *No need to rush. […]*

So, the Politburo authorises further research and consultations. We will return to this later.

GROMYKO. *[…] I am against dropping the idea of "the independent Palestinian state".*

SHEVARDNADZE, YAKOVLEV, DOBRYNIN *argue in support of the proposed plan.*

GORBACHEV. *You should not think that everything we did in the past was wrong. But we risk being late. The USA are trying to do irreversible things… not in our favour.*

So: we do not abandon our policy, and we activate our work. To do that, we must propose something and do something. We must not act recklessly. Nevertheless, it is clear: the Arabs are interested in involving us in the Middle East affairs in order to oppose the Americans. And yes, we should get involved. Because if we do nothing, the US and Israel take advantage of that.

We need the [international] conference - if nothing else, simply to unmask the US duplicity. [...]

Begin the movement in that direction. Destroy the US monopoly in the Middle East.

Arrange consultations, bilateral as well as multilateral. Keep the course and preserve our interests.

Research, consult, and then report to the Politburo. I am sure there will be corrections... We certainly must talk to Algeria... Talk to Iraq...

[...]

Edit the material to show that our policy has been right, we have been defending the independence of the Arabs and the PLO.

GROMYKO, *again, insists on keeping the idea of "the independent Palestinian state".*

SHEVARDNADZE *objects.*

GORBACHEV. *Let's decide this during consultations.*

This document suggests a number of interesting conclusions. One of them is that Moscow was not so much interested in actually imposing its terms of peace as in "unmasking the United States". Whether Israel would actually be undermined was not nearly as significant as the process of holy war against Zionism and Imperialism, under the leadership of Moscow and its regional clients. The idea was to mobilize the Arab world against the West, not just against Israel. Since they fought this war, they had to offer some terms of peace, if only as an ultimatum. If those terms were unacceptable - so much the better.

Furthermore, this was another opportunity to try to split the Western allies. In May 1986, Gorbachev told Syrians that it was high time to "activate diplomatic work using divisions in the Western camp", especially the more pro-Arab positions of French President Mitterrand and Italian Prime Minister Craxi[96]. Indeed, later the same year, Mitterrand suddenly supported the Soviet idea of the international conference.[97] In 1987 the whole European Community, as it then was, followed suit. However, the EC position did not entirely satisfy Gorbachev, because they wanted the USSR to restore diplomatic relations with Israel, and Soviet troops to be withdrawn from Afghanistan.

"What will be next?" Gorbachev asked the Italian Foreign Minister Julio Andreotti, "Demands to solve our border disputes with China and to settle the situation around Cambodia?"

Foreign Minister Eduard Shevardnadze added, "Maybe to settle our disagreements with Japan, too?"

Andreotti answered apologetically:

First of all, the EC document does not set any conditions for the Soviet Union. [...] The points you have mentioned, Israel and Afghanistan, were formulated quite separately, not in the document itself. [...] I would like to make it clear that the EC document says nothing about the need to restore diplomatic relations between USSR and Israel. We only asked to convey this wish to the Soviet leadership confidentially, whisper it in your ear, so to speak. That was my idea. I said directly that this was a very delicate problem and we should not make any public statements here.

The delicate problem was this: back in 1967, in the heat of the Six Day War, the Soviets broke relations with Israel as a sign of support to their Arab comrades. The idea was that Israel would be destroyed in the war, so diplomatic relations would no longer be necessary. Ever since then, Moscow had been searching for a face-saving way to restore relations, but a face-saving way did not present itself. At the same time, it was pretty difficult to demand for the conflict to be settled under Soviet auspices if the USSR did not even have diplomatic relations with Israel. Eventually, Gorbachev turned restoration of relations into a bargaining chip.

M. S. GORBACHEV. *[...] Maybe, at some stage of the progress towards the conference, in the framework of that process, we might return to that problem. But not now. It does not seem possible to draw this issue out of the context of the present situation. [...]*

G. ANDREOTTI. *[...] We are not talking about your recognition of Israel now. Maybe, during the preparations to the conference we can use the issue of restoration of USSR-Israeli diplomatic relations to put pressure on [Israeli Prime Minister] Shamir. And then you would solve that problem during the conference itself.[98]*

By the time George W. H. Bush Administration came into the office in early 1989, Israel and the US were practically in international isolation on this issue, while most other governments, with or without reservations, had taken the Soviet-Arab side. Even the US began to drift away from a pro-Israeli position. At the Malta summit, Bush declared:

The United States have now stopped their unconditional approval of Israeli policies. The Intifada, with its violence, had encouraged us to do so. You can see certain changes in our relations with Israel, even though it is still our reliable ally. We must stop the violence connected to Intifada and begin the dialogue as soon as possible.

Gorbachev, of course, re-doubled his efforts to intimidate Bush with the prospects of Arab unity, and make him accept the Soviet terms until it was too late (see above).

Ironically, however, while Bush's presidency was one of the most eventful ones in history, Bush's natural inclination was to do nothing about anything. He would not advance, he would not retreat; his preferred solution was to wait and see. With growing anxiety, the Comrades saw all their cunning peace plans slowly drowning in Washington sub-committees. After years of cursing the Reagan Administration, complaining "*we won't get anywhere with these gangsters*", and anticipating their more flexible successors - they suddenly ended up in a complete vacuum, facing the stone wall of a dull bureaucracy. Gorbachev and Assad complained to each other:

M. S. GORBACHEV. *[...] You are a shrewd politician, you monitor the trends of political life. Haven't you got an impression that G. Schulz was more active on Middle East [than the new Administration]? He succeeded in involving Reagan into the work. Of course, one can agree or disagree with Schulz's ideas and proposals on the Middle East, but in that period, we made some progress with the Americans towards convening an international conference on Middle East. Whereas now we just do not see this Administration showing any interest in the settlement, in the international conference.*

H. ASSAD. This is the main question I wanted to discuss with you. I share your view that the US policy on the Middle East was better under Schulz - even though I met with him personally twice, and we never agreed about his plan of Middle East settlement.

M. S. GORBACHEV. I criticized Schulz's plan even at this table. But at least he tried to do something, searched for some solutions.[99]

This amusing discomfort with Washington's silence can be seen in many other documents of those months and, perhaps, offers some lessons to the future leaders of the West. When they review their options on Middle East, they should not forget about masterly inactivity; at times, it becomes the best course to follow.

In the case of Bush, however, it could not last for long - and within a few months, the comrades saw their chance.

Gorby and the Gulf

The Kremlin's real objectives in the Middle East (like in any other place) were hidden under several layers of camouflage.

The façade presented to the broad world—to the toiling masses of Western diplomats, Arab sheikhs, Jewish collective farmers, and all people of good will— was simple and attractive: the Soviet Union only wanted peace. A fair and stable peace, which would be a triumph for the international community, international law, and international cooperation.

Hidden beneath this propaganda was the second layer agenda: the peace (to be truly fair and stable) had to be made on the Soviet conditions, "in the interests of Arab people, including the Palestinians," as Gorbachev put it. This meant, plainly, the dismemberment and disarmament of Israel.

Hidden deeper still was the third layer. The entire socialist jihad against Israel was essentially a propaganda operation, and Israel was only significant as a bridgehead of Western democracy in the region. The purpose of Operation SIG was to mobilize the Arab world not just against Israel, but also against the entire Western world.

Finally, the hidden agenda behind all other hidden agendas, the real significance of the Middle East, was still the same: threatening the oil lifeline of the West.

Soviet and Arab comrades had rejected the idea of a direct invasion of Gulf states long before Gorbachev's time in office, precisely because they realized it would be fought off by military force. Nevertheless, they never missed an opportunity to get closer to the target, if only one small step at a time, quietly and safely.

Like his predecessors, Comrade Gorbachev never kept that task out of his mind. We have seen above how he masterminded the wide-ranging Soviet-Iranian alliance, including the agreement on constructing a railway from the Soviet Union straight to the Gulf. Nor did he forget about the Arabian Peninsula, where a Soviet satellite - South Yemen - was conveniently located to block Western tankers from entering the Red Sea, if Moscow said so.

In 1987, Gorbachev told the Politburo about his talks with the new communist dictator of South Yemen:

> **GORBACHEV.** *[...] We have little interest in that country itself. But the most important thing for us is the place where it is situated. We are interested to enhance our relations with South Yemen not ideologically, but strategically.*[100]

Indeed, the talks were dominated by plotting to expand the Soviet presence on the Arabian Peninsula. Once Gorbachev had completed the usual initiation sermon on how to govern Yemen according to Lenin, the rest of the Yemeni delegation was discharged, and the new dictator was left alone with his master.

> **M. S. GORBACHEV.** *[...] We believe you should aim for complete normalization of your relations with North Yemen [...] To do that, you should carry out the necessary work with those in your own party who take an extremist view.*

> **A. S. AL BEID.** *[...] We will continue our efforts to improve mutual understanding with North Yemen. In any case, I promise, we will take no steps concerning that country without first consulting you.*

> *[...North Yemen's President] A. A. Saleh thinks his army has not enough missiles. As we know, he has appealed to the USSR with a request for supplies of such missiles. We believe it would be expedient to satisfy his request. Soviet arms supplies to North Yemen would help to strengthen your presence there, which is objectively in South Yemen's interest.*

Besides, this would be better than if he gets weapons in the West.

In connection with that, I would also like to inform you that United Arab Emirates President Zayed Nahayan approached South Yemen's representative at the OIC summit conference in Kuwait - Chairman of the Presidium of the Supreme People's Soviet H. Attas - and asked us to find out whether the USSR could supply air defense systems to his country. We have passed this information to the Soviet embassy in Aden. For our part, we believe it would be in the Soviet interests and our common interests to satisfy the UAE request.

It seems to us that the Soviet Union would be well-advised to use any opportunity to strengthen its presence in our region, including by using the opportunities of military cooperation with countries of the region. South Yemen, for its part, is prepared to give you assistance within the limits of its capabilities. For example, we could develop cooperation in Sokotra Island Area, where we could develop joint fishing ventures, use the island to install communications systems, and also for military purposes.

We are also prepared to offer our territory to build re-broadcasting transmitters for the Soviet broadcasts targeted at the countries of the region. In our view, this question is especially important, because there can be no peaceful co-existence on the field of propaganda and ideological confrontation.

M. S. GORBACHEV. *Among Persian Gulf states, we have good relations with Kuwait. We also have decent ties with the UAE and have recently exchanged ambassadors with them. If I remember correctly, the UAE has already appealed to us with a request for military cooperation, Comrade Shevardnadze can confirm this. We are currently looking into this.*

Your proposal on military cooperation in South Yemen's coastal area seems interesting to us. It deserves a more thorough consideration.

As for construction of re-broadcasting transmitters, we can return to this question when we consider the issue of the radio-technical means assistance to you.

As the Politburo record shows, Gorbachev's subsequent orders were these:

We have to give missiles to Saleh. Otherwise he will take them from the USA.

No objections to military aid by Egypt, insomuch as requested by South Yemen.

(To [Politburo member] Medvedev:) Vadim, try to connect them to East Germany (about the military aid).[101]

Probably, Gorbachev also played his role in the unification between South Yemen and North Yemen in 1990, on which Assad commented:

Yemen is being united now, but they see their unification as merely a step to pan-Arab unity, not a creation of a "Greater Yemen".[102]

While playing his Middle East gambits, Gorbachev always kept an eye on the Gulf oil. That, however, was a highly delicate maneuver—a burglary by deception instead of armed robbery. Therefore, Saddam had no role to play in Moscow's schemes. He was given an entirely different mission in an entirely different area, where his own talents were badly needed.

Chapter 5:
Riddles of the Invasion

After the end of Iran-Iraq war, the CIA produced a secret report entitled *Iraq's National Security Goals: An Intelligence Assessment.* The document (even the very first sentence of its executive summary alone) completely ruins all the conspiracy theories about the CIA being a powerful, or even sinister, or at least competent, organisation. It reads:

> *Efforts to bolster Iraq's defences against Iran will head Baghdad's list of national security goals during the next decade. [...]*
>
> *Saddam probably will try to promote his leadership goals through less radical means than Baghdad has employed in the past. He has softened Iraq's position on the Arab-Israeli conflict and supports the mainstream elements of the PLO. He probably will largely eschew efforts to undermine conservative Arab regimes. [...]War-weary Iraq probably will not undertake significant military adventures in the near to medium term. [...] Baghdad will stress the importance of its oil reserves and encourage the continual growth of bilateral trade with the United States.*[103]

Indeed, it was seriously thought in Washington that the end of Iran–Iraq war did not really mean anything—Iraq would still be a bulwark against Islamic Fundamentalism, and therefore prudent to continue supporting Saddam.

That year-and-a-half period from December 1988 to July 1990 is never prominent in the *official version* of the history of US–Iraq relations. Both Bush and Baker stress in their memoirs that their policy of supporting Iraq against Iran was inherited from the Reagan Administration. Both employ this as a reasonable excuse - as if both of them were not high-ranking members of the Reagan Administration themselves. As if there was no difference between Saddam actually fighting Iran in Reagan's times and their own wishful thinking that Saddam would somehow remain a bulwark against Iran even after the peace was made. As if that Kissingerian experiment of setting Saddam and Khomeini against each other had not failed long before the end of war, since it became clear that it only made both sides stronger.

Though the Reagan Administration was unsuccessful, at least it tried to find a different solution by building bridges to some "moderates" in Iran. Bush and Baker did not even try; they just continued the appeasement of Saddam.

Meanwhile, anyone who knew anything about the Middle East, from the Israelis to the Saudis to the Soviets, realized that Iraq's war with Iran was truly over. They knew Saddam was now up to something else—something dangerous. Nobody could be sure where exactly he would turn. All they knew was that his weapons of mass destruction and the fourth largest army in the world was not just meant to defend "Fortress Iraq" - as the CIA, in its infinite wisdom, predicted.

Saddam's mission

One of the many trophies Saddam had secured from the international efforts to arm him against Iran were the famous Soviet ballistic missiles Scud-B. 600-km range, Saddam's Scuds could be equipped with chemical or, when time comes, nuclear warheads and reach as far as Tehran - or as far as Israel.

After firing a few Scuds at Tehran and then making peace with the Ayatollahs, Saddam promptly built six launchers in Western Iraq, within range of Israel.

On 2 April 1990, he made the infamous "burn Israel" speech, where he boasted of his chemical weapons. *"I swear to Allah we will let our fire eat half of Israel if it tries to wage anything against Iraq,"* he declared. A few days later, Saddam again threatened he would attack Israel with chemical weapons and added that his war against Israel would not end until the Zionist Entity was exterminated and all its land returned to the Arabs.

Gorbachev's and Assad's verdict on this solo was unanimous and clear: far too weak.

30 April 1990

M. S. GORBACHEV. […] And what about Iraq? What is the matter? Are they not out of trouble with Iran yet, or are they already in bed with the Americans?

H. ASSAD. They have been in bed with the West in general and the Americans in particular for quite a long time. […]

M. S. GORBACHEV. I should have thought that, after quitting the war and finding itself in a different situation in relations with Iran, Iraq should become a factor of increasing pressure on Israel. But this does not seem to happen.

H. ASSAD. Indeed. The [recent] statements of the Iraqi leadership only confirm this. If those statements were sincere, Baghdad would need to get closer to Damask to put pressure on Israel, because Iraq has no common border with Israel. […]

M. S. GORBACHEV. I think so, too.[104]

For years, and especially since the end of Iran-Iraq war, Moscow had been trying hard to encourage "Arab unity" between Syria and Iraq. Thus, they attempted to arrange for Iraqi oil, supplied to the Soviets in exchange for weapons, to be transported through Syria.[105] Given Saddam's military power and Syria's friendship with Iran, the possibility of their pooled forces would be a grave threat to Israel. Moscow hoped such a prospect would soon intimidate Israel and the West into accepting the peace under Soviet conditions as a lesser evil.

The Red Arab dictators were not the most agreeable people in the world, but even among them, Comrade Saddam was always reputed as an *infant terrible*. Of course, Gorbachev and Assad were unfair to him when saying that the duplicitous bastard had sold out to the enemy and was not sincere in his threats to burn Israel. However, he was not very disciplined, and certainly not enough to confine himself to his designated place on Gorbachev's chessboard. After all, Moscow wanted him to accept the leadership of his old enemy Comrade Assad and agree to Arab solidarity on the basis of fraternal sharing of oil revenues. That was not the future he had aspired to when he sacrificed his country in the bloodbath of war with Iran - receiving, in exchange, weapons of mass destruction and the fourth strongest army in the world. Now the time had come for the Mother of all Battles: the conquest of the Gulf States.

Geography helped him prioritize: Kuwait was first, Saudi oilfields were second, and United Arab Emirates was third. Eventually, he would control two-thirds of the world's oil reserves.

In this context, his Scuds targeted at Israel were meant as a shield, not a sword. As it had always been planned among Red Arabs, Israel was to become a hostage nation. The threat to Israel, Saddam hoped, could deter the West from countering his invasions near the Gulf.

Arabian Nights

Then Saddam began harassing emirs and kings with all sorts of ultimatums. His demands were devised in the style of Arabian Nights, in which the teller tries to make each story more amazing than the last one. In the subsequent months, Saddam probably had a lot of fun observing how seriously the great powers took those fruits of his literary genius when they were trying to negotiate a solution to the conflict. His ideas became known as "disputed issues," and were moved around negotiations tables in the capacity of change coins, trying to make the ends meet in the projected deals. These infidel idiots never realized they were just tales.

The first set of demands to the kings and emirs was purely monetary: forgive Iraq's $40 billion debt, give Iraq an additional $30 billion, and reduce oil production to double the prices.

Then, more colorful ultimatums followed. Far away in the East, where the red sun bloodies the golden sand in a stormy Arabian desert, lies a great oilfield of Rumaila. Oh, let my tongue wither if I cannot adequately describe its riches! One who has ever spooned petrodollars from it is forever possessed by the passion for them; neither gold of the earth, nor shine of the stars, nor love of beautiful maidens are anymore dear to his heart. He only adores this oil, as clear as a camel's tear, these magnificent fountains of petroleum coming directly from the entrails of earth and promising riches of the universe to the man who owns that land.

The trouble was that the Iraq-Kuwait border went right through the middle of the blessed oilfield; so Saddam, with his socialist efficiency, and Emir al Sabah, with his capitalist malice, had to spoon from the same pool. The problem was that oil, being liquid, did not recognize the state borders, did not care about Baghdad's economic planning, nor even about OPEC regulations, and only obeyed the laws of physics. Consequently, as Kuwaitis pumped oil from their half of Rumaila, Iraqi oil would constantly flow underground across the border, away from Saddam's socialist planning, into the ruthless world of capitalism. Saddam was infuriated by this unfair process, which clearly resulted from an imperialist conspiracy to destroy the Baathist regime and restore the colonial rule in Iraq. For quite a time did Saddam harass the Emir with ultimatums about this oil. The Emir responded meekly enough, but oil kept flowing out of Iraq anyway.

Another tale was about Bubiyan, an island of enormous strategic importance, securing Iraq's access to the Gulf and possibly populated by hordes of powerful efreeti, eager to fulfill any wish of their master. It was unfair, Saddam said, for such a stronghold to be controlled by such an unworthy ruler as Emir of Kuwait. It had to be passed to Great Leader Saddam, who would use it to defend the Arab world against Persians, Americans, Jews, and other enemies.

The actual invasion, however, marked the beginning of a decline in those literary exercises. The tale to accompany the invasion itself was rather hoary and, to be frank, entirely plagiarized from Soviet comrades. It was announced that the oppressed toiling masses of Kuwait had finally risen to overthrow the tyrant, formed a "Provisional Free Government," and invited the Iraqi forces to come and defend new Kuwait from a possible counter-revolution and foreign intervention. This was exactly what the Soviets said whenever they invaded foreign lands - another Saddam's imitation of Comrade Stalin.

The final tale that arrived a few days later, in response to the deployment of US forces in Saudi Arabia, was even worse. Clearly authored in haste, it was quite inconsistent with itself or with the previous stories. It said that during the Ottoman Empire, a Sultan made an edict that made Kuwait part of the Basra Province. Therefore, "historically," Kuwait had always been a part of Iraq, but imperialist British schemes forced its independence.

Comrade Ramadan even tried to sell this idea to the Turks, much to their amusement—it was, after all, their empire and their sultan. By Saddam's logic, they too would have claim to both Iraq and Kuwait.[106]

This tale in its more polished diplomatic version, later told by Tariq Aziz to foreign leaders, was still unimpressive at best.

T. AZIZ. [...] We have no military intentions about Saudi Arabia, and we would never concentrate our forces at a border with a neighboring Arab state without a good reason. Kuwait is a very special case. All the rulers of Iraq, – Kings Feisal I, Ghazi, Feisal II, later [President] Quasem, – with no exception, would treat Kuwait in exactly the same way as we, if only they had adequate abilities and strength. Everyone in Iraq saw and still sees Kuwait as an integral part of Iraqi territory. This fact cannot be ignored.

One might ask, what about international law and legality, for Kuwait was a member of the UN. Yes it was, and we ourselves dealt with it on this basis. However, for us, this circumstance by no means can cancel the historical reality I am talking about.

Nobody would ever think about claiming that Iraq has any rights for Saudi or, say, Syrian territory. And on the contrary, all in Iraq are convinced that Kuwait is its integral part.

King Hussein [of Jordan], whose close relatives were kings of Iraq, can confirm this to you. He knows that the Iraqi kings even conflicted with Britain, on which they themselves were fully dependent, precisely in the Kuwaiti question.[107]

Yet, after listening to all those tales with straight faces, thousands of diplomats and experts from around the world noted the following "concerns of the Iraqi government:

(a) Re-structuring of Iraq's foreign debt.

(b) Economic cooperation in the Gulf area.

(c) OPEC oil production quotas.

(d) Territorial disputes over Rumelia and Bubiyan.

(e) A lack of democracy in Kuwait.

A final point about Iraq's historic rights was impossible to squeeze into diplomatic language, so it was omitted for the sake of tact. But the other tales seemed perfectly plausible.

And so all the power of diplomacy was unleashed...

Disinformation Campaign

In fact, only one of these issues had any real significance to Saddam—the one about the Emir of Kuwait being an undemocratic autocrat, allegedly overthrown by some mythical 'progressive' forces. That might open a way for keeping Kuwait under a puppet government after a withdrawal of Iraqi troops (see below).

As for the earlier tales, they were deliberate disinformation. This is a classic problem of any invasion: massive troop movements are bound to be noticed in advance. Nevertheless, every invader always tries to take the enemy by surprise. One of the typical tricks for achieving this is to invent a plausible false purpose of such a movement, and take diplomatic and political steps to persuade the enemy this purpose is real.

In this case, it worked 100%.

In mid-July of 1990, American spy satellites noticed an accelerating military build-up in Southern Iraq. American Defense Intelligence assessed that was "not a rehearsal," and concluded that Iraq was preparing to grab the disputed territories of Rumaila and Bubiyan by force.[108]

Without long hesitation, the US Administration decided to go along with this. Even though such methods were not welcomed, Iraq was an ally, and the whole 'territorial dispute' was clearly not a big deal. This decision is, so to speak, not very strongly emphasized in the official version of history but it is, really, an open secret.

On July 19, the State Department cabled all US embassies throughout the Middle East:

The United States takes no position on the substance of bilateral issues concerning Iraq and Kuwait.[109]

This caused considerable panic among the defenseless Gulf leaders. They, however, were also deceived by Saddam's fairy tale demands and thought it was still possible just to pay him off. A storm of diplomatic activity ensued, with various mediators - Mubarak being the most active - trying to find out how much Saddam wanted and how quickly the Emirs could raise the money.

It was against this background that, on July 25, Saddam summoned the US Ambassador April Glaspie to his palace in Baghdad. He told her he had a message for President Bush. It turned out to be a rather long speech, accusing the US of supporting Kuwait and other Gulf states in their "economic war" against Iraq, and full of thinly veiled threats:

> *If you use pressure, we will deploy pressure and force. We know that you can harm us although we do not threaten you. But we too can harm you. Everyone can cause harm according to their ability and their size. We cannot come all the way to you in the United States, but individual Arabs may reach you.*

Glaspie—in accordance with her instructions—assured him that the US did not support the Gulf States against Iraq and had "no opinion on the Arab-Arab conflicts, like your border disagreement with Kuwait." Then she asked:

> *Frankly, we can see [...] that you have deployed massive troops in the south. Normally that would not be any of our business. But when this happens in the context of [... – here Glaspie listed a few of Iraq's latest ultimatums – ...] then it would be reasonable for me to be concerned. And for this reason, I received an instruction to ask you, in the spirit of friendship – not in the spirit of confrontation – regarding your intentions.*

Saddam answered gracefully:

> *We do not ask people not to be concerned when peace is at issue. This is a noble human feeling which we all feel. [...]*
>
> *We want to find a just solution which will give us our rights but not deprive others of their rights. But at the same time, we want the others to know that our patience is running out.*

Then Saddam told her about all the recent diplomatic bargaining over the size of the ransom.

Coincidentally or not, at this very moment, the conversation was interrupted by a call from President Mubarak, who said the Kuwaitis were prepared to pay, and the details could be agreed at Iraqi-Kuwaiti negotiations in Saudi Arabia on 30 July.

Saddam went back to Glaspie and told her the news.

GLASPIE: *This is good news. Congratulations.*

HUSSEIN: *Brother President Mubarak told me they were scared. They said troops were only 20 kilometers north of the Arab League line. [That is,* *of the Iraq-Kuwait border which Saddam questioned.] I said to him that regardless of what is there, whether they are police, border guards or army, and regardless of how many are there, and what they are doing, assure the Kuwaitis and give them our word that we are not going to do anything until we meet with them. When we meet and when we see that there is hope, then nothing will happen. But if we are unable to find a solution, then it will be natural that Iraq will not accept death, even though wisdom is above everything else. There you have good news.[110]*

Glaspie came back to the embassy and sent an optimistic report to Washington. It seemed to her that the crisis was now resolved by Mubarak's diplomacy. Mubarak himself also cabled to Washington, "President Hussein was receptive and responsive."[111] "I believe he […] has no intention of attacking Kuwait or any other party," he assured.[112] Mubarak asked the United States to avoid "any provocative action that is liable to add fuel to the fire and render the easing of tensions more difficult."[113]

Simultaneously, the OPEC meeting in Geneva complied with Saddam's demands on reducing the oil production and pushing the prices up.

Meanwhile, Saddam kept increasing his forces on the border, and the spy satellites duly reported this, but nobody was really worried. The build-up was seen as an attempt to put pressure on the Kuwaitis, to extort more money at the negotiations. At worst, it was thought, Saddam could grab the "disputed territories" after all. Either way, the United States was not going to do anything about it.

Even on August 1, when the Defense Intelligence warned that the invasion was "imminent,"[114] the policy-makers would not believe this. Thus, Baker thought the alarm was "too apocalyptic. In the intelligence business, it's bureaucratically safer to be wrong predicting than to underreact and miss the call."[115]

So Saddam had successfully made his surprise. During the last day of peace, President Bush concentrated on golf, not the Gulf. After scoring a bucketful of balls, weary Bush went to undertake a heat treatment in the White House basement - hardly aware that the tensions in the Middle East were also heating. There he sat in his T-shirt, reflecting about the budget deficit, when National Security Advisor Brent Scowcroft suddenly dashed into the room and panted that Mr. President must urgently phone one Saddam Hussein and tell him not to invade a country called Kuwait. It took a few minutes to brief him on what it was all about, and then they got a report that a full-scale invasion had already began. Bush's first thought was that Saddam "intended to bring greater pressure on Kuwait and to force settlement of their disputes, and that he might withdraw, having made his point."[116]

The Italian Prophet

One of the few who suspected the truth during those days was the Italian Prime Minister Julio Andreotti. On July 26 in Moscow, he told Gorbachev this might be the beginning of the Mother of all Battles.

> **J. ANDREOTTI.** *The position of Iraq in recent days causes particular concern.*

> **M. S. GORBACHEV.** *Yes, Iraq is opposing Kuwait, who helped Baghdad in its conflict with Iran.*

> **J. ANDREOTTI.** *Nearly everyone helped Iraq in those times, because they were afraid of Khomeini. [...]*

> *I believe that the support given to Saddam Hussein was too great. One has to be careful with him. He is a very unreliable character. And it seems to me he has expansionist aspirations.*

> **M. S. GORBACHEV.** *Yes, you are right. Look how ruthless he is towards opposition.*

> **J. ANDREOTTI.** *I am afraid of the following scenario. Saddam Hussein may, counting on Saudi Arabia's relative military weakness, proclaim the slogan of re-conquering the holy places and resort to vicious actions. I hope I am wrong, but I think there is such a risk.*[117]

We can only speculate as to where he got the clue. Other documents suggest that Andreotti was close to some of the Red Arab dictators and would even operate as their go-between with the Western world.

> **M. S. GORBACHEV.** *One of the difficulties of the Middle East process is that the leader of every Arab country sees himself as the leader of the whole Arab nation.*

> **J. ANDREOTTI.** *Yes indeed. The present president of Algeria makes a very positive impression. I often went to spend weekends in Algeria*

on his invitations, very confidentially, without even informing our ambassador. He opened my eyes on many things. It was also from him that I received first-hand information about the meeting of the [PLO] Council, and then shared it with my EEC colleagues.

M. S. GORBACHEV. *And look, for example, at the leaders of Syria and Iraq. We tried to make peace between them time and again. In confidence, I can tell you we were prepared to arrange a meeting between them, but nothing came out of this.*

J. ANDREOTTI. *Yes, they both are tough figures. Mind you, Assad at least controls the entire country, even though he relies on a minority [to do that]. But Saddam is an extremely tough leader indeed.*

The situation with Gaddafi is not entirely clear to me. At one point, I went to see Reagan in California and even brought Gaddafi's "Green Book" with me. I know that Gaddafi repeatedly made overtures towards the US Administration, but Schulz took an absolutely irreconcilable position.[118]

At times, these connections only exposed Andreotti to the Operation SIG propaganda; thus, he was convinced that the US government was "tied by the influence of the Jewish community. Two most influential newspapers in the US are owned by Jews, and the financing of political parties is also, to a considerable extent, done by the Jewish banks and businesses."[119]

After the downfall of communism in Hungary, when the new democratic government restored diplomatic relations with Israel, Andreotti said to Gorbachev:

I still think such presents should not be given just like that, for nothing. It would be a different matter if Israel showed preparedness to contribute to the process of [peaceful] settlement.[120]

Perhaps, it was from some of his friends in the Arab world that he learned about Saddam's plans. Someone, somewhere, knew of the upcoming Mother of all Battles and desperately tried to warn the West - but to no avail.

The invasion

So the great day had come.

At 2 am of August 2, the Baathist hordes crossed the Kuwaiti border. Simultaneously, a landing party from helicopters and boats fell onto Kuwait City and headed straight to the royal Dasman Palace. The Emir, his thirteen wives and numerous relatives barely escaped and fled to Saudi Arabia. Within minutes after they left, Saddam's men reached the palace.

At the top of the steps stood Sheikh Fahd, the Emir's brother responsible for Kuwait's soccer team, a pistol in his hand, with a few bodyguards. He and his guards fought to the end covering the Emir's retreat.

Kuwaitis attempted similar acts of hopeless, heroic resistance throughout the city, both in groups and alone.

Within seven hours, Kuwait was under Saddam's complete control. His Soviet-made T-72 tanks now headed towards the next stop: the Saudi border.

Mubarak and "Arab solution"

One of the first things President Bush did after the invasion was what the Western leaders always did - until very recently - whenever a sudden crisis occurred in the Middle East: he phoned Mubarak. The latter, it emerged, was working hard to solve the crisis by making some deal "within the Arab family". It had been a long-standing convention imposed by Red Arabs that outsiders must not intervene in the internal squabbles of the "Arab nation".

"George, give us two days to find a solution," Mubarak said. "I will talk to Saddam Hussein right now. I am also in contact with the Saudis."

"This is very important," Bush replied. "Please tell Saddam Hussein that the United States is very concerned about this action."

Mubarak said he would, and Bush promised to pray for him.

King Hussein of Jordan, who happened to sit next to Mubarak, also implored Bush not to intervene and assured him that Saddam was ""determined to pull out as soon as possible, maybe in days.""[121]

A trinity of Arab leaders worked as mediators in those few days: Mubarak, King Hussein, and President Saleh of Yemen. They arranged to bring Saddam to see the Saudi king over the weekend of 4-5 August 1990.

King Fahd, however, while pretending to keep searching hard for an "Arab solution" along with his dear "brothers", knew better than that. It was all too reminiscent of the days just before the invasion of Kuwait: a crowd of mediators led by Mubarak, arranging negotiations, which Saddam then used as a cover for an invasion. He would not fall into the same trap twice.

King Fahd told the mediators that, of course, he would be glad to see Brother Saddam and to keep it all in the family; he would just check his diary and then phone Baghdad. In Baghdad, they were eagerly waiting, but he never called. Instead, in utmost secrecy, he talked to the Americans about a deployment of their forces to Saudi Arabia. Saudis extracted all sorts of solemn promises from Bush that it would not be like the last time, when the US promised them a squadron of F-15s and then sent the planes unarmed to keep it all peaceful; or like in Lebanon, where US marines were withdrawn after the first major terrorist attack. As soon as Bush had promised, pledged, sworn that, gave his word of honour, and then repeated the whole procedure several times, Dick Cheney was sent to Saudi Arabia for official talks, and the "Arab solution" game was over.

This left Mubarak and his fellow mediators in a rather embarrassing position: the role they had played during those days did not look very good in the new context. Saleh and King Hussein then openly sided with Saddam; but to Mubarak, King Fahd had thrown a rope. He asked the Americans for their troops in Saudi Arabia to be accompanied with some Arab forces, and specifically, to invite Mubarak to join the new alliance.

Mubarak dashed into this escape route.

In the subsequent days, he took energetic measures to exonerate himself. He phoned President Bush and other Western leaders, to tell them that Saddam was now inviting other Arabs to take part in robbing Kuwait. According to Mubarak, Saddam had just sent him an envoy offering twenty billion dollars in exchange for Egypt's support of the annexation; and of course, Mubarak replied proudly, "We won't sell our principles." He would go on to say that he knew similar offers were made to King Hussein and Saleh.

Everyone was, of course, impressed with Mubarak's selflessness and honesty. To compensate him for the money he lost by supporting the common cause, the US forgave Egypt's entire debt. As we remember, Mubarak never intended to repay it anyway.

Another point Mubarak pushed hard in his contacts with the West was that Saddam had explicitly promised to him not to invade Kuwait, and then broke his word. This reached Gorbachev, who took an opportunity to reprimand Saddam through his foreign minister:

M. S. GORBACHEV. *The USA also use the fact that Iraq had promised president Mubarak not to take a military action against Kuwait, but broke this promise, deceived the Egyptians. Now the Americans say that Iraq cannot be trusted.*

T. AZIZ. *This is not true. One may disagree with President Hussein, one may hold very different opinions from his, but nobody has a right to say that the president lied. If he has given his word, he would keep it in any case, no matter how high the price is.*

As you know, my position and my own convictions do not allow me to say anything against any Arab leader. But, to be frank, the rule of today's president of Egypt is a real disaster, not only for Egypt, but for all Arabs.

M. S. GORBACHEV. *Why?*

T. AZIZ. *President Mubarak does not know how the Arab world lives, what its real problems are; he cannot understand the meaning of what is going on. He was simply used during the recent events.*

I was upset to learn that King Hussein of Jordan could not be received in Moscow these days. The King was in Baghdad together with Mubarak on the eve of the events and has first-hand knowledge of what really happened. As a reasonable and experienced statesman, he could have given you an objective account of everything.

For my part, I can quote practically verbatim the words President Hussein said to Mubarak and then to King Hussein. The President first said them at his tête-à-tête meeting with Mubarak, and then repeated them in my presence. "I will not take any action towards Kuwait," the president said, "before the Iraqi-Kuwaiti meeting in Jeddah on July [30]. However, Brother Mubarak, I beg you not to reassure the Kuwaitis."

You understand that no Arab leader can tell another one in plain language that he has to start a military action against an Arab country. But any sensible person should have understood what the president meant.

Just like with the other details of those events, it is still the word of Mubarak against the word of Saddam. I wonder, though, what would King Hussein have said? (He adamantly denied that Saddam paid him for his support, which was taken in the West with understandable scepticism).

Be that as it may, Mubarak"s true role in the events around the invasion remains largely shrouded in mystery and may never become fully known.

In the subsequent months, Saddam made a point of treating Mubarak as a traitor. He would rather negotiate with Americans, or Saudis, or any other Arabs, but always single out Mubarak as someone who cannot be trusted at all. This could have been genuine, or this could be simply an attempt to split the coalition. This could, indeed, be another "lesser evil" game: perhaps Saddam thought Mubarak was now most useful as a mortal enemy, which would strengthen his position in the coalition and enable him to restrain the Americans. In the misty world of Middle East intrigues, there are all sorts of possibilities.

Faint accompli?

In Washington DC, the Mother of all Battles came as a bolt from the blue. The White House had a plan in case Saddam successfully extorts so many billions from the Kings and Emirs (do nothing) and a plan in case Saddam invades Bubiyan and the Kuwaiti part of Rumaila oilfield (do nothing). But it was hardly possible to find a plan in case he starts a Mother of all Battles.

At the meeting of the National Security Council the next morning, Brent Scowcroft writes, "*I was frankly appalled at the undertone of the discussion, which suggested [...] adaptation to a fait accompli.*" Asked by journalists about the possibility of a US military intervention, President Bush ruled it out.

It was only after his meeting with Margaret Thatcher the next day that Bush changed his position and confirmed that the "military option" was, after all, on the table.

Meanwhile, the threat to Saudi Arabia seemed more and more real, and King Fahd requested a deployment of US troops (see above). Interestingly, later the following rumour went into circulation:

> *From the transcript of the meeting between Mikhail Gorbachev and Felipe Gonzales, Prime Minister of Spain*
>
> *(With foreign ministers)*

Madrid, 27 October 1990

[…]

M.S. GORBACHEV. *Americans are telling us this: we, they say, believed our Arab friends, especially the Saudis, that Saddam would not be able to hold on for more than three weeks after the US forces appear in the Gulf and the embargo becomes operational. And it is now three months since then… Anyway, we were against the deployment of US forces there in the first place.*

E. SHEVARDMADZE. *They made that decision without even asking for our advice.*

[…][122]

It is not clear whether Gorbachev told the truth here—he did that only on occasions and, as one of his Politburo colleagues later said, "Gorbachev is the kind of man who is lying even when he is telling the truth." There is no reference to that story in the transcripts of Gorbachev's meetings with Bush and Baker.

The US deployed forces. Their tasks at that stage were limited to the defence against a possible invasion of Saudi Arabia and the enforcement of the embargo against Iraq.[123] Later, that operation received the name Desert Shield. Those forces were neither intended for, nor thought capable of, an offensive.

This situation was still very distant from Desert Storm. At the initial stage, all steps for ousting Saddam out of Kuwait were limited to the embargo and diplomatic representations.

Chapter 6:
New World Order

I've always known that I was more a man of action than of reflection.

State Secretary James A. Baker III

State Secretary James A. Baker III writes in his memoirs that Saddam's great mistake was poor timing. Saddam had overlooked what Baker was doing. If Saddam had been smart enough to wait for another three weeks, when Baker would be on vacation, the whole course of history could have been different direction.

Unfortunately for Saddam, Baker was alert and sober on August 1st and 2nd, fishing in Siberia with Eduard Shevardnadze. As a result, they learned the bad news together. The next day, after Baker's stop-off in Mongolia, they made a joint statement against Iraqi aggression, which laid the foundation of the global anti-Saddam coalition.

Baker certainly sees that moment as the greatest success in American diplomatic history. The entire first chapter of his memoirs, preposterously titled "The Day the Cold War Ended,"[124] is dedicated to issuing that joint statement with the Soviets. Though it may seem like easy business issuing joint statements, this one, Baker reveals, resulted from a titanic battle between Soviet hard-liners and soft-liners, the latter led by Shevardnadze. The soft-liners supported Baker's hard-line draft statement, while hard-liners were lobbying for their own soft-line drafts—indeed, the final dramatic battle of the Cold War.

According to Baker, the Arabists in the Soviet Foreign Ministry were hard-liners and Saddam's sympathizers, so they wanted neither a joint statement with Baker nor an arms embargo against Iraq. Gorbachev was at his summer resort away from Moscow and could not help, because he was too scared of the powerful Arabists. However, decisive Baker sent his friend Shevardnadze into battle, and gallant Shevardnadze single-handedly called Arabists to order. Then he took the responsibility to sign Baker's draft statement without waiting for Gorbachev''s instructions.

The Soviet documents, however, tell a different story.

First, there was no resistance within the Soviet leadership to this idea of issuing a joint statement. The proposal was casually approved without any debate before Baker even landed in Moscow.

Second, Baker forgets to mention that the Soviets had unilaterally declared an arms embargo the day before. There was no question that arms supplies to Iraq would stop—the debate was over whether the statement should mention this.

Third, the initial reluctance to include that reference in the text of the statement came not from the mythical Arabists, but from Shevardnadze himself.

Below is a memo to Gorbachev from Anatoly Chernyaev, his aide on international affairs:

Mikhail Sergeevich!

Eduard Shevardnadze just called and told the following. Baker is cutting short his visit to Mongolia and flies home via Moscow. He offers Shevardnadze to make a joint statement on Iraq and Kuwait.

E. S. believes this is good from all points of view. But he has doubts about Baker's suggestion to mention the embargo on arms supplies to Iraq in that statement.

E. S. thinks (and I believe he is right) that doing that in a joint statement would be inconvenient. It would be better to do that in a different way: to announce that we, the Soviet Union, are freezing the supplies today, in the "Vremya" [official news TV] program. This means that is our unilateral action rather than a joint one with Americans. And we should not include this point in the joint statement.

E. S. has already summoned the Iraqi Ambassador. E. S. told him that the Soviet leadership is under great pressure from our public, from the [Supreme Soviet] members, that the issue may emerge in the Supreme Soviet, that we are receiving a lot of appeals from the other countries, including Arab ones. In a word, he has prepared the ground with the Iraqi.

E. S. said that he is going to act according to what is said above unless you express different considerations.

[signed] Respectfully, A. Chernyaev. August 2, 1990.

There is a handwritten note at the bottom of the page:

M. G. "s approval is passed to E. S. at 19:30.[125]

Apparently, when Shevardnadze saw how important to Baker the reference to arms embargo was, he changed his mind—understanding that this would make no difference to the Soviets. Moreover, no matter what Baker believes, either Gorbachev or his assistant authorized the decision. As Chernyaev writes in his diary:

> *Meanwhile, the Iraqi crisis was developing. [...] Shevardnadze acted strictly in the spirit of new thinking. Though he asked, by telephone, Gorbachev's authorization for everything, starting from his consent to a meeting with Baker in Moscow and a joint statement with him. But sometimes, if he called at night, I did not bother Gorbachev. I undertook responsibility to authorize it myself, assuring Eduard Amvrosievich that Gorbachev would agree.*[126]

So, Baker's estimate of his role in world history is slightly exaggerated. His lobbying of assistant advisors to deputy ministers in Moscow was, of course, important. But the Cold War was fought elsewhere by other people.

Baker's legions

"Coalition-building," to use Baker's term, is a typical *modus operandi* of US foreign policy in a time of a crisis, though it is difficult to explain why. Obviously, both the military and economic strength of the US is sufficient to defeat any enemy alone. Any alliance is only as strong as its weakest member. Most allies in these coalitions contribute very little to the common cause, and they only get aboard after their numerous and preposterous conditions are met. Then they raise all sorts of objections to anything that needs to be done. After the victory, they want rewards for their participation. Nevertheless, whenever there is an international crisis, "coalition-building" suddenly becomes a top priority.

This time, Baker felt destined to create the hugest coalition in human history. Moscow was only the beginning. From day one, Baker enlisted every country that was fortunate enough to catch his eye.

It happened that, after fishing in Baikal with Shevardnadze, Baker was due to visit Mongolia the same evening. On the plane to Ulan-Bator, the State Secretary had this idea to construct an unprecedented, monstrous mega-coalition led by him. Being a man of action, not of reflection, Baker went out of the plane and immediately created a coalition with Mongolia. After that, he already felt more confident, aware that the might and glory of Chingis-Khan were squarely behind him. Baker began getting aboard country after country, just like nuts. Soon, the number of coalition members exceeded any reasonable limits. With a little more time and effort, it could have grown to outnumber the United Nations.

Coalition-building, Baker reveals in his memoirs, may seem like an easy business to a layman; in fact, it is a complex and demanding art. A good coalition is not just a formless crowd of allies—the more, the better. There are allies of various sorts, and you have to structure your coalition carefully, based on sophisticated considerations and priorities.

The most important one was this: United States cannot send troops anywhere just to defend its interests and allies. We don't do this kind of things in the new world order, this looks too much like Vietnam. The conflict is not about America fighting its enemies, it is simply about good versus evil or, to be more precise, the new world order versus an old local disorder. Even if it helps US interests or allies, this is a pure coincidence; and in fact, such suspicious coincidences better be avoided.

To emphasize this new philosophy, it was important to avoid alliances with traditional allies, and seek alliances with traditional enemies. Nearly every country, from Mongolia to Syria, was welcome in the new mega-coalition, but Israel became the only exception. On the other hand, the Soviet Union—as the global antagonist of the West and the principal sponsor of Saddam's regime—was the most valuable ally.

The Soviets, for their part, had a very limited range of options and very strong reasons to join. They did not ask Comrade Saddam to invade Kuwait. His little escapade came exactly at the wrong moment—at the peak of Gorbachev's grand operation to save socialism at home and abroad. As Gorbachev once told the Turkish President, Saddam's action "contradicted everything that had been going on recently in the international relations."[127] Indeed, Gorbachev had just successfully charmed his opponents, seduced them with the prospects of eternal peace, and inspired the shining utopia of a "new world order." His foreign policy was like mass hypnosis. Slowly, like in a dream, the West was disarming, opening all the possible gates and handing more and more money over to the Soviet Union. In this situation, the most important thing was to avoid sharp moves that would scare the victim away. This was hardly the time for a Mother of all Battles in the Middle East.

Besides, Saddam's standing in the socialist camp was quite low by that time. As we remember, Comrade Gaddafi had been lobbying Moscow to depose him, and Comrade Assad dropped transparent hints that, if Iranian Ayatollahs wanted to get Saddam's head as a condition of peace with Red Arabs, he could see no reason why this was not a price worth paying.

So, the option of backing Saddam's invasion of Kuwait was not given a moment's consideration in Moscow. The USSR had no resources to support another round of the Cold War, and no desire to sacrifice its own complicated global schemes. All it could do was take the Western side, ensuring it would have a say in solving the crisis. Then it would use this position to minimize the damage Saddam caused, and to advance its own agenda in Middle East. If an opportunity presented itself to save that damned idiot in Baghdad, then he would survive. If not, it would be his problem.

Another priceless recruit for Baker's coalition was Comrade Assad, still sitting with his machine-gun at the Middle East road junction. Again, Syria was hitherto the main enemy of the West in the Middle East, the favorite satellite of the Soviets, and on the top of it, a Baathist regime like Iraq. It was important to demonstrate that, while opposing Saddam, the United States did not have anything against Baathism, but only fought for the new world order.

On his way to Damask to perform another masterpiece of coalition-building, Baker once again popped into Moscow, and sagely confided to

Gorbachev:

> *A very big problem for us is that he supports terrorism. And not only in the past.*
>
> **M. S. GORBACHEV.** *Talk to him about this. But I know what he will tell you: the US supports Israel, supply it with huge quantities of weapons, which upsets the balance in the Middle East. He has very detailed information about this. He keeps asking us to help him with weapons.*
>
> *In general, he is a serious statesman, free from Islamic ideologization. As for terrorism, I don't think he sympathizes with it. Maybe there was something in the past, maybe some people around him…*
>
> **J. BAKER.** *Absolutely definitely, at least in the past. Even now, so-called ""People's Front of Liberation of Palestine General Command"" (Jebril's group) operates from Syrian territory. It is implicated in the explosion of Pan-Am aircraft.[128]*

So the State Secretary concluded his lecture and was off to welcome Syria aboard his coalition.

Another founding principle of Baker's coalition was the supremacy of the United Nations. "Almost by definition," Baker writes, "the first stop for coalition-building is the UN."

Likewise, at the regional level, supreme importance was attached to the Arab League, with Mubarak as its chairman.

In the UN, the coalition priorities were these: first, the permanent members of the Security Council with their right of veto and, second, the temporary members of the Security Council (Cuba, Yemen, Zimbabwe, etc.)

In this regard, the Soviet Union was again the most important ally. If the Soviets joined the coalition, Baker calculated, France would not want to "appear softer than the Soviets" and China would join out of fear of isolation.

Indeed, at that time, China had different concerns about the Middle East. About a year before, the Chinese government had slaughtered a few thousands peaceful demonstrators in Tiananmen Square, and were still very upset that the world reacted without due understanding. They were in international isolation and needed to get out. The deal was simple: China supports the US against Iraq, and the US forgives them for the massacre. Baker would offer this to his Chinese opposite number quite cynically. "I'd offered him an incentive proposal," he writes, "The President would see him for a yes vote [in UN Security Council], but I would meet him if China abstained."[129]

At later stages, further incentives would be offered:

M. S. GORBACHEV. […] We can see that the Chinese are beginning to manoeuvre. However I don"t think they will veto the proposed resolution.

G. BUSH. I think, if we adapt this approach, the Chinese will follow us. You know, we have problems with the Chinese, but we work on the basis that they do not want to be in isolation.

M. S. GORBACHEV. I think you should lift your sanctions against China.

G. BUSH. There are legal difficulties. I have vetoed the Congress resolutions against China, and I've managed to defend my position so far. Actually, I agree with you, but under our crazy system…

M. S. GORBACHEV. It is no longer just yours.

G. BUSH. Anyway, if you talk to the Chinese, tell them that our administration is persistently seeking a normalisation of relations. Solidarity in the UN framework would help us to do even more in this respect.[130]

The price of support from the USSR and France was, in a sense, even higher. Both Gorbachev and Mitterrand had their own agenda in the Middle East, and would use their role in the coalition to promote it. As Gorbachev confidentially told the Egyptian Foreign Minister, what worried him most in the Gulf crisis was this:

If we don't untie the Kuwaiti knot and there is a regrouping of forces in the region, Americans will strengthen their positions. It will complicate the arrangement of the peace process in the Middle East.[131]

Gorbachev added that the French also shared this approach. Indeed, his discussions with the French during that period provide an interesting insight into their hidden agenda. The French, like the Soviets, joined the coalition in order to restrain its other members. They were Trojan horses. It is necessary to get behind someone before you can stab him in the back.

A few weeks later, the leader of Italian communists cheered Gorbachev:

A. OKKETTO. *[…]We highly appreciate the Soviet Union's role in this conflict. Your actions in the UN have been a real masterpiece of diplomacy. If the Soviet Union condemned the US action in the first place, it would not have so many trump cards to restrain the aggressive intentions of the US now. […]*

M. S. GORBACHEV. *[…] For the first time, we formed a united front in the United Nations. This is a great achievement. Now everything is being done under the UN auspices. This was achieved not without our influence, and the US duly appreciate that. This enables us to restrain them from unilateral actions.*[132]

""Prototype of the world government""

The night after the invasion, Bush was asleep and having dreams about the new world order. Baker was in Mongolia considering his personal role in its history. Scowcroft was sending cables around the world urging everyone to cut arms supplies to Iraq; and Shevardnadze was on his way back from that famous fishing expedition at Baikal, fed with black caviar by a beautiful Aeroflot stewardess. Meanwhile, an emergency meeting of the UN Security Council convened. After exchanging an appropriate number of platitudes, the Ambassadors unanimously voted for a resolution condemning the invasion, demanding a withdrawal, and calling for negotiations.[133]

Normally this would have had no significance whatsoever. The UN exists to pass resolutions that hardly anybody reads or takes seriously. It had been universally disregarded as a by-product of a failed experiment, a decaying monument to President Roosevelt's utopian dream about a world government. Another co-founder of the UN, the more cynical Comrade Stalin, then adapted it as a cover for Soviet espionage. That was about the only meaningful function the UN performed ever since its inception; the rest became purely ceremonial.

However, this time was different.

Anyone who reads Baker and Bush's discourses on the process of coalition-building cannot help noticing that their strategic thinking went in circles, and rather narrow ones. It was necessary to involve the UN in order to build a large coalition; a large coalition was necessary to pass unanimous UN resolutions, which in turn preserved and enlarged the coalition.

What was really behind it was their idea of a "new world order," the vague but sinister Messianic concept that only a select few could possibly comprehend. Indeed, what is the new world order? Does this mean world laws and a world government capable of enforcing them? As Baker told Gorbachev:

> *Now we have a real chance to make the United Nations work in the way planned by its founders. Indeed, this is a chance to lay foundations of the new world.*[134]

We will probably never find out if Baker knew anything about the founders of the UN and their plans. Gorbachev, however, did know. Furthermore, one of his closest aides, Georgy Shakhnazarov, had been responsible for developing the Soviet project of a world government for years, as well as handling this category of fellow travellers in the West.

Shakhanzarov was a very unusual character for a Soviet apparatchik. A witty, sarcastic intellectual and poet, a cynic as well as a dreamer, he spent his free time writing science fiction short stories. One story is about a meeting of a global Supreme Soviet in the distant future, discussing a groundbreaking technology that allows a space satellite to read and record the minds of all people on the planet. The global Soviet is split equally on the issue: the good guys want to install this technology for the benefit of future historians, the bad guys make all sorts of libertarian objections. In a surprise ending, the characters learn that a working model of the system had been installed in the building, recording their thoughts. Next moment, the entire Soviet—good guys and bad guys alike—rush, in panic, to the exit.

The Communist Party found a practical use to Shakhnazarov"s imagination: to invent scenarios of the global future, and to engage like-minded Western futurologists and other "social scientists". Unsurprisingly, the whole work turned around the idea of a world government. Soon, the communists began to play with that idea in practical politics. The leaders of the Italian Communist Party – the biggest in Western Europe – were particularly enthusiastic:

A. OKKETTO. The UN shall become an instrument of the world government.

A. RUBBI. Berlinguer spoke about the world government as early as at the 15th Congress of the ICP.

A. OKKETTO. At that time, many in the audience smiled at this.

M. S. GORBACHEV. We also have many people smiling at this.

Maybe, indeed, it is worth thinking about arranging for the communists, social democrats and someone else to work out an agreed constructive proposal. It should be not propaganda, but a real policy.

A. OKKETTO. [The leader of West German Social Democrats, Willie] Brandt wants to involve representatives of parties, statesmen and other major figures in this work, to discuss the problems during seminars and conferences.

M. S. GORBACHEV. Let us arrange all this, and also consult Brandt and others.[135]

After Bush and Baker subscribed the United States to the "new world order", the idea of UN becoming a world government was seriously discussed at the level of summit-meetings – perhaps, for the first time since Roosevelt"s death. On October 25th, 1990, Gorbachev told Argentinean President Carlos Menem:

M.GORBACHEV. [...] But we should go further. Further progress will depend on the actions in Europe, in Latin America, in the Asian-Pacific region. After European home is built, many other homes of co-operation must follow. [...]

C. MENEM. [...] speaking of integration, everyone agrees with it. We in Latin America intend to act along the same lines as Europe. In general, the humankind has no other choice. And then, after integration, we will concentrate on conquering the universe.

M.GORBACHEV. One of my aides has written sometime ago that we need to create a world government. People were laughing at him at that time. But now?

C.MENEM. *Some 40 years ago Peron was speaking of continentalism which would enable us to go for a world government.*

M.GORBACHEV. *I suppose we should think about enhancing the UN role. It could not realise its potential for 40 years and only now did it get such an opportunity. Here is a prototype of the world government for you.[136]*

In this sense, the significance of the Gulf crisis went far beyond the future of Kuwait. This was a precedent. This was just a start. This was the first rebellion faced by the UN in its new role. The apostles of the new world order could not afford to be seen defeated.

R. DUMAS. *Unfortunately, the situation we are facing is utterly simple. We cannot afford mistakes. We must not, directly or indirectly, legalize the action committed against Kuwait. Because that very world order which we aspire is under threat now.*

M. S. GORBACHEV. *Unless we are successful, it would seem like everything we've achieved worth nothing.*

R. DUMAS. *You are absolutely right.*

M. S. GORBACHEV. *Someone would even be able to use the flaws of the new order to argue for returning to the old one.*

R. DUMAS. *Yes, they would say that the old order was better. But we must not get into the trap.[137]*

Baker was of the same view:

J. BAKER. *[...] We are talking about a new international order which can now be created thanks to what we, the US and the USSR, have already done together. And now we face the first real crisis after the "Cold War". The problem is that we are facing a man who recognises no moral values. If such a man prevails over the will of the whole international community, this would mean we cannot create this new international order.*

M. S. GORBACHEV. *No, we won't let this happen. Saddam's victory would create a very bad precedent at the start of this new period in history.[138]*

At the same time, they could not let the "global policeman" of the "old world order" – the US – simply come and solve the problem. It was for the UN to decide how to deal with the crisis, and for the US to obey its command.

The Doves' Agenda

Therefore, from the very start, the American-led coalition included a powerful anti-American faction. Of course, in this context, anti-American did not necessarily mean anti-White House. On the contrary, more often than not, Bush and Baker were useful to them. So, to avoid this confusion, let us just call that faction "Doves."

Their priorities in the situation were so convoluted that one could hardly make head or tail of them without a good deal of expertise in Marxist dialectics.

First, it was important to support and preserve the "new world order" and keep everything within the UN.

Second, as a consequence, it was necessary to push the US to the margins, as far as possible. The US was not the "global policeman" anymore. It was just one of the members of the UN Security Council.

Third, the military action had to be avoided, for it would inevitably bring the US back to the forefront, back to its "global policeman" role. The crisis had to be solved by diplomacy. Only this way, it could be solved by someone other than the US.

Fourth, on the other hand, the crisis still had to be solved. If, and only if, nothing else worked, the force would have to be used.

Fifth, whichever way the events develop, at every stage, they would push their own regional agenda: undermining Israel, helping the Red Arabs.

Sixth, this meant they did not want Saddam to be beaten too hard, and were determined to prevent an overthrow of his regime.

The significance of the Franco-Soviet axis was not just that Gorbachev and Mitterrand could block any decision in the UN Security Council.

Their approach reflected the views of the European Left (and possibly even worldwide Left), as well as the position of the Soviet Empire.

Thus, in a conversation with the then Socialist Prime Minister of Spain, Gorbachev said:

M. S. GORBACHEV. *[…] At this new stage which the world community now enters, we cannot allow a precedent which would put in question our ability to solve such problems with the new means. Otherwise, numerous dangers await us in the future. We cannot idealize the world around us. Such threats may arise again. This is why we have agreed to a close cooperation with the US and Europe. From the first hours of the crisis and at all its subsequent stages, we sought cooperation – and we cannot retreat from this now. We cannot afford a split of the world community on this issue. This is the most important thing.*

My approach to the situation is based on two principles. We must achieve the goals declared by the UN in a peaceful way. First, this will demonstrate the United Nations' ability to enforce implementation of its decisions by peaceful, political means. Second, we all must understand that the military way is fraught with very serious consequences.

[…]

We must hold the course of firm resistance to the aggressor. Otherwise, the path to a new international order will be blocked.

F. GONZALES. *May I be brief: I absolutely agree with your analysis in all its nuances. I believe we have been absolutely right in all our actions towards the aggressor to the day. This is a new factor in the international relations. The Soviet Union has a particularly important role in providing a permanent dialogue, by preserving a communication line to [Saddam] Hussein.*

Like you, I have been persistently telling Bush that we should not rush things. I absolutely agree that the solution of the Iraq-Kuwait conflict should cause - though not directly, not immediately - a serious progress in the resolution of Arab-Israeli conflict.

May I just add two or three considerations in addition to what you have said.

First, it is very important to preserve the unity in our approaches to the UN"s role in this conflict. Even if we fail to avoid use of force, this decision must be certainly taken in the UN. In general, we need to improve the machinery of settling international conflicts within the UN framework. I have a very strong impression that there is too much of improvisation this time, including the build-up of military presence in the conflict zone. We need to avoid creating an impression (which is arising in certain quarters) that the US and other forces here play the policeman role.[139]

The influence of the Doves faction was no smaller out of the UN than in the UN. Indeed, Gorbachev's talks with the French over that period would typically begin from boasting how influential he was now in Washington.

M. S. GORBACHEV. *For example, we are warning [the Americans]: be careful, they are provoking you, trying to make you use force in the Persian Gulf. And the Americans feel that we are frank and that they can trust us. Mind you, in the old times they would rather act contrary to our advice, just because it come from the Russians.*

Interestingly, just two days ago we particularly emphasized this point in our contacts with the American president and state secretary. And today we receive classified information that certain Iraqi circles would very much appreciate if the American ground troops move towards Kuwait and use force. By that, the responsibility for escalation of tensions in the Persian Gulf would rest with the USA.

[…]

I fully share [President Mitterrand's] opinion that all of us must show vigilance and solidarity. […] We must aspire cooperation, accord, and show firmness. However, our experience of dealing with Americans demonstrate that they always make emphasis on flexing the muscles, because this gives "return" in domestic politics. The more determination the president shows in terms of military power, the greater his popularity is.

However, Gorbachev continued, it would be irresponsible to suck up to the stupid and aggressive American crowd.

If we manage to overcome the conflict, to prevent a military clash, only then we shall have a right to call it victory. […]

R. DUMAS. *[…] From the very beginning, we took an independent* *stance towards our allies and, first of all, the USA. This "autonomy" does not mean an automatic disagreement. We are talking about liberty in assessments, decisions and actions. On many occasions we, like you, had to restrain the United States' dynamics. And I could use a more precise expression instead of the word "dynamics."*

[...]

The Soviet Union's and France's independence and freedom of action provide special significance to their cooperation in present situation.

M. S. GORBACHEV. *Yes, this cooperation is useful not only for our two countries, but also for the others, including our American partners.*

R. DUMAS. *First of all, for our American partners.*

We told them many times: you must not be the only country which is at the frontline in this situation.

[...]

Besides, this conflict by no means should develop into a clash between the industrial countries, on one hand, and the Arab world on the other. Therefore, we fully agree with your view about the need to take some steps towards the Arab countries. [...] Probably, the contacts with Arab countries concerning this problem might also become a matter of our countries' coordinated activities.

M. S. GORBACHEV. *Such an approach is welcome. Somewhere we should act in parallels, somewhere – jointly. In any case we should exchange information.*

R. DUMAS. *For example, we are united by the belief that the Palestinian problem is central in this region. Our positions are practically identical. We believe that an International conference on Middle East is the place where this problem ought to be discussed. It is necessary to return to this idea.*

There is a real danger, which we must avoid. This local conflict, caused by a breach of international law, might transform into a global confrontation between the developed countries and poor ones.

We must act in a balanced way, allow no failure, and be loyal to each other. For this is the only way to force Saddam Hussein to retreat.[140]

I do not know how sincerely Mitterrand and Dumas believed in that danger of antagonizing the Arab world or even all the "poor countries." Was it a real concern, or just an excuse to shift the coalition closer to Mitterrand's own Middle East agenda?

Nevertheless, their search for an "Arab solution" would never stop throughout those months. The key figure here was, of course, Mubarak, who joined Gorby and Mitterrand in the triumvirate of the leading Doves.

Two days after Dumas, Egyptian Foreign Minister Ahmed Esmat Abdel Meguid also visited Moscow. When Gorbachev learned about that, he re-shuffled his schedule of urgent measures for the salvation of Soviet empire – only to free some time to see Mubarak's envoy.

Two key considerations concerning current situation in the Persian Gulf area[, Gorbachev said]. We have already shared them with the French and met understanding.

First. The irresponsible actions of Saddam's regime might result in an escalation of situation and an explosion in the region. To avoid that, it is necessary to activate the Arab factor. The cooperation of our Arab friends leaves a huge room for improvement.

I am saying this because here is a representative of Egypt in front of me, and I know the potential of your president. Even if you don't appeal to us, we will do our best to make the Arab factor influence the outcome of this situation. [...]

There are two reasons why the activation of Arab factor is necessary. The very nature of the conflict, involving two states which belong to the Arab world, requires the Arabs to consolidate and contribute to the settlement. We need the whole world to see that the Arabs can consolidate quickly. If the world sees that the Arabs can be easily divided, they will abuse that. If the Americans feel this weakness, they will try to consolidate their position in the region. And this is serious. I am talking not about tactical issues, but about big strategy.

Now the second consideration to be conveyed to Egypt's president. As you've probably noticed, the solution of the Middle East problem, of the Palestinian question, is moved to the background in the current situation.

And, if we don't untie the Kuwaiti knot and the regrouping of forces in the region happens, Americans will strengthen their position. It will complicate the arrangement of the peace process in the Middle East. What happened between Iraq and Kuwait once again confirms the urgency of the problem of Middle East settlement. It must be solved. It would be appropriate to raise the issue of the need to call an international peace conference on the Middle East.

ABDEL MEGUID. *We fully support the view about the necessity to call an international conference, and will act on this direction.*

[...]

I fully agree with the way in which you've outlined the significance of the Arab factor in current situation. Egypt believes that the Arabs as a whole must make every effort to prevent the escalation of tension into a full-scale military conflict. For that purpose, a meeting of the Arab states' foreign ministers will take place, on Egypt's initiative, in Cairo on August 30. [...] We don't call to confrontation with Iraq at all. On the contrary, we are ready to search for a way out of the present situation together with it. When reporting to President Mubarak about the contents of my talks with you, I shall emphasize that you've paid special attention to the Arab factor.

You were absolutely right to note that the Middle East settlement, especially the Palestinian problem, has receded to the background now. We must admit that this happened not as a result of some outside forces' actions. It is a fault of an Arab state. It is done by Arabs themselves. We see our duty as to correct the current situation jointly with the Palestine Liberation Organization.

A week ago Arafat sent his envoy to Cairo, whose mission, as we understood, was to excuse the PLO"s pro-Iraqi position this way or another. Palestinians have really made a mistake taking Iraq's side. It is still difficult for us to understand Arafat.

M. S. GORBACHEV. *We must rescue Arafat. And he must consult the Arabs more often.*

ABDEL MEGUID. *[...] Just like the Soviet leadership, we are convinced that even in the current situation it is necessary to move towards convening the international conference on Middle East. [...]*

M. S. GORBACHEV. [...] But some Americans and Thatcher, as I've noticed, doubt that a peaceful solution in the Persian Gulf region is possible. The situation is so important that we need more dynamism, especially from our Arab friends.

ABDEL MEGUID. I fully agree with you. Our position is that all the available political means must be tried first. They still have not been tried. We cannot resort to other means as long as there is some hope for a political settlement.

M. S. GORBACHEV. And before resorting to military measures, we must think a thousand times.

ABDEL MEGUID. [...] Now that a number of Security Council resolutions are passed, sanctions against Iraq are introduced, its sea blockade is practically established, we must give some time for these measures to start working effectively. Iraq must feel their burden. At the same time, we must think about giving Saddam Hussein some way out of the present situation.

M. S. GORBACHEV. I agree. We should help Saddam to find an exit from the deadlock. He seems to be unable to find it himself.

Only in the end, some tone of bitterness about stray comrade Saddam intruded into this businesslike conversation.

ABDEL MEGUID. [...]

President Mubarak was extremely alarmed and upset with the invasion of Kuwait. It was exactly he to whom Saddam Hussein had promised, in late July in Baghdad, that he would not use force against Kuwait. Mubarak passed these words to the emir of Kuwait, and then to the king of Saudi Arabia. Now it has transpired that at that time the Iraqis had already worked out the plan of capturing Kuwait.

M. S. GORBACHEV. This is perfidious and simply indecent. But politics is politics. We have to put emotions aside and search for a reasonable solution of the problem.[141]

Doves and Hawks

One year before the invasion of Kuwait, when the Bush Administration was still new, Mitterrand and Gorbachev discussed ways to advance their influence in the White House.

F. MITTERRAND. *[...] Perhaps, Bush is a kind of politician who always speaks in the way similar to his latest collocutor? [...] Undoubtedly Bush is a man of good will. But the whole question is whether he has a strong character. If not, he will probably do what his associates tell him.*

So, who in the new administration could be useful to the socialist Franco-Soviet axis in terms of influencing Bush?

F. MITTERRAND. *You know, among the president's associates, Baker seems to be an open-minded figure.*

M. S. GORBACHEV. *But he is not Shultz.*

F. MITTERRAND. *Baker lacks experience.*

M. S. GORBACHEV. *Not only experience, but also imagination.*

F. MITTERRAND. *Yes, he lacks these things so far.*[142]

Only a great utopian could believe that a man in his sixties may lack imagination only for a time being. Ironically, however, it later emerged that Baker did have an awful lot of imagination. Whether it had any limits at all is something known only to Gorbachev.

Long before the war erupted on 2 August 1990, Bush Administration increasingly resembled a royal court in an Arab Emirate, dominated by sophisticated intrigues of various national and international cliques. Hawks and doves, eagles and chickens, socialists, capitalists, mondialists, and all others were engaged in an everlasting struggle for influence over the kind-hearted Emir and his imaginative Grand Vizier.

As the war began, the Grand Vizier mounted his magic carpet and began an unprecedented round of shuttle diplomacy to construct his global coalition. Under the carpet, however, the coalition was torn apart by a silent and furious factional struggle.

The "hawks" faction was dominated by those who were in the coalition for practical reasons: Britain as the main geopolitical ally of the US (especially before Margaret Thatcher"s resignation in November 1990), President Ozal of Turkey (which is bordering Iraq), and of course all the Gulf States, led by Saudi King Fahd. On the very first day after the invasion, their positions were made abundantly clear. In the words attributed to King Fahd, "perhaps Allah has contrived these events to rid us of Saddam."[143] The hawks liked to compare Saddam to Hitler, were convinced that the only solution was to use force, the sooner the better, and would have liked to go the whole way until Saddam"s regime was removed from power.

On the other end of the spectrum, the "doves" were in the coalition for "new world order" reasons, e.g. due to their positions in the United Nations and Arab League. This faction was led by a trinity of bankrupt socialists of different shades - Gorbachev, Mitterrand, and Mubarak. They were against a military action, wanted to find a compromise with Saddam, and above all, feared a long-term increase of US influence in the region - and in the world.

Both factions had powerful allies in Washington.

In the middle of all that sat George W. H. Bush, the President without a vision, surrounded by crowds of professional visionaries, each pointing in a different direction…

Chapter 7:
First secret of Helsinki summit

Saddam had committed a crime: an aggression against Kuwait.

However, under the new world order, Saddam was charged with an entirely different crime: he had disobeyed the UN Resolution number 660. He had been ordered to withdraw his troops, *immediately and unconditionally*, to wherever they had been on 1 August 1990, not an inch to the South, not an inch to the North. He failed to do so.

He was ordered to seat and talk to the Emir of Kuwait *immediately*, and the talks had to be *intensive*. He failed to do so, intensively or otherwise.

Under the new world order, you may do what you like. If you like to invade Kuwait, Godspeed. However, once the UN Security Council has told you to withdraw, you must withdraw. Once the UN has told you to seat and talk, you must seat and talk. The Security Council giveth and the Security Council taketh away. Blessed be the name of the Security Council.

Such is the logics of the new world order. Saddam failed to follow it—and for that, he would now be punished.

◆ ◆ ◆

Naturally, Saddam would not miss the opportunity to exploit the political inadequacy and moral weakness of the "new world order" utopia.

A toothless condemnation in a UN resolution was precisely the response he had expected from the weak, fat, sentimental, impotent West. However, within the next few days, it became clear that this particular resolution was not like the others. It had real consequences: the embargo, the deployment of US forces into the region, and this seemed to be only the beginning...

OK then, Saddam announced, if it is now a new world order where UN resolutions are taken seriously, be consistent. There are 659 other UN resolutions, most of them never implemented. There are, for example, resolutions demanding that Comrade Assad withdraws from Lebanon. There are numerous resolutions on dismemberment of Israel. Enforce all those (at least in the Middle East) one by one, and when you reach number 660, then I will happily consider whether I should comply with it.

Such was the "peace initiative" Saddam proposed to the world on August 12. In effect, it offered a simple exchange: I will withdraw from Kuwait if Israel withdraws from the "Palestinian territories" first.

This was obviously unacceptable, and he certainly did not expect this to be accepted. He was trying to expose the hypocrisy and double standards of his opponents. From the point of view of UN resolutions, he was perfectly right.

Of course, it was obvious to everybody that Saddam's crime was the aggression against Kuwait, not disobedience to a UN resolution. It was equally clear that eventually, it would be for the US troops – not UN sanctions – to punish him. It was a job for a global policeman, not a global psychotherapist.

Yet, the world leaders were too keen on playing the childish game of being a world government.

Saddam reminded them of its rules.

Then something extraordinary happened—something that has been kept top secret by a number of governments across the world ever since, and is now revealed for the first time.

Publicly, Saddam"s "peace initiative" was rejected within a few hours after publication.

Secretly, leaders of the Coalition began negotiations with Saddam on the agenda he had offered to them.

Doves at work

It all began in early September, as Gorbachev was given a real chance to increase pressure in favor of his own agenda. Bush asked him for an urgent meeting to discuss the situation. Gorbachev immediately agreed, and the summit was arranged to take place in Helsinki on September 9.

The remaining days were spent in laborious preparations. Gorbachev instructed his experts (Baker's favorite "Arabists") to work out the best arguments as to why a military action was unacceptable, why economic sanctions were a deadlock, and why only a compromise would be a solution. Mitterrand and Mubarak were asked for advice. Gorbachev also sent a message to Saddam, asking him if he had anything new to say.[144]

Saddam was the first to reply. The next day he asked Gorbachev to receive his foreign minister Tariq Aziz before meeting Bush. Aziz came on September 5, passed Saddam's ""best greetings"", and then Gorbachev made a short speech.

M. S. GORBACHEV. The meeting in Helsinki is Bush' initiative. We agreed to it, understanding it would be useful. We keep insisting to the Americans on our own assessment of the events in Persian Gulf and the course of action we deem optimal in present situation. We are going to do that in Helsinkli, too.

As for Iraq, we have cooperated with you in the past and we would like to preserve that cooperation. Even the fact of our meeting today clearly shows our interest in that. At the same time, it is perfectly clear to us that if Iraq takes constructive part in the political efforts to untie the tight knot of problems which have emerged in the Persian Gulf, that will have certain results. But if there is no such participation, that may end badly.

Bearing in mind our past and present relations, I would like to say quite clearly that there is a grave danger in the conflict which has now erupted. You might say this assessment stems from the lack of courage in the Soviet Union's position. We don't think so. Our position is strong enough. But I cannot say the same about Iraq''s position.

The last thing we want is to lose everything which has been created in our bilateral relations during the years of cooperation. For this very reason, even in this extreme situation, we insist on the dialogue, with Iraq taking part in the search for a settlement.

In a recent speech I noted that President Hussein's actions were unacceptable for us. But a massive and prolonged stay of US troops in the region would also be unacceptable. We want a return to the original situation, with provision of necessary security guarantees to all sides involved in the conflict. Naturally, we would prefer the process of search for political solutions to go on with active participation of the Arabs. However, it is becoming more and more obvious that the Arab states are unable to reach an agreement.

What will you say to me? As your friend, I advise you to start searching for political ways out of the crisis as soon as possible. For the voices calling for "tough measures" against Iraq are sounding ever louder on the international stage. We know what it means. Does it suit you? I cannot believe that the Iraqi leadership will agree to expose their people to such a malevolent fate.

I have thought over President Hussein's statement that this conflict is rooted in the clash of strategic interests of the West, Arabs and other states in this region of the world. We know that is true. However, even if the problems really exist, solving them in such a way is absolutely unacceptable for us.

Now three possible scenarios have come forward. The first is the military way. In our view, anyone making choice in its favor makes a very dangerous mistake. It doesn't matter whom we mean, President Bush, Prime Minister Thatcher who has made a lot of statements about that, or President Saddam Hussein.

The second scenario means the blockade of Iraq, which would continue and, most probably, be tightened. Naturally, this would put a very hard burden on the Iraqi people. After all, it is anti-humanist and simply cruel towards the Iraqis. This way would mean bitter suffering to the people, even though the Arabs' sympathies might be leaning towards Iraq ever more. But even if the Arab countries are sympathetic towards the Iraqi people's sacrifices, this way is very hard and, most importantly, it does not contain constructive elements. It does not lead to a resolution of the crisis.

To be brief, only the third scenario can be discussed realistically: serious search for a political solution. We are convinced that only this option is in Iraq's best interests.

In Helsinki and otherwise, we are going to oppose the military option persistently, persuading President Bush it is dangerous and pointless. But, to be frank, we need constructive and realistic moves on your part for that.

That is exactly what we wanted to hear about when we asked President Hussein if there were any new elements in the Iraqi position. Do you have any new suggestions?

So far, the Americans don't want us to be mediators. But we've told them that the search for solutions may involve some mediatory missions, without specifying whose missions we meant.

We appreciate the fact that even in this harsh situation our dialogue with Iraq goes on. We do not wish Iraq anything bad. But there is the logics of history, the logics of development, and both we and you have to accept it.

In reply, Aziz declared:

I am very grateful to Your Excellency both for the content of your ideas and for the form of their expression.

For many years I literally live Soviet-Iraqi relations. […] I know for sure how high the Iraqi leadership values the relations with the Soviet Union. President Saddam Hussein shows his great personal interest in these relations. Especially valuable for him are his personal relations with you. You and he are political leaders of the same generation, and I am sure that mutual understanding between you on many issues is very much possible.

Then Aziz sentimentally recollected quite a few of high-level Soviet-Iraqi meetings, and finally confided:

We in Iraq are very upset when we hear stern remarks about us from the Soviet leadership. […] Our government is neither aggressive nor adventurous in its nature. While in power, we have created a solid basis for the existence of our state. We have also played a constructive role in our region. A good programme for joint actions of the Arabs was worked out at the pan-Arab summit conference in Baghdad a few months ago.

Due to the lack of time, I cannot go deep into the reasons which urged us to take actions we are discussing here today. But trust me, we would have never done that without serious reasons.

We were in a very real danger, comrade President. The problem was that the USA and their allies among Arab regimes had seriously sat a goal of crushing Iraq. I am not trying to excuse us, I am stating the facts. The responsible decision we took was based just on these facts.

As for today's situation, its essence is the confrontation between the USA, their NATO allies and some Arab regimes – on one side; and Iraq, Arab states and people's masses – on the other. I assume the full responsibility to say that neither leadership nor people of Iraq are afraid of that confrontation. The potential of hatred and anger towards the USA and their pro-Israeli policies, after accumulating for years not only in Iraq but all over the Arab world, has now reached the critical point. All Arabs are ready for that confrontation. The USA deceived the Arab world for decades, took Israel under their wing, supported the Israeli aggression against us, pocketed our riches.

We in Iraq are quite confident of our strength and not afraid to oppose the Americans. We know that this confrontation can lead to a broad-scale conflict along all the lines. The consequences of this conflict may affect not only our Arab region, but the whole world. But we are not afraid of such a future.

When the Americans talk about their ability to conduct a so-called "surgical operation" against Iraq, they are making a mistake. If they do anything like that, the result will be a long and very bitter – for them – conflict. It may turn everything upside down in this region of the world.

Naturally, we, being revolutionaries, are not afraid of such an outcome. We are prepared for sacrifices. But if it is possible to avoid this scenario, we will do our best for that. Peace is a sacred goal for us. We mean peace which would provide our security.

Now they are threatening us with war. But the Americans' assumption that they can intimidate us with their threats is absolutely wrong.

Now, about our approach to a political solution. Trying to restrict the whole complexity of our region's political, economic and other problems to one single issue of Kuwait is absolutely unrealistic in current conditions. The life itself has put the whole complex of problems on the agenda, so they should be solved together.

I mean the Palestinian problem and the Israeli occupation of Arab lands; stifling economic conditions many Arab states find themselves in; the outrageous gap between the rich and the poor in the Arab world, the tragic situation in Lebanon and a lot of other problems. The whole Arab world, from Iraq in the East to Morocco in the West, is boiling. The

Arabs are unable to wait any more. Therefore, no decent Arab leader can say that the issue of Kuwait and its Emir is the most important one now. To pull this question out, to bring it to the forefront means an intolerable simplification of the state of affairs.

I am telling this to you because I know that you can understand us. We don't tell this to Americans. It would be pointless to count on their understanding. They have created this situation with their own hands and bear full responsibility for it.

Our political course is based on the initiative proposed by President Hussein on August 12. You know it.

M. S. GORBACHEV. *Yes, we do.*

T. AZIZ. *The West rejected it immediately. Washington did that literally in two or three hours after it was made public. The motives behind the US behavior are absolutely clear to us.*

Nonetheless, the Iraqi initiative works, enjoys attention of the Arab leaders and the Arab public.

On the Soviet side it was said, by my dear friend E. A. Shevardnadze, that you in Moscow can see positive elements in this initiative. However, the Soviet side stopped at this point and did not develop its attitude towards our proposal any further.

We are going to keep basing our policy on the president's statement. At the same time, we are prepared to discuss any other considerations. Of course, our positions would consolidate if you, for your part, support our proposals.

You've been speaking about Arab part in the solution of the current problems. I can tell you that the Arabs make serious efforts even now. But the Americans block the way for these efforts. Sure, there are also some Arabs who don't want to make a constructive contribution. However, in my view, the Arabs' potential is not exhausted and they will be able to contribute to the search for a solution.

I would like to stress that, no matter how the situation develops in connection with Kuwait, we shall remain friends of the Soviet Union. But those on the opposite side have never been, and shall never be, your friends.

The situation around Iraq has been critically deteriorating since February. It was then that President Saddam Hussein, at the summit of Arab leaders in Amman, proposed to withdraw huge Arab capitals from the West and invest them in the economies of the Soviet Union and East European states. This idea was a reflection of our principal strategic course.

We do understand the situation in which the Soviet Union operates. We do understand why you have taken your current position. We do not count on the Soviet Union to defend Iraq. We are able to do that ourselves. What we would really ask the Soviet leadership to do is to restrain and, if possible, oppose American extremism in military sphere. We would like the Soviet Union to take a more balanced position, take the political initiative in its own hands, avoid restricting the whole complexity of the region's burning problems to one single issue.

Yes, we are upset with the Soviet leadership's reaction to the events in the Persian Gulf area. But we shall never change our positive attitude towards your country. Moreover, no matter which political position the Soviet Union takes, we shall never doubt benevolence and sincerity of its intentions towards Iraq.

As for the USA, nothing can ever expiate their aggressiveness, their cruelty towards Arabs and their patronage of Israeli aggression. And on the other hand, we shall never forget the noble position of the Soviet Union. In our view, now is a historical moment when this position can be dramatically strengthened if the Soviet Union takes a more balanced course towards the events in the Persian Gulf.

However, Gorbachev believed he was already doing his best, and it would be too dangerous to shift to a more pro-Iraqi approach. Therefore, he kept insisting that, by invading Kuwait, the Iraqi comrades had played into the enemy's hands.

M. S. GORBACHEV. *For many years we have been persistently seeking a solution for the extremely important problems of the Middle East. These are, first of all, the Palestinian problem, Arab-Israeli conflict as a whole, the complicated interlacing of the Lebanon crisis. Now, after Iraq has done what it has done, it became many times harder to find the solution of the region's problems.*

In effect, you have given the Americans very strong excuses to increase their military presence in the Middle East and the Gulf. The American troops won't leave so easily from there. We know that now Japan and Saudi Arabia are getting involved into financing them. Therefore, the United States have achieved their objective.

T. AZIZ. *There would be no problems, including that of Kuwait, if the Americans give at least a part of the money they are spending for military preparations for the Arabs' needs.*

M. S. GORBACHEV. *The fact that Kuwait was occupied and then declared the nineteenth province of Iraq gives an additional excuse to secure the American military presence in Arab lands and to involve the US' Western partners.*

A[LEXANDER] N. YAKOVLEV *[Politburo member]. This is a good excuse for the Americans to achieve their goals.*

For quite a time onwards, the Soviets kept trying to persuade Aziz that the Iraqi invasion was a wrong move in their common chess game.

You are trying to link everything, [Gorbachev said,] including the Palestinian problem, the liberation of Arab lands, and Lebanon. Your position is constructed in such a way that nobody can stomach it. Therefore, the USA will remain on Arab land for a long time, while the ring of blockade will be tightening around Iraq. You will get into a difficult situation. It will become increasingly likely that the Iraqi leadership, counting on the Arabs' solidarity and compassion, will resort to an escalation of the situation in order to break away from the grip of difficulties. As a result, a huge explosion may happen, and the control over the situation will be lost. Even if you are courageous enough, just think who could find such prospects attractive?

T. AZIZ. *We are grateful for your genuine concern with Iraq. Believe me, we appreciate everything you've said.*

At the same time, I must say that we are not novices in leading our country and in the affairs of international politics. We look forward without pessimism. We clearly see that the USA are trying to intimidate us, but their efforts are in vain. We are defending our land, where they are strangers. I have already mentioned the reserve of hatred accumulated by the Arabs. Psychologically, Arabs are ready for a vigorous confrontation with the US, and this readiness would be enough for a thousand years. These are not only feeling of the Iraqis, but also of Arabs of Jordan, Palestine, Algeria, Tunisia. Today only someone who opposes the USA most vigorously, be he even inferior to them in military force, can be the leader of the Arab world. In this, we cannot betray ourselves.

[...]

We are sure that the current confrontation between Iraq and the US will, in the end, bring us success. Of course, we do not expect that the Soviet Union unreservedly takes our side. We only ask the USSR not to embarrass us, to keep a balanced approach, to give us an opportunity to prove ourselves. You will benefit if we win, and you will suffer if we lose. The only thing that just cannot happen is that you benefit from our defeat.

M. S. GORBACHEV. *[...] I am afraid it is not as simple as you think. We know from our own experience that something you can easily do today becomes very difficult tomorrow, when you have to pay a much greater price for it.*

What comes to my mind in connection with this is the year 1967, when we had to save President Nasser's regime, literally to rescue it with all possible means. [...]

T. AZIZ. *By no means do we want the Soviet Union to suffer any damage because of our actions. We have no intention of shifting political, military or economic costs onto you. We only ask you to avoid speaking the same language as the USA. We also beg you not to let new resolutions of the Security Council put us in a humiliating situation. Give us a chance to solve our problems ourselves. I am ready to come to Moscow as often as every fortnight, openly or – if you wish – secretly, and consult with Eduard Shevardnadze on any issues that may interest you.*

Let me assure you again that we do not fear American threats and can face our future confidently. We have got the necessary experience to solve difficult problems. We are deeply convinced we can stand it this time. Just don't put too much pressure on us, leave us at least a small window.

M. S. GORBACHEV. *I cannot agree that we speak about Iraq in the same language as the Americans. You can accuse anyone that they speak others' language: the Chinese speak ours and we speak someone's else. That is not the point. With regard to what happened in the Persian Gulf, the whole* *world speaks approximately the same language. To be frank, you have left no other option to us.*

It looked like Gorbachev was getting angry, and Aziz tried to appease him:

T. AZIZ. *By no means did I want you to think that we see no difference between the Soviet and American positions.*

However, Gorbachev was still so angry that he even referred to God, which in Bolshevik mouth, is one of the rudest swearing words:

Perhaps, he said, you are getting instructions from the Almighty, but anyway, I want to give you an advice. It is up to you whether to follow it. We believe you should not decline from seeking a political solution on a realistic, constructive basis. I feel so far you are not mature enough for this. But you should take into account that the situation is going to worsen in the future.

There is a limit beyond which the people cannot make further sacrifices, cannot sustain more miseries and hardship. Then they may call their leaders to account. I don't think that is an outcome you want.

There is a play "Brest Peace" by Shatrov on the Soviet theatres stages, where the director has used a touch. Lenin is persuading Trotsky, who led our delegation at the negotiations in Brest, to make peace with Germans. Lenin says that he is almost ready to knee before Trotsky. It was a critical moment of history, when it was necessary to save our revolution. Later, they had to make peace anyway, but on much worse terms. Lenin even called that peace "obscene."

This was an even worse insult than a suggestion that Saddam's government was getting instructions from God. In communist worldview, God is enemy number two—after Trotsky. Comparing a comrade to Trotsky, even indirectly, was the worst curse a Soviet communist could make. However, Aziz reacted calmly:

I know this story. It is irrelevant to us. Our position is reliable, it is fundamentally different from the situation of that time. Just give us a chance to stand this confrontation.

There was no agreement, and the conversation seemed to have ended with nothing. Though Aziz kept insisting it had been great to see comrade

President, and that he was delighted with such an interesting debate, Gorbachev stated he was deeply dissatisfied with the meeting's results. Then he asked Aziz to pass his greetings to Saddam Hussein, and they parted.[145]

◆ ◆ ◆

The next day, Mitterrand called and declared solemnly:

This is President of France Francois Mitterrand speaking.

M. S. GORBACHEV. *My cordial greetings. Did you have a good rest during your vacation?*

F. MITTERRAND. *Unfortunately, it was very brief.*

M. S. GORBACHEV. *I've already forgotten those two or three weeks of my vacation, too.*

F. MITTERRAND. *So. I'm very glad to talk to you, Mr. President. The situation in the world is very complicated now. We are experiencing a difficult period. In this sutiation, it is particularly important for me to know your assessment of the matters.*

M. S. GORBACHEV. *I fully share your concern. I agree that we must constantly keep in touch, consult each other, in order to keep the situation in our hands. There is a danger that the events get out of control.*

F. MITTERRAND. *I agree.*

M. S. GORBACHEV. *[...] I constantly bear in mind the present situation in the Persian Gulf zone. In this respect, you and I have a very good mutual understanding. I am acting now, and I am going to act in the future, precisely in the spirit of this mutual understanding. I am going to arrange the discussion of these problems with G. Bush, during our upcoming meeting, in the same spirit. By the way, the fact that he has resorted to such a meeting is very important.*

F. MITTERRAND. *Thank you for such an approach. [...] What, in your opinion, should be our further actions concerning this conflict?*

M. S. GORBACHEV. *We must show firmness and unity, strictly obey all the decisions of the UN Security Council, and search for political solutions. At the same time I have to note that, so far, our contacts with*

Baghdad offer little prospect. It looks like they still have a space for manoeuvre.

F. MITTERRAND. *You are right.*

M. S. GORBACHEV. *Now, even at the political level, some suggestions are made about use of force. I am very critical about them, and even reject them.*

F. MITTERRAND. *Yes. First of all, we must achieve a successful implementation of the embargo policy. This is the only way to avoid an open war.*

Then Gorbachev briefly told him about his yesterday's talks with the Iraqi minister:

Saddam Hussein's representative constantly hinted that Baghdad hopes for understanding on our side. I felt he did not mean the USSR alone, but also France, as these two countries have special relations with Iraq. I replied that nobody would support Iraq. Indeed, what can they count on? That the Arabs rebel and support them? But this is unreal.

F. MITTERRAND. *I've got an impression that Iraq does not seek any other solution than war at all.*

Gorbachev went on with his story, while Mitterrand inserted approving comments from time to time. Gorbachev explained how he was accusing Iraq of playing into the enemy's hands, of providing an excuse for increasing American presence in the Middle East.

F. MITTERRAND. *Of course.*

Gorbachev went on to describe his further accusations, that Iraq was jeopardizing all the prospects of re-organizing Middle East, including the solution of ""Palestinian problem"".

F. MITTERRAND. *Precisely.*

M. S. GORBACHEV. *So, my conclusion is: we must show firmness.*

F. MITTERRAND. *My opinion is the same. We must be firm towards Iraq to force it to make concessions. But this policy of firmness towards Iraq must be complimented with a single policy towards the United States. The problem is that the American leadership is under pressure* *from a very significant part of their public opinion which demands to use military force quickly and harshly.*

M. S. GORBACHEV. *Yes, we must help our friends in Washington to understand where the true solution of this situation lies, how we can benefit from it.*

F. MITTERRAND. *As far as we are concerned, our analysis of the situation is the following.*

If there is another aggression by Iraq, which is unlikely at the moment, the French forces will take part in the conflict alongside the American ones.

In the second place, we can consider a following hypothesis: these are the US who strike first, without the UN decisions. In such a case, a priori, we won't take part in any action of this kind. [...]

But there is also the third hypothesis, for which we must struggle. If we manage to keep the blockade really strict, this might open a way for negotiations.

I am familiar with these plans and programs which exist in various Arab countries, and I am coming to conclusion that there is some field for negotiations. But these negotiations can only begin after the moment when the UN Security Council's resolution is implemented. This includes restoration of Kuwait's sovereignty.

Speaking of restoration of Kuwait's sovereignty, I mean only the country. I would like to tell you that I've taken upon myself no particular obligations concerning the exiled dynasty. Unlike many of my allies, who are in favor of their restoration, I've never insisted on such a demand.

My personal opinion is that Iraq may get certain advantages as a result of these negotiations. But of course, not so much as annexation of Kuwait.[146]

Gorbachev did not argue, even though this soft-line approach was at odds with the UN resolutions, which demanded a complete and unconditional restoration of the situation that existed before August 2. Hence were the important limits to the possibility of compromise, which both Mitterrand and Gorbachev understood. Mitterrand continued:

We should act in a way which would not damage the authority of the

UN. We have put the UN"s authority at stake in this conflict. If we waste it, this would significantly complicate UN"s peace-making activities in the future. If, on the contrary, the UN's authority strengthens as a result of settlement in the Persian Gulf region, the UN's abilities to settle other conflicts would strengthen as well.

At the moment, everything must be done to avoid a military attack by either side.

Now, we need Saddam Hussein to understand: the hostages story he has brewed is a colossal mistake. Everything I've said before concerns, so to speak, Saddam Hussein's rational actions. But his actions concerning the hostages rather belong to the sphere of the irrational.

All Saddam Hussein has achieved by that is that the public opinion in countries such as the USA, France or Great Britain is overexcited, is very hostile towards him. [...]

As a result, most reasonable plans may be overthrown by the irrational elements in Saddam Hussein's policy. So, we must force him to understand that the hostages do not protect him at all. On the contrary, the very fact of such a problem's existence is very dangerous for him. And obviously, in case he frees the hostages his credibility with the world public would increase.[147]

Gorbachev could only try to persuade Saddam. At the moment, however, it was George Bush (senior) rather than Saddam Hussein whom Gorbachev was preparing to meet. So, Mitterrand returned to this business. How could the damage done by Saddam to both Soviet and French policies in the Middle East be minimized?

M. S. GORBACHEV. *I have another small, but important consideration. Admittedly, the Arabs disappoint us. For you and I have had mutual understanding that the Arab solution would be the most acceptable.*

F. MITTERRAND. *Exactly. It would be very desirable if the UN gives Arab countries the mandate to undertake temporary responsibility for the settlement of the Kuwaiti problem before the full-scale negotiations begin. Unfortunately, in my view, the Arabs are incapable of that at the moment.*

M. S. GORBACHEV. My opinion is the same.

F. MITTERRAND. You have mentioned the Palestinian problem. Are you going to continue pushing forward the idea of calling an international conference on the Middle East?

M. S. GORBACHEV. This idea, which you have once suggested, is still in the air. I am going to talk to Bush about that. But I would like that to be a confidential exchange of opinions. If these discussions are made public and any disagreements are out, this will only please Saddam Hussein.

F. MITTERRAND. Yes, you're right.

We have voted for the known resolutions together. Therefore, we must preserve our unity and act in a common front. No divergence from our resolutions to either side can be allowed.

M. S. GORBACHEV. You're absolutely right.[148]

The two presidents said goodbye and hung up. In two days, Gorbachev was off to Helsinki, accompanied by a team of advisors, including his Foreign Minister Eduard Shevardnadze, his main expert on the Middle East Yevgeny Primakov, his chief aide for international affairs Anatoly Chernyaev, and the head of Comintern Valentin Falin.

In Helsinki, on the night before the summit, Gorbachev convened them all for the last brainstorming. Chernyaev writes in his diary:

Shevardnadze took refuge in silence, Primakov was correcting [the strategy of negotiations] bearing the Arabs in mind. Falin was after the "class struggle," referring all the time to the conference of European "leftists" in Tampier. I called for "realpolitik": we should prefer America to the Arabs. Our salvation and our future are here.

To my amazement, at the meeting with Bush M. S. [Gorbachev] was 95 per cent after my line. Five per cent he left for the Arabs.[149]

Interestingly, all the American memoirists (Bush, Baker, Scowcroft) assess Gorbachev's behavior at Helsinki summit as a sign that he was driven to the corner by "Arabists." Once again, it shows how little they understood about the Kremlin decision-making. If there was any pro-Western advisor near Gorbachev, it was Chernyaev. By his own assessment, his "realpolitik" advice was followed by Gorbachev in Helsinki 95 percent of the time. If there was any "Arabist" there, it was Primakov. His influence, as assessed by his main opponent, was no more than five percent. That was not an "Arabist" victory. Any alternative would be much worse.

In the morning of September 9, Gorbachev and Bush finally met, accompanied respectively by Chernyaev and Brent Scowcroft. According to Chernyaev, Bush looked very nervous, was eager for support, and scared of the Soviets' possible disagreement.[150] Gorbachev's impression was that his American colleague was "in a state of uncertainty and even confusion on what to do now."[151]

New Mid-East Order

"Glad to see you, Mr. President," Bush began.

"And I'm glad to greet you," Gorbachev replied, "Glad we've met, though I must say it was not easy to escape—a lot of work at home."

"It is good," Bush kept mumbling, "that we've arranged in Camp David we would meet whenever necessary, just as we are doing right now. The fact that we've arranged this meeting is taken positively all over the world."

Gorbachev answered with something equally meaningless. Bush agreed with him. Uneasy silence hung in the air before Bush finally asked:

What order of discussion do you prefer? Of course, I would like to tell you about our ideas. At the same time, I very much wish to listen to you. But at the onset I want to stress: it is good that the Soviet Union and the United States have shown to the whole world that now, during the crisis in the Persian Gulf, we are together, side by side.

So, maybe, you want to start? Or should I first tell you about my view of the Gulf situation?

M. S. GORBACHEV. *I agree to listen to you first, Mr. President. You see how easily you can reach an agreement with me.*

G. BUSH. *Very well, to the business, then.*

You and we have had good cooperation on the issue so far. We realize you had had long relationship with Iraq and therefore it was pretty difficult for the Soviet Union and for you personally to take this position.

Looking at the situation in a wider context I see a real potential of a new world order to emerge. Just in that way, new opportunities are looming because of this crisis, this tragedy.

But the new world order should be based on an explicit principle. We must prevent Saddam Hussein from capitalizing on his aggression. I am not sure he has realized that we, the United States, are fully determined to do that. I know, from a number of sources, that he questions my determination. Hope you will try to reason him out of this. We will not be reconciled to the failure of our efforts to reach the goals set by the United Nations.

We have worked out a strategy targeted at this and I believe that this strategy has good chances of success. We prefer the sanctions as means of achieving this goal – Iraq's withdrawal from Kuwait and restoration of the Kuwaiti leadership. I don't want the conflict to escalate. I don't want military force to be used. I know that you share this approach. But Suddam Hussein must realize that, unless he withdraws from Kuwait, we are prepared to use force. It is unacceptable to keep the status-quo. [...]

Saddam Hussein's actions concerning the innocent civilians, possibly including Soviet citizens, cause particular indignation. If you happen to contact him, I'd ask you to let him know the following. Using innocent people as a "shield" won't force me to change our policy in the slightest. I believe such actions might be a reason to conduct a Nuremberg-style legal trial.

And just two more points. When flying here, journalists asked me in the plane: are you going to ask Gorbachev to send troops to the region? I told them I had no plans to address you with such a request. But let me assure you that if you take such a decision, the United States would welcome this.[152]

Scowcroft shuddered.[153] His imagination pictured the Workers' and Peasants' Red Army appearing in the Gulf, all the stock markets subsequently collapsing, and other apocalyptic pictures. Luckily, Gorbachev did not react. Bush got away with that, and continued:

And the other point is, probably, particularly important for you. We have no intention to keep the American troops in the Gulf on a permanent basis. There are no such intentions behind the current American presence in the Gulf. Certain arrangements should be made to prevent repeat of aggression and possible use of nuclear weapons, in case Saddam Hussein remains in power. But these should be international arrangements rather than American ones. We have no plans to keep American forces in the Gulf area either in direct or indirect form.

Now, to show down all my cards, I wish to say this. For many years, during the Cold War, the United States policy consisted of preventing the Soviet Union from playing any role in the Middle East. Certainly, the Soviet Union disagreed with that line, was displeased with the U.S. attitude. Even though I am sure that it would be a great victory of Saddam if he managed to add the issues of the Arab-Israeli conflict to the crisis caused by his aggression, I want to assure you that the old concept, old U.S. attitude towards the Soviet Union's involvement in the Middle Eastern affairs, have changed. The new order, which, I hope, might be established after all these troubles, implies both the United States and the Soviet Union will make more positive, common efforts to resolve not only this particular problem but also other problems of the Middle East.

And the last point. The closer views we have by the end of this day the more favorable will be the prospects of the new world order, of the development of the Soviet-American relations, and certainly of the present crisis, the liquidation of consequences of Saddam Hussein's aggression. Mr. President, I speak to you as to an honorable friend, an equal and important partner, as a party in affairs whose role is vital. Let's look forward realizing that not only this particular problem but also grand matters are in question. Whatever small differences in our approaches were – and I should say those differences have significantly narrowed owing to the Soviet side's efforts in the framework of the United Nations – it is very important to appear together, with a common attitude at the coming news conference. On Tuesday I will address the American people on television. I want the tone of my address to be positive and optimistic. I would like to say that we have turned the page of the Cold War, done away with it once and for ever...[154]

In the context of what we know about the basic parameters of the Cold War in the Middle East, those were astonishing concessions. The West had always aimed to contain the Soviet influence in the Middle East—and for a good reason. The objectives of the Soviet policy in the region were well-known: an international conference under UN auspices to determine the conditions of peace based on relevant UN resolutions. Those objectives did not change under Gorbachev—not until the very last day in the Soviet Union's life.

Bush's apparent agreement to those terms was a logically inevitable consequence of his "new world order" ideas. The question raised by the invasion of Kuwait was this: who shall be the "global policeman" to protect the brave new world from gangsters such as Saddam? Under the old world order, that role was performed by the American troops. Under the new one, it had to be the "international community," acting through the UN, and naturally included the Soviets. Therefore, the Soviet presence—perhaps even military presence—in the Middle East was not just permissible, but necessary. Furthermore, Soviet presence would mean a Soviet part in decision-making; Soviet decision-making meant the Arab-Israeli issues would be settled in a way that would satisfy Soviet allies in the region (such as Syria and the PLO). This, in turn, might very well mean the end of Israel.

If we look at the UN resolutions, which would provide the basis for peace, the horrid implications of the new order proposed by Bush become abundantly clear: First, Israel would have to withdraw from the "occupied territories" of Gaza, Samaria-Judea, and Eastern Jerusalem, which would be turned into a Palestinian state. Second, Golan Heights would be returned to Syria, leaving the Northern half of Israel defenseless. Third, the "Palestinian refugees" from all over the Arab world, well-organized and trained to kill as they were, would be given a "right of return." What survived of Israel would be effectively invaded by the PLO army.

Bush's wiser predecessors knew that they could not make concessions on Israel: you either make none or surrender the whole country. What Israel has is the minimum it needs for survival. There is no space to retreat.

Did Bush realize this?

Fortunately, all these dreams of a "regional security system" under UN and Soviet auspices were gone with the Soviet Union. However, the fact that this new American policy on Middle East was promised begs many questions. For example, who else, apart from Gorbachev, was it promised to? Was it promised to Arab allies? After all, Bush and Baker had to reward them, too. It would be only reasonable to promise the same reward to all the allies, rather than a separate one to each. To make one concession is better than to make several dozens. The single concession that could satisfy the majority of allies— from European socialists to Arab kings—is Israel.

That was not a bluff - Bush was serious. In the final chapter of this book, we shall see how, as soon as the Gulf War was over, the anti-Israeli hidden agenda was put into operation.

Anyway, forget the hidden agenda - just look at what happened in the Arab-Israeli 'peace process' over the past two decades, with Israel forced to make one concession after another. Had the Soviet Union survived and taken the place in the Middle East which Bush had promised to it, it could have been even worse.

As history shows, whenever you start with new world order, you finish with final solution of the Jewish question.

However, all this was only the beginning of that extraordinary summit meeting.

Chapter 8:
Second Secret of
Helsinki summit

One who has never lived in America during a period of "sammitomania" can hardly appreciate the scale of the disaster… If it was in my power, I would ban [summit-meetings] by law, like selling alcohol to the underage or to Indians. For there is no ally or principle which the great American nation, drunk with its own progressiveness, would not give away to its newly found brothers.

Vladimir Bukovsky. USSR: from utopia to disaster

Naturally, the price of involving traditional enemies into the coalition was higher than that of involving traditional allies. However, Bush and Baker decided that the new world order was worth it.

The logical conclusion of this policy was to ally with Saddam himself, thus eliminating all the remaining problems. After all, Bush had already agreed that the price of Kuwait's liberation would be the "solution of other problems in the Middle East." That was exactly what Saddam demanded in his "peace initiative." The only difference was that Saddam wanted to have Palestine first and discuss Kuwait later, while Bush preferred it the other way round. However, the general outline of the deal sought by both sides was clear enough: Kuwait in exchange for Palestine — oil in exchange for Jews.

What remained to be negotiated were the details, the timetable, and the mutual guarantees. Just one last step remained to be made, and the coalition would be complete.

Beating around George W. H. Bush

Then, in Helsinki, Gorbachev began from far away:

> *The question is, are we able to act on this new stage of global politics which we have entered after the end of the Cold War? And, most importantly, how shall we act? [...] In fact, we are facing a global choice. You speak of a new order. Indeed, we must live in a new way, construct our relations in a new way. The price of that is very high.*

As an example of the high price he himself had to pay, Gorbachev recalled the collapse of communist regimes in Eastern Europe and unification of Germany. He implied it had cost him enormous efforts to resist the temptation to start a Third World War because of these events. Gorbachev said:

> *Given the level of military opposition in Europe, such a mess could be caused which we would probably be unable to clear.*
>
> *And now, we are facing a no less difficult challenge.*
>
> *You probably agree that the events in Eastern Europe and German affairs were more difficult for us than for the USA. I can tell you frankly that literally overcoming ourselves, overcoming the old approaches which had seemed immovable, acting in a way which the changed realities required cost us colossal efforts, great exertion of political will. [...]*
>
> *Now, this Gulf situation is more difficult for the United States than for us. [...] People want quick victories from their president. [...] We realize how difficult your, as the President, situation is [...] and feel sympathy.* [155]

In this way, Gorbachev led Bush to the idea that he should sacrifice everything to the friendship with the Soviet Union, just like Gorbachev himself, he claimed, had sacrificed Eastern Europe to the friendship with the US. Of course, he was lying: he simply had had no means to keep Eastern Europe under control, no matter how hard he did try. What happened in reality had nothing to do with his good will.

On the other hand, what exactly was so difficult in the "Persian Gulf situation" for the United States? In fact, it was Gorbachev who was in difficulty again, as he had to preserve his friendship with the both sides in a war.

Bush, however, swallowed all this without arguing. Gorbachev went on:

Without hesitation, we condemned Iraq's aggression against Kuwait. We are going to follow the UN Security Council's resolutions strictly.

Though, I must say, we had certain difficulties on the initial stage of the conflict when you took a decision first and informed us about it later.

G. BUSH. *Which decision do you mean?*

M. S. GORBACHEV. *I mean the decision to send American troops to the region. We were informed about it not before these forces began to move. I don't want to say this changed our political approach. But this complicated the situation to some extent. Probably, this happened because our new relations are still in the process of formation.*

G. BUSH. *This is an interesting point. We sent our troops to the region on Saudi Arabia's invitation. The situation was very tense, as Iraqi troops were already to the South of Kuwait's capital city. However, I'm accepting your words as constructive criticism. Probably, I should have phoned you then. I want to assure you that we did not want to act behind your back.*

M. S. GORBACHEV. *In general, we have managed to act together, shoulder by shoulder. We have managed to mobilize the UN Security Council, practically the whole world community. And this is a great achievement. In this light, even the US presence in the region is seen differently.*

G. BUSH. *I agree.*

M. S. GORBACHEV. *Obviously, the world community cannot move forward towards the new peaceful period of its history without certain machinery arranged to protect this peace process from such problems, without machinery of response to such conflicts.*

In today's situation, you have taken upon yourself the main mission of opposing the Iraqi aggression. And now I am coming to the central point of my discourse, which will be followed by suggestions on what to do now.

Look where we are, what has been achieved. The threat to Saudi Arabia is eliminated. The whole world has condemned Saddam Hussein's aggression, put him in the pillory. The infrastructure which provides world oil supplies from the most important source is preserved and secured. So, the US President and the whole world community have something to be proud of. Important strategic objectives have been achieved, though not all of them. The problem of Kuwait is not solved, and of course, it is necessary to solve it.

[...]

What you've just said is very important for me. In my view, three points of what you've said are most significant.

Firstly, like us, like practically the whole world, you want the problem of Kuwait to be solved. Secondly, you've made an important statement concerning the US presence in the region. You've said you don't want to keep it on a permanent basis. And thirdly, you've said that you prefer a non-military solution of this problem.

I do realize that all of us, and you in particular, are sort of under pressure right now. People expect strong actions from you. Indeed, we need strength. But if this means use of military force, this is too dangerous.

So far we have acted together, on a multilateral basis. But a unilateral military action by the USA would lead to consequences unacceptable for you as well as for all of us.

I don't want it to look like I am declaring some maxims. But the logic of our considerations is the following. Unless Iraq attacks Saudi Arabia or Israel via Jordan, the United States would look like the initiator of military actions. What happens if military action is taken against Iraq now, when it is still keeping the status-quo?

G. BUSH. *Do you mean, if we launch a military action without a provocation from Iraq?*

M. S. GORBACHEV. *Yes. Look how Iraq acts now. Marshal Akhromeev showed this to me on the map of Iraqi forces' dislocation. The main contingents are located deep within the country, rather than in the area near Saudi Arabian border. If you start a military action against these forces this would inevitably lead to huge casualties. The memories of Afghanistan and Vietnam are still fresh in our countries.*

Gorbachev realized this was not as true about Vietnam as about Afghanistan and quickly corrected himself:

Now it is already deep in people's minds. And very soon they will start to say that the president has chosen not the best option, that he got involved in military actions which cost thousands, tens of thousands of casualties. No, we have to seek different ways.

Apart from casualties, we should not forget economic consequences either. […] If this region is basically destroyed, can you imagine the financial losses? We are talking not about billions, but about trillions of dollars. All of us will be going to the dogs.

Another consideration. Even now we can see and must admit that Saddam enjoys certain sympathy from some people in the Arab world, from a significant part of the Arab masses. To them, he is a hero, a fighter for the Arab cause, the man who is not afraid to oppose the United States. The Arab world will turn against you if a big war, with a lot of destruction, begins in this region, where the Arab nation possesses huge riches. You will be accused of acting inadequately to the situation.

We have to bear in mind that the Muslims' mentality is quite a different matter from yours or mine, from the mentality of Americans or Europeans. Everything is uncertain there. To them, all of us are Barbarians, infidels. You would look like enemies, like desecrators of Arab sanctities.

By the way, I would like to note that now both you and we are well aware of the great dangers inherent in Islamic Fundamentalism. This is a great threat and we must cooperate to oppose it…

At this point, Bush politely interrupted him and pointed out that, in fact, there was little support for Saddam in the Arab world. Most of the Arab countries condemned the aggression. Egypt, where the majority of the world's Arabs lived, was among its firmest opponents.

Gorbachev dismissed the argument, saying that the toiling masses were quite a different matter from the ruling circles; the masses were Islamic and therefore on Saddam's side. He hinted that anti-Saddam Arab leaders might face fundamentalist uprisings in case the conflict escalated.

Amusingly, that was the very argument that Aziz advanced and Gorbachev vigorously opposed at their meeting a few days earlier. Gorbachev rubbished and ridiculed this idea on many occasions over those days, when talking to Mitterrand and others. It is highly unlikely that he really believed in the slightest possibility of any such uprisings. Now he was just throwing all the available arguments, true and false, at Bush:

I have to be frank with you. Probably, you have noticed the caution being expressed in a number of Western countries. If the events develop in a wrong direction, they will probably have to distance themselves from you.

G. BUSH. *I know.*

M. S. GORBACHEV. *And another important thing. The unity in the Security Council might be broken. For example, we can almost be sure that the position of China would change. And China is a country which has the right of veto.*

I suppose, all of this would be hard for the American society, too.

Therefore, we have to seek a different way.

It is obvious, of course, that Saddam Hussein won't withdraw from Kuwait so easily. In recent exchanges of opinions with all our partners, everyone emphasized the need to strictly obey the embargo introduced by the UN. And it should be mentioned that the situation inside Iraq is changing. Saddam Hussein himself is in a difficult situation now. No matter what statements he makes, eventually he will have to take a sober view of the situation.

We have a lot of strong experts on the Arab world and particularly on Iraq. We've discussed the situation with them. They've done a detailed situation analysis and came to an absolutely clear conclusion. The use of force against Iraq would be acceptable only if it attacks Saudi Arabia or Jordan. In any other case the use of force should be out of question.

G. BUSH. *Well, what if, for example, they strike at Israel with a couple of Scud missiles?*

M. S. GORBACHEV. *This would be a different situation. However, I don't think they can do it now.*

It is really impossible to accept the status quo. We cannot allow the aggressor to benefit from his aggression. But all our experts think Saddam Hussein should not be driven into a corner. It will bring no solution. It is necessary to look for an option allowing him to save his face at least partly. This is the reality. It is not pleasant in moral sense. But we should act on the basis of realities of the situation, look what options are possible, what options are feasible.

Whose face required saving?

As we shall see in a moment, Gorbachev's real plan was sinister and clever. Yet, pausing here, everything he said to Bush in the course of advancing the argument was propaganda nonsense, or disinformation.

The chief Arabist in the Soviet Foreign Ministry at the time, Deputy Minister Alexander Belonogov, led the team of experts who had briefed Gorbachev for the meeting. In his book about Kuwait crisis, Belonogov gives a summary of Gorbachev's above arguments and then comments:

To add weight to the above, the President referred to the opinion of some unnamed Soviet Arabist experts and the data received from some situation analysis.

I must make it clear that the Foreign Ministry brief given to the President contained nothing like that. Later, reading the transcript of the negotiations, I was surprised that Mikhail Sergeevich resorted to "horror stories" of this kind, so reminiscent of the then Iraqi propaganda, in a serious conversation. [...] I was also surprised by another Gorbachev's argument: he claimed that using force against Iraq would look like an aggression, and that use of force was permissible only if Iraq attacked one more country. Here, Mikhail Sergeevich was clearly at variance with the international law and, indeed, with logics - as if one had to commit at least two murders, not just one, to be liable for it.[156]

Nor did the Soviet Arabist-in-Chief ever advise Gorbachev that, if driven into a corner, Saddam would do something terrible rather than "lose face". "I thought then and think now," Belonogov writes, "that Saddam Hussein was exactly a man to whom saving face was not an end in itself."[157] He then gives a detailed account of all earlier situations where Saddam had a choice between saving his face and saving his skin (though Belonogov uses more diplomatic expressions to explain the dilemma). Saddam had always saved his skin, and then instructed his propaganda department to explain why this had been his heroic victory. It was Belonogov's view that, in any

Stalinist regime, saving the dictator's face is not the dictator's problem and does not affect his decisions. It is entirely a problem of his propaganda department to present his every decision as a victory.[158]

Undoubtedly, his view was known to Gorbachev at the time. When he attributed the "face-saving" nonsense to his Arabists, he simply lied.

In fact, it was President Bush, not Saddam, who sought a face-saving exit for himself.

The gist of Saddam's position was this: I may withdraw from Kuwait in exchange for Israel's withdrawal from Palestinian territories. Is this a deal?

The gist of Bush's position was this: Saddam must withdraw or be driven out of Kuwait. This done, the "world community" would take a deep sigh of relief, declare emphatically, "Now, to change the subject completely...", and make Israel withdraw from Palestinian territories. In other words, the deal can and will be done, but it must not be seen to be done. In the secrecy of summit-meetings, Bush solemnly pledged that America would adhere to its side of the bargain even though the deal remains secret.

Whose position looks more like a face-saving capitulation?

It is impossible to conceal—not even in the *official version*— that compromise proposals linking the two issues together were in circulation during the fall of 1990. Such proposals are always referred to as proposals to give Saddam a face-saving exit. The official version asserts that all of them were firmly rejected by the United States.

The truth was that Saddam did not seek a face-saving way to surrender. The Bush Administration did.

It was Bush, not Saddam, who was seen in this period to be nervous, scared, or (in the words of a different witness) to be "in a state of uncertainty and even confusion on what to do now."[159] Indeed, Saddam was never seen to be in such a state in his entire life.

The critical disagreement between them—the issue that eventually made an amicable settlement impossible and led to the armed conflict—was whether the deal would be done openly or in secret.

This considered, let us return to the conversation in Helsinki on September 9, 1990.

To the business

Having told Bush all his "horror stories" about the Fundamentalist revolutions, the world-wide jihad, many thousands of casualties and many trillions in financial losses—all that inevitable consequences of an attack on Saddam—Gorbachev proposed a solution:

What if we make a series of interrelated steps, a complex of measures? In particular:

If Iraq announces that it is going to free foreign citizens it is holding and to withdraw its troops from Kuwait, the United States and other countries would make a statement in the Security Council that they are not going to attack Iraq, to strike at Iraq.

Next. If the both statements are made, the withdrawal of the Iraqi troops and their replacement with inter-Arab forces of agreed structure, under UN flag and control, begins, the United States would cut their military presence in Saudi Arabia, probably at a symbolic scale initially. The withdrawn troops would be replaced with the inter-Arab forces under UN auspices, both in Kuwait and Saudi Arabia.

Then, the UN Security Council might vote for suspension of its resolution regarding the embargo against Iraq. After the withdrawal of Iraqi forces is completed the appropriate resolutions would be repealed.

G. BUSH. *And this is conditioned by the withdrawal of all Iraqi forces from Kuwait?*

M. S. GORBACHEV. *I will say about that a bit later.*

G. BUSH. *My question is, of course, hypothetical.*

M. S. GORBACHEV. *There are some other elements in this plan. By the way, we tested it on Arabs. If Saddam rejects this plan, he will unmask himself in the eyes of the whole world, in the eyes of Arabs. And this would prevent the growth of sympathy towards Saddam Hussein in the Arab world.*

You've mentioned that Saddam Hussein wanted to pile all problems, to interlink the Arab-Israeli conflict, Palestine, Lebanon. It is so, and he scores on it. It is necessary to face the fact that the problem of Israeli occupation of Palestinian lands is sensitive. Therefore we find it necessary to knock this card out of his hands and play it in our common interest.

You probably thought of it, too.

An international conference with the Security Council members' and Arab states' participation might discuss the problem of the restoration of Kuwaiti independence and other problems of the region including the problems of Palestine and Lebanon. But they should start from the problem of Kuwaiti independence. The conference might also discuss the issue of establishing a system of security guaranteed by the Soviet Union and the United States, by five permanent members of the Security Council.

It should be mentioned that they in the European capitals express some interest in this idea, bring forward parallel proposals. If Israel agreed to take part in such a conference, not at the first but probably at the second stage, perhaps we would be able to re-establish diplomatic relations with Israel as a quid pro quo.

This plan seems acceptable for many Arabs. Of course, Saddam Hussein may reject the idea of withdrawal. But – since we connect it to the discussion on the problem of Palestine, of Arab lands – for the public opinion, it would be Saddam to blame for the continued Israeli occupation, for the lost opportunity to solve this problem. He would show to Palestinians and all Arabs he is just exploiting that problem.

We believe that, combined with the embargo, offering the settlement plan would put him in a difficult position and significantly restrict his space for manoeuvre.

We asked our experts what they think about the idea of blockade of Iraq. But it is impossible to keep this blockade without using military force. Hence, war may start at any moment. This would mean the end of any hope for peaceful settlement.

At the same time, we believe that a tougher economic embargo is possible. So far Saddam Hussein has successfully exploited the thesis about the Soviet Union and the United States joining forces against him, starving the Iraqi people, and this being almost a genocide against Iraq, against Arabs. This argument has certain influence on the Arab masses. We should bear this in mind, too.

And another significant point of the plan we are considering. The present government of Kuwait, the government in exile, and Saddam

Hussein's government should enter into negotiations to discuss the future relations between the two countries, financial problems the countries had discussed before. Later, elections, referendum or some other option could be provided.

What Sabahs were supposed to negotiate with Saddam were his Arabian Nights demands — all these oil prices, oilfields, money, and islands - which he used as an excuse for the invasion. Now Sabahs would have to continue these negotiations in exile, in an even weaker position than before. Gorbachev probably thought that Sabahs would have to agree with anything Saddam demanded in exchange to the future restoration of Kuwait's sovereignty. Yet, the question of the Sabahs' own future would still remain open.

Gorbachev went on:

We believe that such an approach would allow us to snap up the initiative, to deprive Hussein of his glory of Arab nation's hero, of the image points he is scoring in the Arab world. If Saddam accepts this plan, a comprehensive solution would become possible. But, most probably, Saddam will reject this plan, at least at the beginning. Anyway, once this or another such proposal is put forward, you and we will be viewed in a different light, as true advocates of a political solution. Yes, we've shown determination and solidarity in condemning the aggression. But, at the same time, we are giving him a chance. We knock Saddam Hussein out of his current position, from which he can get certain dividends. We are protecting the UN resolutions and everything we've already achieved, but also allow the new process to begin.

[...]

You, Mr. President, have expressed a lot of interesting considerations which we are taking into account and to which we will certainly answer. Indeed, it is very important to make demonstration of cooperation between our countries and our joint determination to correct the situation, to restore justice, the result of our today's talks.

But here before me lies the text of Saddam Husain's yesterday speech, in which he addresses both of us. He says: Iraq has invaded neither of your countries. Iraq has no intention to cause any damage to your interests. Then he speaks about Kuwait's history, that Kuwait is an offspring of British colonialism. He says: in his time, Iraq's Prime Minister Said, a friend of the West, told the Englishmen that Iraq wouldn't agree with the establishment of that state. Prime Minister Quasem, a friend of the Soviet Union, used to say the same thing.

The UN Security Council kept silence, Saddam says further, and so did the Soviet Union, when the American forces invaded Panama. But suddenly everyone protests now, when the events take place in an Arab land, when the problem concerned is ours. The White House and the Kremlin must know they are dealing with a nation able to stand up for itself. Then he speaks about the Arab nations unity, that the Iraq's people are chosen by God and deserve support of all Muslims. And so on.

G. BUSH. *All of this is rank nonsense.*

M S. GORBACHEV. *But it is well-calculated.*

G. BUSH. *The only truth in his statement is that Bush is not a Muslim, that he eats pork. The rest of it is rubbish.*

Now, about your plan. I think he will accept this plan, even jump on it. But the majority in the world would consider it to be our great defeat. For in that way he would manage to shift the focus of the situation. He would manage to link it to Israeli-Palestinian problem, and that is exactly what he wants. That problem has remained unsolved for years and we cannot allow the Iraqi aggression to be linked to that problem.

I have no doubt that your experts know more than ours, but I would not agree with them on one point. I don't think Saddam has managed to become a symbol of Arabs' fight against the infidels. First, the aggression has undermined his prestige and this is clear to many in the Arab world. Second, he hasn't managed to get Assad, Mubarak or the majority of the Arab League to his side. Saddam would like us to believe that he represents the whole Arab world. But the Arabs tell me this is not true. So, whatever he says, I don't believe he is such a giant.

If the plan leaving the Kuwaiti issue open to some extent was adopted, it would be a great defeat of the United Nations, a blow on the new world order.

M. S. GORBACHEV. *But the heart, the benchmark of the plan is the suggestion that Iraq should withdraw from Kuwait.*

G. BUSH. *Yes, there are some points I agree with.*

M. S. GORBACHEV. And it is very likely that he will not accept the plan.

G. BUSH. Why not? He would get almost everything he wants. His strategic goals in Kuwait would be achieved. And American troops would leave the region with no guarantees.

M. S. GORBACHEV. No, the Kuwaiti issue would be settled, the inter-Arab forces would be brought in, and certainly the international guarantees backed by the USA, the USSR, permanent members of the Security Council would be provided.

G. BUSH. This is positive, I agree with that.

M. S. GORBACHEV. The present Kuwaiti dynasty would be restored as Iraq would have to negotiate financial and economic issues with it; as for the prospects, they are the problem of the Kuwaiti people who would settle their internal affairs themselves.

G. BUSH. Do you mean elections?

M. S. GORBACHEV. Yes.

The fact that elections in an absolute monarchy are, by definition, a regime change somehow escaped Bush's attention.

G. BUSH. Yes, given that, I think Saddam would reject such a plan. Of course, he would like to interlink his aggression with the Arab-Israeli problem. But he has put on stake too much by capturing Kuwait, and he wouldn't want to lose the fruits of his aggression.

I want to assure you once again: we are for a peaceful solution.

Keep it secret

So, perhaps without Bush even noticing it, they were now discussing the details of Gorbachev's plan, taking for granted that it was acceptable in principle. Gorbachev skilfully kept the conversation on this ground now:

So, let's think over this plan, consider scenarios, so to speak. Many considerations expressed by Arabs themselves, particularly Maghreb and other countries, are taken into account here.

I am firmly convinced of one thing. It would be mad to launch a military action against Iraq unless it makes any new military steps itself.

G. BUSH. *You are right. But, as I've mentioned, Saddam is now energetically destroying Kuwait. He is dismantling this country step by step, machine-tool by machine-tool. Not to mention human casualties, great sufferings of the Kuwaiti people.*

M. S. GORBACHEV. *That is why we need to act quickly. And this is the essence of the plan.*

One would imagine that Bush instinctively felt he was being fooled somehow. Yet, no matter how hard he tried, he could not figure out what was wrong.

G. BUSH. *At first, as I was listening to you, I had an impression that the question of restoration of Kuwait's current rulers remains open in the plan.*

M. S. GORBACHEV. *This is an important issue. But we provide that negotiations are resumed between Iraq and Kuwait's current government on the settlement of financial claims, and so on. So, this issue is taken into account.*

Now Saddam exploits the subject of Arab-Israeli conflict. We should seize this element, propose the conference. By the way, this idea meets interest in West European capitals. Then he has either to accept this plan, including his withdrawal from Kuwait, or to reject it. But by doing this, he will also reject that very idea he is trying to exploit in the eyes of Arabs.

G. BUSH. *Supposing he rejects the plan – what happens next?*

M. S. GORBACHEV. *Then we have to go on with embargo and political pressure. But he would be deprived of support which he admittedly has now. For he would reject what he himself is offering. This will expose him in the eyes of Arab peoples. The result will be strong isolation of Saddam Hussein.*

G. BUSH. *But if he agrees to this plan, though he has to withdraw from Kuwait and current Kuwaiti leaders are restored to power, he also achieves a conference on the Palestinian problem and withdrawal of American troops.*

M. S. GORBACHEV. *Once the Iraqi forces are withdrawn from Kuwait, American forces would be withdrawn gradually and replaced* *with inter-Arab forces. And only when international guarantees are provided.*

Bush was completely lost. He did not know what to say. For every his word Gorbachev had a dozen. What could he do, someone without a "vision" dropped by the destiny into this club of professional "visionaries" known as "top level international politicians"? He could only try to escape from responsibility.

G. BUSH. *I am concerned with one more thing. Whatever is proposed, it should not be a Soviet-American plan. If two our countries develop the settlement of this issue it would seem very strange to many in the world. Probably it should be a UN move.*

But I must say that the considerations you've expressed are very interesting. We shall think them over seriously.

Gorbachev did not mind that. The more secrecy there was in Bush's co-operation with the Soviets, the better, as the difference between open and secret collaboration is more or less the same as between a partner and an agent. So, Gorbachev was quite easy-going on that point:

Can we take decisions on any plan here? – he asked. No. But why do we meet? Surely not for doing nothing. That is why I think if any idea emerges between us that seems fruitful, we might think about a machinery of launching that process. As a result, some plan or a complex of measures might emerge. And then it is no longer important who suggested what, and when. The important thing is the result: multilateral efforts, the creation of machinery for settling the problem.

G. BUSH. *I agree. I wouldn't like to send the others a message that we two are sort of working on the problem. It is important just to start the search for solution and to reach an agreement about the acceptable approach in the end. I agree with you in this respect.*

M. S. GORBACHEV. *Today we might just say that we've conducted a broad discussion on the problem and believe it is possible to find an approach allowing to untie this dangerous knot. In order to avoid escalation of this problem into a more dangerous crisis, it is necessary to act jointly now.*

> **G. BUSH.** *I agree practically with everything you've just said with the exception of one formula. I would say "we shall look for a solution" rather than "we believe it is possible to find a solution." For I am still not sure that a solution is really possible.*

No more did Bush try to conceal how afraid he was of going to war, of a situation when he would have no other choice. He well remembered Saddam's threat to his ambassador about terrorist attacks against the US. He confided to Gorbachev:

> *What worries me is that we're dealing with an unstable man, who may resort to some provocation – against the USA rather than against the Soviet Union. For example, he might organize some terrorist attack which would guarantee we have to take responsive measures. If he wants to provoke us, he will do that.*

> *All the Arab leaders say the same thing: he is a cruel, unstable and ambitious man, capable of any provocation. And this worries me because we cannot do nothing if we face an obvious provocation, we cannot restrict ourselves to words.*

Of course, Gorbachev could not miss the wonderful chance to exploit Bush's fear. He said Saddam, indeed, had the potential to be dangerous if he was driven into a corner, but:

> *He won't resort to a provocation if we do not, so to speak, bring him to his knees before the whole world, if we give him an escape route. I mean a political process which would, at least partially, make an impression that there are no winners and losers. Such is the opinion of people who know him personally for decades.*

Poor Bush! All he had wanted was to demonstrate that he had support of Gorbachev, who was the world's highest ranking idol at the time. Saddam claimed he had support of Allah, so perhaps the US President thought he needed some counterbalance. As a result, he suddenly got committed to some secret negotiations of a sinister, controversial deal with Saddam. He did not mean it. In fact, he did not mean anything controversial at all. Therefore, he took the last, desperate attempt to reduce his obligations:

> **G. BUSH**. *I like the idea to show to the world that we are ready to go our half of the way, and even more, towards the peaceful settlement. But we*

must act very cautiously to avoid undermining the collective efforts made within the UN framework.

Some people in our country also suggest possible compromise solutions. For example, on the basis of holding elections in Kuwait to determine Kuwait's future and who's going to govern Kuwait. Of course, if this leads to restoration of the situation, to restoration of the ruling regime – very well. But if holding such elections is supposed to be an agreed condition of the settlement, this, in my view, would undermine the collective position we've taken. It should be absolutely clear that an aggression must be in no way rewarded. If there is an impression that the aggression has brought at least some benefits, that this outrageous act has led to even a partial success, we can well face a similar problem in two or five years.

M. S. GORBACHEV. *But if Saddam gains nothing and finds himself driven into a corner, we shall pay a very high price. This is a man who can strike so badly that we lose much more than if we give him some hope, some escape route. Therefore, we cannot bring him on his knees. This would result in no good.*

G. BUSH. *Do you believe it was possible to achieve a compromise with Hitler?*

M. S. GORBACHEV. *I believe these are incomparable phenomena. There is no similarity.*

G. BUSH. *I agree that Saddam Hussein is not a phenomenon of global scale. But as for personal cruelty, they are comparable.*

Gorbachev felt he was no more on a safe ground, so he took a serious look and said solemnly:

M. S. GORBACHEV. *Mr. President, Mr. George Bush, I am addressing you as a friend. We have to make a choice. A choice between the options we have, and I do realize that the list is neither long nor pleasant. But I believe that if the President, having already achieved the main strategic objectives of the US in this situation, acts on a basis of avoiding America's engagement in a colossal conflict, which might lead to a destruction of structures providing world's oil supplies, this would be considered as a great victory. I believe everyone would agree with that.*

Of course, now they are palming off an idea that your prestige is on stake, etc. Yet, we must act wisely. We must save both men and oil. Of course, we can just blow it up... But we have to make a choice.

Indeed, we are dealing with a paranoid. Just for this reason we have to give him some carrot. In the end, all of us will benefit if the aggression's consequences are eliminated, international law is restored, justice is restored.

G. BUSH. *I agree with everything you've said. We do not seek laurels of individual or collective victors in the fight against Saddam Hussein. But both you and I want the new order to prevail in the future world. For this, we need to find such a response which provides guarantees against an aggression in the future. As far as I see, that is exactly what many provisions of your plan are designed for.*

The only problem is the inclusion of Israeli-Palestinian problem into this plan. This is a carrot which might make an impression that the aggression is successful. I would be very alarmed with a result like this.

M. S. GORBACHEV. *This is not the carrot I mean. The carrot is that we recognize him as a partner.*

If we do not include Israeli-Palestinian problem into our plan, he may say: I've suggested a comprehensive solution which was ignored, was not even considered.

If we do include the Israeli-Palestinian question and he rejects this plan, he would discredit himself in the eyes of all Arabs. All of them will see that he had bluffed, just played on this issue, which is very sensitive for Arabs.

If he agrees, Kuwait will be restored, order in the Gulf will be restored and the process of Arab-Israeli settlement will begin. We might restore our relations with Israel on the first stage, without waiting for the final settlement of the Palestinian problem. This would be a serious move on our part, a kind of compensation.

But I should repeat: inclusion of the Israeli-Palestinian problem is not a carrot for Saddam Hussein. If he rejects this plan, he will expose himself to the Arabs and receive no support from them.

At the same time, by including this issue, we are supporting the moderate forces among the Arabs, such leaders as Mubarak.

G. BUSH. But in fact, we already have a conference dealing with the problem of Iraq-Kuwait conflict now. I mean multilateral efforts taken in the UN Security Council.

M. S. GORBCHEV. And this plan is also going to be under the UN auspices, in the UN format and with participation of UN Security Council members and Arab countries.

If Saddam rejects this plan, we win time, while he goes into isolation. He will look like a maniac, with whom the world cannot do business.

But in fact, he is not a maniac. Yevgeny Primakov, member of Presidential Council, knows Saddam personally for a long time. He says Saddam is not schizophrenic, but a person we must take seriously.

"Try to sound him out"

Now it was time for Gorbachev to ask the crucial question: so, is the plan on? Are we just going to think and talk about it only in our own narrow circle of Coalition leaders for the time being? Or do you want me to go and talk about it to him?

Maybe, we should sound him before talking to the others. We can send someone to him, perhaps, without telling him the essence of the plan.

G. BUSH. I suppose, you should try to sound him anyway. We have no access to him. It would be very constructive if you, with your history of relations with Iraq, could sound him out somehow.

If you talk to Mubarak, he would say: Saddam cannot withdraw from Kuwait now. Too much is at stake, he has already suffered too great losses.

M. S. GORBACHEV. Assad says the same.

G. BUSH. If he withdraws from Kuwait, he is finished.

One can imagine that at this point Gorbachev winked and lowered his voice:

M. S. GORBACHEV. That is what the whole process should be based on.

G. BUSH. If there is any disagreement between you and me, it is this. I do not think we need any additional evidence that he is crazy. But your argument is, at least partially, based on the idea that his true intentions are yet to be revealed.

M. S. GORBACHEV. We need to call his bluff. But if he accepts this plan nevertheless, a process will begin, which is eventually good for all of us.

G. BUSH. I would like to clarify… Is your idea based on a suggestion that Iraqi, American and all the other forces are withdrawn first, and the international conference is called after that?

M. S. GORBACHEV. An agreement on the conference and its format is yet to be achieved. The process will start on the basis of this arrangement.

Iraq's declaration that it releases the hostages and withdraws from Kuwait will be tied to the US declaration in the UN Security Council that the US won't attack or invade Iraq.

At the first stage, Iraq would withdraw its troops from Kuwait, and inter-Arab forces would be stationed there. The United States would also withdraw some symbolic number of troops, which would also be replaced by inter-Arab forces.

As for your military presence in general, this should be measured carefully. American forces can leave after structures and guarantees to provide security in the region are created.

G. BUSH. Will the ruling regime of Kuwait be restored?

M. S. GORBACHEV. Yes.

G. BUSH. Well, let's think this over, let's discuss this. I would like to ask my aide Brent Scowcroft whether he has any questions or comments in connection with this?

B. SCOWCROFT. No, not as yet. But the main question remains anyway. If he rejects this plan, can we indefinitely tolerate the current status-quo, this stalemate?

M. S. GORBACHEV. If he rejects this plan, we shall keep putting pressure, increasing Iraq's isolation. Some internal processes may start in Iraq, when the people see there is no way out with this man. Then, for the Iraqi people, it would be rather he than we to blame for all the hardship.[160]

While Gorbachev remained fresh, optimistic, and capable of speaking on and on, the Americans were completely exhausted. The talks had already continued three hours over schedule. Bush gave up resistance and went away for a break before the plenary session.

According to Baker, when Bush told his team what had just happened, they were shocked.

"You can't do that!" exclaimed Dennis Ross of the State Department, "This will absolutely undercut what we're trying to do! We'll put the moderate Arabs in a position where Saddam is delivering for the Palestinians and they're not! If we create linkage, he can claim victory! And if he does that, we're going to face a Middle East that is far more dangerous than we've ever seen!"

"Well," Bush replied, "I just don't think he's gonna accept anything less than that."

The argument continued for a while and concluded with the President's rather touching monologue:

"I put all these kids out there. Nobody else did it—I did it. And I've gotta take every step to be sure that I don't put their lives at risk needlessly. If I can get them out of there without fighting, I'll do it."

The room was suddenly very quiet, Baker remembers:

The president had spoken from the heart about the loneliness and responsibility that only a commander-in-chief can ever feel.[161]

If what Baker writes is true, this episode is quite important. It means that Bush took Gorbachev's plan quite seriously, thought it had a chance to succeed, and was prepared to accept all the consequences.

The problem is that Baker contradicts himself. On the same page, he writes that the whole disagreement concerned the public joint statement the two presidents were supposed to make after the meeting. Gorbachev insisted on mentioning Israel and the international conference there, and Bush nearly surrendered. It was Baker himself who saved everything. While Gorbachev and Bush were arguing, he persuaded his own man in the Kremlin, Foreign Minister Eduard Shevardnadze, that such a joint statement would be a disaster. Therefore, Baker and Shevardnadze wrote a draft without mentioning the international conference. Gorbachev—for some mysterious reason—signed it without asking questions.[162]

Scowcroft also expresses his astonishment with such "an amazing—and exceedingly reassuring—turnabout."

"Gone," he writes, "virtually without a trace, was the Gorbachev of the morning, defending his Iraqi client."[163]

The question is: if the whole argument was about joint statement, how could it help Bush save the US Army from doing its job?

The above transcript gives a solution to all these riddles we find in the memoirs. In fact, what Bush and Gorbachev negotiated was not a public statement, but a secret deal. The last thing they wanted was to make it public just after the meeting. In case they would need to make it public later, they agreed to disguise it as a UN plan. However, judging from what they said, they would hardly make it public before getting Saddam's preliminary agreement to the plan.

It looks like Baker's and Scowcroft's memories let them down, at the same time and in the same way, and not for the first time. This demonstrates beyond any doubt that US foreign policy in 1988-1992 was handled by a truly united team of truly like-minded statesmen.

All this, however, was not yet the end of the Helsinki Summit.

Mitterrand's amendment

Pausing here, that eclectic proposal on the future of Kuwait, also accepted by Bush (a period of UN control through Arabs, negotiations between Saddam and the Emir in exile, elections in Kuwait) had a story behind it.

One compromise solution that seemed likely to satisfy Saddam was to withdraw his troops, but leave Kuwait under a puppet government. After all, Comrade Gorbachev had just withdrawn from Afghanistan in this way, and the whole world applauded the champion of peace.

Therefore, as soon as the UN resolution demanded to withdraw Iraqi troops, on August 3, Saddam announced the withdrawal would, of course, begin the day after tomorrow. However, the "Provisional Free Government" would, of course, stay.[164]

On Sunday August 5, indeed, Baghdad television showed some Iraqi troops leaving Kuwait. They were supposedly replaced by the newly formed People's Army of Kuwait.

Three days later, however, glorious Iraqi historians (best in the world) made that groundbreaking discovery that Kuwait had always been a part of Iraq. Accordingly, the virtual Provisional Free Government (which, in fact, never quite materialised) appealed to citizens:

Dear brothers, the crystal-clear historical fact is that Kuwait is a part of Iraq, its people are Iraqis, and throughout their history they drank the waters of the Tigris and Euphrates rivers; they grew up on the shores of Shatt al-Arab. […] Prompted by our deep-seated faith in unity and belief that supreme pan-Arab interests take precedence over all other considerations, and for the sake of beloved Palestine and holy Jerusalem, which will only be returned to its owners when the banners of Arabism and unity are held high and when higher pan-Arab interests take priority over selfishness and parochial interests […] the provisional Free Kuwait Government has decided to appeal to […] the honorable, generous, chivalrous guards of the eastern gateway of the Arab homeland, led by the knight of the Arabs and the leader of their march, the hero leader President Field Marshal Saddam Hussein – to approve the return of the sons to their big family, the return of Kuwait to great Iraq, the motherland, and to achieve the complete full unity merger between Kuwait and Iraq, so that the hero Saddam Hussein will be our leader and the leader of our march in his capacity as the President of the Republic of Iraq, just as he is Chairman of the Revolution Command Council… etc., etc., etc.

So the Provisional Free Government died without being born.

However, the idea to resurrect it in some form and give Kuwait to Saddam's puppet regime survived. King Hussein of Jordan, intimidated or induced into collaboration with Saddam, advocated it openly. Saddam's much more enthusiastic collaborator, Yasser Arafat wrapped it into a more diplomatic form of the following "plan for an Arab solution": Saddam would withdraw (in exchange for territorial concessions and so many billions of dollars), but the Emir would not come back. The new government of Kuwait would be elected by popular vote, while Comrade Arafat's 300,000 Palestinians in Kuwait would undertake to arrange for the necessary result.*iii And then, eventually, it all goes back to Saddam's Plan A.

Naturally, all such publicly made proposals were firmly rejected by the West.

But now we see this scheme had its powerful advocates within the coalition itself. The one who would make it the central point of the proposed compromise was Mitterrand. As we have seen in the previous chapter, he believed that a "restoration of Kuwait's sovereignty" need not include the restoration of the Emir. In further conversations with Gorbachev, he developed that point:

F. MITTERRAND. *Our main task is this. We must find a solution which would enable Saddam Hussein withdraw from Kuwait after all those things he has promised to the Iraqi people. If he does not withdraw from Kuwait, the war in inevitable before the end of this year.*

M. S. GORBACHEV. *In any case, Saddam will make reservations about the borders and access to sea. All this is negotiable.*

F. MITTERRAND. *Yes, but first of all, he must withdraw from Kuwait and free the hostages.*

In the best-case scenario, two variations are possible. One is that the US Security Council decisions are fully implemented. Or, the control over Kuwait could be temporarily taken by Arab states, in order to create the conditions for negotiations over the future constitution of that country. The question on the role of Kuwaiti dynasty would also be decided in that period.

The problem is that the UN Security Council has, in my view, carelessly passed a resolution which says it is necessary to return to the situation before the Iraqi aggression, i. e. return Kuwait to Emir al Jaber. Saddam Hussein will never agree to that, and therefore, there will be war.

[…] If Saddam does not withdraw from Kuwait, the war will inevitably begin before the end of this year [1990].

The question is: who should "takeover" Kuwait? If we are talking about

---

* It was not yet widely known at that time what Palestinian elections are like, even if fought between PLO's own factions or splinter groups

the Emir, that will be too great a humiliation for Saddam, and he will never agree to that.

We might consider a scenario which, in my view, is possible, with Kuwait being placed under a temporary control of some committee of Arab states. That would let the Arab states carry out negotiations and work out some solution. Subsequently, a question of Emir's restoration in accordance with the relevant UN Security Council resolution may arise. In that case, too, there will be an issue of some territorial concessions to Iraq.[165]

Indeed, Mitterrand even thought this might be an answer to the whole problem of Saddam's reluctance to keep the Kuwait-Palestine "linkage" secret and the West's reluctance to admit it publicly. At the darkest moments of Gorbachev's mediation, Mitterrand would advise him:

Let me speak metaphorically. We need to get over a wall which seems to be absolutely plain. To do that, we should find some jut, some asperity we could clamber to. In other words our task is to find correct tactics.

In my view, we should outline the long-term and short-term perspectives.

The long-term perspective should be discussion on, and solution of, the whole complex of Near and Middle East problems. This would be a conclusion of the whole settlement process.

It is necessary to give the Arabs some hope to motivate their actions. Naturally, it does not mean we are trying to deceive them. For, to the final account, all our actions are designed precisely for giving Saddam some perspective, a sort of alibi, to make it possible for him to agree with us.

As for the short-term perspective, there are difficulties with our allies. The Americans especially insist on the liberation of the hostages and entire Kuwait, and we fully agree with them. But I have some doubts on how expedient it is to demand restoration of the ruling Kuwaiti dynasty.

The problem is that we have sort of a following dialogue with Saddam Hussein. We tell him: we are not prepared to talk to you before you withdraw from Kuwait and give it back to Emir as-Sabah. But we give Saddam no guarantees either about the international peace conference, nor about Kuwait's future status.

As you and I have already said, he would never agree to this. This means that there will be war. Hence, the UN resolution about return to the situation which had existed before the aggression means war.

That is why I believe it is necessary to introduce the temporal dimension in our course. It means this. Iraq withdraws from Kuwait. In connection with this, the decision about restoration of the regime in Kuwait is taken. Simultaneously, the negotiations begin. Kuwait would be passed to the new regime not from Iraq, but from, say, the UN. And the subject of the negotiation, which would begin meanwhile, would include the possible concessions to Iraq, particularly in the questions of its access to the Persian Gulf, of the oilfields, and so on.

This would satisfy Saddam's pride. He would never agree to pass Kuwait to the Americans' hands. Neither would he pass it to the hands of Emir al-Jaber. This would be a loss of face, fatal both for Saddam and for his regime. He can leave Kuwait only if that country is passed to the Arab forces. They could perform the government functions there, undertake the responsibility for this country for the period of negotiations.

Saddam will be able to start negotiations if such an "Arab scenario" is being implemented, or if the UN SC fully undertakes the settlement process, or if the international conference convenes. In my view, two latter options mean quite cumbersome structures. In any case, Saddam must be given a hope to achieve a compromise on the territorial question. However, we have not yet reached that point. Still, it is necessary to give Saddam a hope for approximately such a scheme. Otherwise, the use of force is inevitable.

The difficulty you and I have is to make our partners agree that such a transitional stage of establishing a temporary authority over Kuwait is necessary. May I repeat: in the long term, it is absolutely necessary to aim for the settlement of all problems of Near and Middle East through negotiations. Whereas in the short term, there will be negotiations, involving the Arab states, on the territorial status and other territorial aspects.

Such an approach would let Saddam save face and avoid humiliation.

In such a case, he will be able to tell his people: it is thanks to me that the negotiations on all problems of Near and Middle East have begun. It is thanks to me that you have got this and that.

Personally, I can envisage no other plan. In my view, any other scenario will lead to war.[166]

Chapter 9:
Re-distribution of wealth

Believe it or not, after all these extraordinary concessions from Bush, Gorbachev still expected to get money for his support. And Bush was morally prepared to pay. A different matter is that he had no money at that time: the budget deficit and all that. Now he had to find a way not just to eat a pie and to have it, but also to share it with his friend Michael.

At the plenary session in Helsinki, after Gorbachev absent-mindedly approved the notorious joint statement, the participants passed on to other issues.

G. BUSH. Now, if you don't mind, we might discuss the economic situation in the Soviet Union. I would like to see how we can help you.

Gorbachev briefly outlined the dreadful present and the bright future of the Soviet economy, and then concluded:

In this situation, your understanding of our problems is, in itself, already not enough. We need help. We need additional financial resources for manoeuvre at the stage of entering market economy. The West must help us with goods and in financial sense. The numbers are not terribly big here. We are asking not for non-repayable grants. We shall repay everything, and repay with interest. However, we need clarity regarding your intentions right now, before October 1.

I hope, when Mr. Baker visits us [4 days later] we will be able to specify our approaches to cooperation and clarify the American position. For the US approach sets an example for other countries, too. This is the moment when we need clarity.

G. BUSH. In some fields, we are ready to start immediately. Thus, I believe that there is a huge potential in our cooperation on the issues of energy. We are prepared to pass you such technology, which, for obvious reasons, we denied to you before.

State Secretary Baker is instructed to discuss all these problems in details with Minister Shevardnadze. But you and I also can touch upon them right now.

In particular, I'm interested: what do you need immediately in terms of aid? I have to tell you in advance: we have no extra money. The deficit of federal budget is close to its record high. In this situation, the Congress shall never give the president a "card-blanche" to spend billions.

At the same time, the increasing trust between us helps cooperation. Frankly, our statement on Iraq shall be a great help to my administration in pushing forward the projects of economic cooperation with the USSR. But, again, I don't want to make a false impression that I am free in my actions. We have great restrictions.[167]

Indeed they had, even besides the budget deficit. Even if Bush had money, it would be illegal, under US legislation of that time, to lend them to the Soviet Union.

J. BAKER. As a lawyer, I would like to underline two obstacles. First, tell your negotiators to work seriously on reaching an agreement on Tsar's debt. We are prepared to be satisfied with a minimum here. A breakthrough in this issue would help to cancel the congress's restrictions on loans to the Soviet Union.

Second, it is very important to launch the trade agreement you've signed in Washington as soon as possible. And for this you must, at last, pass an emigration law.[168]

With all these difficulties, Bush and Baker smartly found some ways to help their friend. On one hand, they could use the American influence to persuade some third countries to provide a few billions. On the other hand, they apparently had some ways to encourage private businesses to invest in Soviet Union – no matter how hopeless such investments might be.

J. SUNUNU. We are encouraging the American companies to cooperate with you directly. But the problem is they don't know who to deal with.

The republics disavow the center, and the center disavows the republics. It is risky to sign contracts if you don't know who is going to fulfil them on the opposite side.

M. S. GORBACHEV. *Yes, this is a real problem.*

This was a right moment for smart Bush to try to compensate his financial impotence with political help. He offered Gorbachev to send some governors, or other representatives of States, to the Soviet Union. Their mission would be to persuade the Soviet republics' leaders to be more loyal to Moscow. Gorbachev said this might be useful some other time, but now he needed money.

In spite of all the difficulties, the White House managed to enlist some twenty two big businessmen for this hell-bent adventure. All of them would visit Moscow, led by Baker and Secretary of Commerce Robert Mosbacher, four days later.

J. BAKER. *Mosbacher and I will bring to Moscow the true captains of American industry, who are ready for serious businesslike discussions. I see great opportunities, first of all, in the sphere of energy. We should be more daring in implementing new forms of cooperation. Will you give our businessmen real concessions in Siberia?*

M. S. GORBACHEV. *We have some specific projects. In particular, an international development of Tengiz fields offers great prospects. [...]*

We also need your approval for such a major initiative as development of a new civilian airplane on the basis of Soviet-US-Israeli cooperation. [...]

G. BUSH. *Yes, this looks promising. What is going on here on our side?*

B. SCOWCROFT. *The interested businessmen, according to my information, are included in Mosbacher's delegation.*

G. BUSH. *Fine.*

I'd like to add that our business circles are known for great sensitivity and understanding of partners' problems, particularly as far as development of natural resources is concerned. You should not worry: our cooperation in the field of energy is not going to look like exploitation of your riches.[169]

It looks like the whole Bush administration was mobilized and every official had to subscribe some businessmen. Scowcroft happened to know some aircraft constructors, Baker – some energy merchants, etc. How exactly they managed to seduce these businessmen into investing in the collapsing Soviet Union is anybody's guess.

Probably, it was easier with those from oil industry: instability in the Middle East usually encourages search for alternative sources of oil. Even Gorbachev's Soviet Union no more looked particularly unstable against the Gulf background. Therefore, 40% of the businessmen brought to Moscow on September, 13 "represented the energy sector". One Mr. J. Merphy was so quick that could be congratulated with "an important contract on petrochemical machinery-producing" at the reception with Gorbachev the same day.[170]

They others still had to be persuaded. So, chairman of Gosplan* Yuri Maslukov made an impressive speech, boasting how wasteful the Soviet economy was. One could make many billions by just utilizing its garbage.

A specific feature of our economy[, Maslukov said,] is a huge share of the mining complex. More than 30% of industrial power is concentrated here. Admittedly, as much as one ton of mining resources is spent for each rouble of national income. The effectiveness of raw materials' usage is extremely low. For example, at Sokolovsko-Sarbaiskoe minefield of metal ores only iron is mined, while 25 other metals go to burrow.

If the American side makes investments to increase effectiveness of mining and raw materials' usage, this might give billions in income to the both sides.

As for other kinds of raw materials, the effectiveness of mining and depth of handling are also very low. Huge quantities of raw materials remain in soil or go to burrow. For example, 70% of mined potassium saline remains in soil. The level of extraction of minerals is 20-40% in the USSR. Meanwhile, according to our data, in the USA it reaches 90%, and in Japan – 92%.

Americans disagreed: as far as they knew, their level of extraction was lower. There must have been some different methods of evaluation. But Maslukov continued:

---

* Gosplan (State Planning Committee) was the body responsible for economic planning in the Soviet Union and largely controlling the Soviet state-run economy

Anyway, if you manage to increase the effectiveness of extraction [in the Soviet Union] just by 5-6%, the investments would pay off very quickly.

We have a lot of well-explored, but not mined, deposits of zinc, titanium, tin. For example, we cannot start mining the Udokanskoe deposit of copper because we lack money. We have a list of 25 such deposits, regarding which we would like to establish contacts with interested companies and persons.

At last, oil. We have big reserves – 4.5 billion tons of viscid oil. But we don't have technology for more effective production and handling. We have big reserves of oil-containing bitumens, from which huge quantities of light petrochemicals could be produced. We have experimented with technologies of mining these bitumens, but, so far, unsuccessfully.

The problem of depreciation of oil refinery industry's basic funds. 70% of them are out-of-date morally or physically. Introduction of hydro-cracking would allow to get 25-30 tons of aviation turbine kerosene, etc. Given we share profits equally, it would recoup the investments in 2-3 years.[171]

Maslukov continued his tale about treasures concealed in Soviet garbage heaps, and, probably, eventually undressed everyone of the 22 businessmen. Meanwhile, Gorbachev. Shevardnadze, Chernyaev and Baker quietly left, feeling that the business affairs were in reliable hands now.[172]

However, all these far-reaching projects were not enough for Gorbachev. So, as soon as the four friends were alone, he promptly returned the conversation to the problem of cash.

M. S. GORBACHEV. I would ask the president and you, [...] in spite of all the problems you're facing, to find a way to give us 1-1,5 billions of dollars as an unbound interest-free loan. [...] We need a one-time support. We are also arranging this with Kohl and Andreotti now. [...] I do understand that you have no extra money, but you have to understand us. We will repay it after some time.

E. A. SHEVARDNADZE. In some cases, loans can be given through private channels, while the governments just guarantee them.

J. BAKER. I shall pass this to the president immediately. I can promise that the President, I and other leaders of the administration will try to find a way to help you.

But I must explain something to you, regardless of any political issues.

The problem are not these issues. The problem is not, for example, Cuba. Let's put them aside. I would like to tell you about other things.

There are laws, passed during the 45 years of the Cold War, which bar us from doing this. To do what you ask us to do, we need the Congress to pass new legislation. And this would raise political controversy.

Besides, we cannot raise the issue of new legislation before the problem of so-called "Kerensky's debts" is solved. Otherwise, it is impossible to cancel Johnson"s law on liability. We are prepared to show maximum of pliability on this issue. Our delegation can talk to your experts even before the scheduled meeting in October. But, as a state secretary, I am obliged to press for a solution of this problem.

Another problem is Stephenson-Bard amendment. While Johnson"s law prevents you from searching for money at private financial markets, for example, by issue of rouble bonds, Stephenson-Bard amendment prohibits loans of Export-Import Bank, i. e. governmental loans for projects in the Soviet Union.

I know that the president will regard your request with great sympathy. But I must tell you frankly: we don't have such opportunities which exist in Italy or Germany. The problem is not economic – we would be able to find money. The problem is that we have to go to the Congress, and this would provoke a political debate at home.

Besides, we need a ratified trade agreement in order to act. And this depends on the immigration and emigration law being passed in your country.

M. S. GORBACHEV. *This law has been passed in the first reading. But we have agreed with you not to rush things. It is against your interests to boost this before November 4.*

J. BAKER. *I would prefer not to say publicly that we have any mutual understanding in this respect. If the debates in Congress begin, it would re-open the problem of Baltic states, and so on.*

M. S. GORBACHEV. *I understand you. Going through the Congress in this issue would take a lot of time. It would be unrealistic to count on that. But maybe, with your great experience, you might help us to get this money through some third country.*

Mentioning Baker's great experience did help.

J. BAKER. Yes, I thought about that immediately. Let me see what we can do along these lines. These days I've been busy raising money to finance our expenses connected to the Persian Gulf crisis. I got some experience of asking for money.

M. S. GORBACHEV. Maybe, something could be done for us, too. What is one billion for an Arab prince who has 104 or 105 billion dollars?

J. BAKER. Absolutely right. I have managed to mobilize 12 billions of dollars in three countries within just four days. Half of these money will be spent for aid to the countries which are most affected by the crisis – Egypt, Jordan, Turkey.

[…]

I promise […] to look what can be done to provide you with a loan from some third country.

M. S. GORBACHEV. The Foreign Minister of Saudi Arabia is visiting us next week. By the way, the Israeli minister of science and energy is also going to visit us.

J. BAKER. Please, don't ask anything from Israelis. Their money are, in the end of the day, our money. (Laughter)[173]

When Gorbachev and Chernyaev were leaving Kremlin in the same car that evening, Chernyaev asked:

If so, why do we need these Israeli ministers at all?!

Gorbachev only laughed, leaving his loyal aide to speculate about his intentions. Chernyaev guessed correctly, and organized the Soviet-Israeli meeting respectively. 'I have managed to insert economist (!) Petrakov into this meeting with the Israelis', we writes in his diary.[174]

According to Chernyaev, Gorbachev believed he would eventually get 10 billion dollars out of the Israelis.[175] And, as we shall see in the next chapter, he had some reasons to think so.

◆ ◆ ◆

Indeed, money was yet another odd aspect of the coalition-building. Baker was travelling all over the world, collecting billions in some of the allied countries and allocating them among the others.

Of course, as far as military expenses were concerned, it was only fair that the interested parties (particularly the Gulf states) shared the financial burden. What seems strange in not fund-rising side of this activity, but the spending. For some reason, Bush and Baker felt obliged to pay their allies. I don't know exactly how much the overall cost was, but these were evidently many billions. Thus, as Baker mentioned just above, in those three days he raised 12 billions and planned to share half of them between Turkey, Egypt and Jordan. This gives us some idea of his proportions. So, in financial terms, this coalition was pretty wasteful.

Please note that the list of the beneficiaries included Jordan, which was hardly an ally. At that time, Jordan"s position was, at best, neutral, or even pro-Saddam. Precisely for this reason, Western countries were competing in bribing it to switch sides. Alongside Baker, European Community also provided unconditional financial aid to Jordan these months. Naturally, since the pro-Saddam position surprisingly appeared so profitable, Jordan had no reasons to change it.

By the way, if we believe Mubarak, Jordan was at the same time receiving many billions from Iraq, precisely for the same reason of its pro-Iraqi position. Rightly or wrongly, Bush and Baker did believe Mubarak. So much so that they made him their principal Arab ally, gave him many billions of dollars, and wrote off all his debts.

Poor Mubarak probably felt very jealous about Jordan. If we believe for a moment that Saddam had really offered him 20 billions for support, now Mubarak should have regretted that he did not take them. As the case of Jordan demonstrated, support for Saddam was not at all an obstacle for Western aid. But even if he did not lose these mythical 20 billions he should have regretted his heroic pro-Western stance nonetheless. It appeared no more profitable than Jordan's pro-Saddam position.

Probably, Bush and Baker understood this delicate diplomatic nuance, and that is yet another reason why they tried so hard to comfort Mubarak with more money.

On the whole, this re-distribution of wealth against the background of growing dark holes in the US budget was rather ridiculous. The justification for it was this: such countries as Jordan or Egypt lost money because of the embargo against Iraq, and therefore needed compensation. This, however, did not sit very well with the idea of "new world order" where, as Bush once joked, "the rule of law supplants the rule of the jungle."

After all, the embargo was introduced by a legally binding act of international law: a UN Security Council resolution 661. And the law, be it even international, is supposed to be obeyed by everyone regardless of how unprofitable this is.

Probably, Bush and Baker reasonably feared that the embargo, even introduced by an international law, might be violated. Nevertheless, bribing potential violators was obviously not a good solution. Paying or receiving money for performing one's legal obligations is corruption.

So, like many utopians before and after them, Bush and Baker had to find some compromise between the utopia and the reality. Their utopia implied that every country must obey, or be forced to obey, a UN resolution. The reality was a bit different. A country would obey these resolutions, but only if that paid. Therefore, Bush and Baker – as the only party interested in new world order – had to pay.

With the benefit of hindsight, it is now clear that the money were simply wasted. In the end of the day, it was military force – not an embargo – that solved both the practical problem of Iraqi occupation of Kuwait and the ideological problem of Saddam's disobedience of UN resolutions. But at that time, Bush and Baker did not see the embargo as a supplement to war or a prelude to military action. For many months, before this approach proved its fruitlessness, they still hoped that the economic sanctions might serve as a substitute to an attack.

Needless to say, this view was constantly abetted by Gorbachev and his comrades in the coalition's anti-American wing.

As for getting money for Gorbachev himself, the story developed in the most predictable way. Bush and Baker asked Saudi Arabia to help their friend; and of course, generous Saudi king sent him four billions fairly soon.

But then, in Helsinki, Bush also provided Gorbachev with another rich source of money. This source did not depend on anybody's generosity. This aid to the Soviet Union would be far from voluntary. One can be sure Bush did not understand what he was doing – but his moment of weakness opened a door to a very sinister blackmail.

Chapter 10.
Victorious Gorbachev

....

It seems to me that Jews value their lives higher than Syrians or
Russians do (laughter).
Mikhail Gorbachev to Hafez Assad, 28 April 1990

....

As we remember, in Helsinki Bush and Gorbachev agreed to keep the
linkage between the problems of Kuwait and Israel in strict secret. And
I wish I could say that Gorbachev honestly kept his word. But, alas…

One might expect they he hurried to his anti-war allies, such as
Mitterrand and Mubarak, to boast about his diplomatic triumph. But in
fact, he did the opposite. He went to the "hawks", his main opponents, to
let them know who was winning now.

Gorby and Brits

On September 14, UK Foreign Secretary Douglas Hurd came to Moscow,
full of enthusiasm about the new Grand Alliance. Apparently, all he knew
about Helsinki was the public joint statement.

*D. HURD. [...] For our part, we are going to follow the course
determined by you and President Bush in Helsinki and in the UN
Security Council.*

*Our countries have certain links with the Middle East and some
experience of contacts with the countries of this region. We suppose that
now we may share some information which was previously considered
as secret. Now that we've established so good relations, we are quite
prepared to cooperate on this matter, as well as on other ones.*

But there was something about the "course determined in Helsinki" which the British still did not know.

"The Helsinki summit exceeded any expectations – both our and the Americans", Gorbachev started. Then he told Hurd about the details of the summit, including the Soviet "plan" and the American reaction.

> *We described this plan in details. At first, it caused some confusion. But then, as we began discussing it in elements, we reached an agreement about the necessity to continue exchange of opinions on this issue.*

Now, Gorbachev added, Baker and Shevardnadze are finalizing the details of the "plan".

Hurd weakly protested against the controversial linkage, but Gorbachev rebuffed him in a way pretty similar to how he rebuffed Bush. His "horror stories" (to use the expression of his chief Arabist) were now even more picturesque:

> *If military action bursts out, the Arabs will undoubtedly take Saddam's side. The whole Moslem world will start moving. The moderate leaders, such as President Mubarak, Assad or even Guddafi, might find themselves in difficult situation. [...]*
>
> *In fact, Iraq alone has one million people under arms in this region: 650 thousands in the army and more than 250 thousands in the [Republican] Guard.*

Gorbachev"s strategic calculations were even more misty than purely numerical ones:

> *Having defined two or three points in Saudi Arabia, Saddam concentrated all his bases in Kuwait and in his own territory. If the war bursts out, this means destroying the whole population. The whole civilized world would protest against that.*

Apparently, unlike simple mortals such as I and perhaps the person who wrote the transcript, Hurd was smart enough to understand what this meant. He did not argue against Gorbachev's opinion, but insisted that British position was not very different. The UK, he said, was also in favor of peaceful solution, and Thatcher's tough rhetoric was designed only to intimidate Saddam.

Before leaving, Hurd gave Gorbachev a piece of good advice:

'If the Soviet Union restores its [diplomatic] relations with Israel and Saudi Arabia on the same day, this would demonstrate your excellent sense of balance.'

'We, like you, are also for balance,' Gorbachev confirmed.[176]

Gorby and Jews

However, Gorbachev immediately broke the suggested balance. The Soviet Union restored its diplomatic relations with Saudi Arabia within three days after this conversation. The precious four billions were looming at the horizon, and Gorbachev wanted no barriers to block their way to his treasury.

As for Israel, it still had to deserve his mercy.

Yet, even without diplomatic relations, Gorbachev and Israelis had what to talk about. Just after receiving Hurd on September 14, Gorbachev saw two Israeli ministers.

After mutual greetings, M. S. GORBACHEV says: as ancient Greeks used to say, panta rei.* Indeed, everything changes, as you and I are sitting at the same table now. That is good.

Then he told them about Helsinki summit, but in a different manner from how he pictured his plan to Bush or Hurd. This time Gorbachev omitted his usual "horror stories". He understood that, unlike Bush, Israelis knew something about Middle East. Hence, he did not hope to deceive or persuade them – he just presented them with a faint accompli.

By contrast to conversations with Bush and Hurd, Gorbachev did not even mention that the whole "plan" would be strictly conditioned by Iraq's withdrawal from Kuwait. He just said that "all the problems of the Middle East, including the Arab-Israeli problem and the Gulf crisis", would be considered by "a wide international conference".

"Such a conference would start the process of peace settlement in the Middle East," Gorbachev added. Israelis surely knew what it meant.

As for Saddam, Gorbachev continued:

I insisted that we must act firmly and strongly, but avoid driving Saddam

---

* Everything flows

Hussein into a corner, like a beast. In such a case he might resort to such steps which would have severe consequences not only for the Middle East region, but for the whole planet.[177]

I would imagine that the Israelis might have taken Gorbachev's account rather sceptically at first. After all, the Soviet dreams about international conference had always been as well-known as the American opposition to the idea.

To clear any doubts, Gorbachev mentioned that Bush accepted his "plan" not immediately, but only after a considerable effort on his part to civilize and enlighten his American partner.

I felt that the US president was under powerful pressure of public opinion. For the Americans are educated in such a way that they expect obedience from other nations. They expect that other nations knee before them, like Grenada or Panama did. The Americans would like to see similar development in this case.

I suppose, I've helped the president to understand that the right strategy now is just to continue to do what is already being done. [...] We should not give way to those who shout about the necessity to support prestige and advocate an attack. What we need is not an attack, but a solution of the problem. Therefore, we should find other, political methods. Fortunately, in today's world there is common understanding that we are on the right way.

As we know, [a few days ago] the NATO has also supported the political methods of solving this problem.

In general, probably, the greatest meaning of what is going on is that we look for a new approach in this situation. The matter is the new quality of cooperation between the USSR and the USA, cooperation in Europe and practically all over the world.[178]

Gorbachev's message was clear enough: the consensus in the world is such that there will be no war. Rather, Saddam's "peace initiative" would be accepted with some small corrections.

Of course, the Israelis tried to explain him some Middle Eastern realities:

[Israeli Finance Minister] Y[itzhak] MODA'I. [...] Israel is situated within a range of Iraqi missiles. There are rumors (and not only rumors,

but also reliable information) that Iraqi missiles did hit targets in Iran within a greater range than between Iraq and Israel. There missiles may be equipped with chemical, or maybe even more powerful, warheads. No one, neither USA nor USSR, can want peace and stability in the Middle East more than Israel, which is situated there. We fear that if the USSR, the USA and the world community as a whole allow this huge and powerful arsenal to remain in Saddam's hands, time may come when Saddam resorts to unpredictable actions with irreversible consequences. Our small country is concerned with this perspective. Of course, I must add that we are not afraid of this. We are capable of defending ourselves. But who needs war for defense?

M. S. GORBACHEV. *Yes, I suppose we should resolve this conflict with political means and provide reliable guarantees. It is important to make sure that this man does not get into such a position when he can go beyond what is reasonable. So, we must look for adequate solutions.*

Then Gorbachev, once again, described his theory about the necessity "to play Saddam's trump cards against him" and to ruin his image of Palestine's liberator by liberating Palestine without his help. Gorbachev stressed that he and Bush discussed this in Helsinki and agreed "to continue thinking about this". In conclusion, he generalized:

What happened in Helsinki is very important. The United States needed a lot of time to understand (as President Bush has confirmed in Helsinki) that they have to cooperate with the Soviet Union in the Middle East (as well as elsewhere).

Hitherto, American politicians – Brzezinky and Kissinger, for example – tried to oust the Soviet Union out of the Middle East region. But why? And is it possible?

Today the Americans think differently.

Moreover, in today's world the United States are unable to be a leader or a policeman even in one region. […] Helsinki [summit] demonstrates a great breakthrough in the understanding of what our world is and how we should live.[179]

So Gorbachev, quite clearly, told the Israelis that they had been betrayed. Sure enough, he did it neither out of mere indiscretion, nor for stupid boasting.

Rather, he was driving them to certain conclusions.

Indeed, since the Soviet role in the Middle East would increase, it was now vital for Israel to ensure good relations with the Kremlin. Translating from diplomatic language, life or death of Israel were in Gorbachev's hands. Therefore, now he could dictate, and they would have to obey; he could blackmail, and they would have to pay. Israel's submissiveness would have direct impact on how different the Soviet-American "peace settlement in the Middle East" be from Saddam's one.

Indeed, immediately after he made the situation absolutely clear, Gorbachev passed to dictating and blackmailing. Generous soul, before solving his own problems, he started with his Arab friends' concerns.

> **M. S. GORBACHEV**. *[…] Recently, President Mubarak told me […] that if the Israeli government settles immigrants from the USSR in Israel-occupied Arab lands, Arab leaders would address the Soviet government with a plea to stop, suspend, or abandon altogether the issue of permissions for the Soviet citizens to go to Israel for permanent residence. Perhaps, he is right. […]*

> **I. ZEMTSOV**. *Our government fully agrees with you. As you know, our Prime Minister has assured you in a cable that the immigrants would not settle beyond Israel itself, even if this means some infringement of the citizens' democratic rights and freedoms.*[180]

Once Mubarak's problem was successfully solved, Gorbachev could pass to his own problems. We already know them: he urgently needed a lot of money.

> **M. S. GORBACHEV**. *It is not a very big sum which we need – 15-20 billions of dollars. […]*

> *As you see, they immediately found money to finance stationing of troops in Saudi Arabia. But it is more difficult to get a comparable sum for us.*

> *We would like to invite you to take part in these efforts. This would be a good sign and a good symbol. I hope that your visit shall give a start to our cooperation on the new stage. We would welcome such cooperation.*

In Gorbachev's situation, it was quite fortunate to suddenly get a few millions of Jewish hostages to his custody. There was enough of rich Jews all over the world to pay a good ransom.

Y. MODA'I. *[...] Ever since my first meetings with your representatives, I've been asking myself how small Israel might help great Soviet Union. [...] Our own economy receives support – and, to be frank, aid – from the Jews who live abroad. In this respect, our economy is in unique situation. Therefore, apart from all the other things, such as directing its investments and specialists to the Soviet Union, Israel can organize foreign investments from the third countries.*

Clearly, the Israeli finance minister had understood Gorbachev well.

In addition, significant direct aid from Israel was promised. "I am sure that we might help the Soviet Union, for example, in agriculture," Israeli minister of energy, science and technology Yuval Ne"eman said. "I mean both direct supplies of agricultural production and help in organization of respective branches of agriculture in the USSR."

Moda'i widened the sphere of Israeli aid beyond agriculture, offering to help "urgently increase the production of consumer goods".

You have enough of qualified workforce, [he explained enthusiastically,] enough of raw materials, and with our experience and our technology you can easily organize wide-scale production of consumer goods immediately, not in 5-10 years. our technology is not very complicated and not the most advanced one, but it is efficient.

Gorbachev replied:

Let's consider our today's conversation as a prologue. I would ask you to arrange the practical side during your further negotiations with our representatives. Please bear in mind that [...] we are [...] interested in receiving money and goods [by October 1, according to Gorbachev's current schedule of economic reforms].

When already leaving, Ne'eman suddenly had yet another wonderful idea:

Maybe, as a symbol of starting normal commercial and other links between us, Soviet Union might sell some quantity of oil to Israel?[181]

Gorbachev did not reply. It was up to Israelis now, how they are going to pay their ransom. After personally outlining his threats, Gorbachev could safely leave the collection of tribute to subordinate Soviet officials.

Now we can see his reasons to expect as much as 10 billions from Israel. Blackmailing has always been many times more profitable than begging.

Gorby and Sheiks

Actually, the combination of these two is probably the best. Do not forget the American-inspired generosity of Saudi king towards Gorbachev. All the more so as Gorbachev was expecting a Saudi foreign minister's visit in three days after the Israelis.

While the Saudi prince is saddling his Arab horse to go North, and Gorbachev is building cloud-castles in anticipation of his petrodollars, let's have a wider look at the role of Saudi Arabia in the whole story of the Gulf War.

In the diplomatic games around the crisis, the United States were a prize rather than a player. Saudi Arabia was a player, unlike the US and like the Soviet Union, but its goals were exactly the opposite to the Soviet ones. If Gorbachev needed to keep the US out of the war, or at least to prevent their victory, King Fahd needed the Americans to enter the war and to win it.

In a sense, his task was not easier than Gorbachev's. Of course, common sense was on Saudi side. But global political climate, with all its "new world orders" and universal enthusiasm about "the end of the Cold War" were against him. Therefore, making the common sense to prevail in Washington also required a tricky diplomatic game.

We have already described the first round of this game, which took place in August 1990. Then, King Fahd openly supported Mubarak's efforts to find a compromise "Arab solution", thus confusing Saddam and preventing his invasion of Saudi Arabia. At the same time, he invited the American troops, and extracted from Bush a word of honor that they would not leave before solving the problem.

Now he needed these troops to attack, and preferably to destroy Saddam's regime altogether. As we remember, this was directly opposite to what Gorbachev needed.

Such was the situation when the Saudi foreign minister Prince Saud al-Feisal visited Moscow on September 17, 1990 to restore the diplomatic relations.

◆ ◆ ◆

After the appropriate greetings, pleasantries and (on Saudi side) florid curses of Saddam Hussein, Gorbachev took the floor. He wanted to make it clear that he understood the Saudis" intrigue well and did not believe them on the slightest. On the other hand, he did not want to spoil the relations, which just had been restored after so many years. "Who knows," Gorbachev thought, "one day they might give me four billions."

M. S. GORBACHEV. *Did you really, on the basis of the available information, think that Iraq would attack Saudi Arabia?*

S. AL-FEISAL. *Iraq planned to capture a part of our territory. And, if not for His Majesty the King's quick appeal to our friends and their positive response, this would happen. Although Iraq had a non-aggression treaty with us, we received intelligence about concentration of Iraqi forces with an evident intention to invade the kingdom's territory.*

M. S. GORBACHEV. *I noticed that Iraqi forces were situated in central regions of the country, far enough from Saudi Arabia's border, although big forces were concentrated in Kuwait. Saddam Hussein was sort of sending a signal that he was not going to move towards Saudi Arabia.*

However, when dealing with such a man, who neglects the relationship which existed between you and Iraq, you have to be prepared to anything. That is why we, from the very beginning, took a position of condemning the aggression, of rendering such actions unacceptable.

[…]

I told President Bush that we should stay firm, but not allow the whole region to get into the fire of war. Iraq will surely try to provoke this. Nonetheless, in the interests of the Arabs, of the countries of this region, of the whole world, it is important not to get involved in a wide-scale military conflict.

We have to search for a political solution of the problem. We need some formula which would give Saddam Hussein an opportunity to "save face". Obviously, the occupation is unacceptable, Kuwait must be liberated,

Kuwaiti government must return. But apart from the problems which ought to be discussed between Iraq and Kuwait, there are also problems of the whole Middle East.

If we drive Iraq into a corner, try to put Saddam Hussein on his knees, he may resort to an adventure. It is important to prevent an impression that Saddam is a hero, a great martyr, from emerging among the people's masses. This would make the Arab masses lean to him. And this would also justify adventurism in his actions. He would seem to have no other choice but to defend Iraq and the Arab nation.

Therefore, we have to arrange some process. A key to that might be found among the Arabs. It is their land. This gives a chance to arrange talks between the Arabs and agree about something. The Arabs are divided at the moment, but this can be overcome. It is an important question: how the Arabs should act?

S. AL-FEISAL. *Thank you for frank expression of your vision of the situation. I'll be as frank.*

Saudi Arabia is interested in peaceful settlement more than any other country. If nothing else, in case of a military solution, no one, except Iraq itself, shall suffer more than we.

Our state has never showed any inclination to adventures in its policies. The King never makes steps which might have unpredictable consequences.

From the very beginning of the conflict we did our best to achieve a common Arab position. Unfortunately, we did not succeed, because some Arab countries do not want to put positive influence on Iraq.

Not to repeat what I've already said at the meeting with Mr. Shevardnadze, I'll say briefly that we welcome the role of the Arabs, be they governments of Arab countries, or non-governmental organizations, or politicians.

But we are sure that Saddam Hussein has no intention of withdrawing from Kuwait. Therefore, we have only one choice in front of us: either to accept the aggression and its results or to drive Iraq out of Kuwait by the forces of international community.

We are sure that consequences of driving them out would be softer and lighter than if we accept the occupation. If Iraq remains in Kuwait, this would lead to a split in the Arab world and a threat of total war in the region.

M. S. GORBACHEV. *But what if Saddam does not want to withdraw from Kuwait? We cannot agree that only a military solution remains.*

Political pressure on Iraq is growing now. The embargo is in force. The situation in Iraq is going to escalate. The people suffer difficulties. In these conditions, Saddam Hussein might resort to a military adventure. But this scenario is unacceptable to us.

Perhaps, we should not wait for such a development, but offer Iraq some solutions?

S. AL-FEISAL. *If only it was possible! We are trying to do that all the time. But there was no sign that Saddam would make concessions.*

The war in the region is already unleashed. We did not choose the military way. Iraq has done that.

M. S. GORBACHEV. *This does not make things better. Even if Iraq suffers a defeat, it will be bad. It will be bad for all of us. The whole world will suffer huge damage.*

S. AL-FEISAL. *We don't want Iraq to suffer any damage. As I've already said, Saudi-Iraqi relations used to be the most solid and developed in the whole Arab world. I might exemplify it in such a way: if a son has firmly decided to commit a suicide and nothing can be done, it does not mean that his father should kill himself out of solidarity.*

[...]

If Saddam agrees to withdraw from Kuwait and restore the legitimate government in that country, Iraq won't suffer. Its regime will remain, and preserve its strength and dignity.

However, in order to achieve a peaceful settlement, the world community must demonstrate that the aggression is completely unacceptable, and we are prepared to pay any price to achieve our goal.

A split of the Arab world into two parts does not meet the interests of the world community, including the Soviet Union. In such a case, every country will have to make a choice: which Arabs it is going to cooperate with?

This would lead to a split at the international scene, too. This would threaten the new world order, which is now emerging on the basis of the values common to all mankind and of the balance of interests. We have to avoid this. We are going to support the Soviet Union in its activities in the name of establishing this new order.

Suppose that all the attempts to persuade Iraq to withdraw from Kuwait, by political, diplomatic or economic means, fail. Is it possible that then we have to reconcile with the aggression and the split in the Arab world. Or should we demonstrate our readiness to resort to other means? We need full clarity on how far we are prepared to go to achieve the goal.

Gorbachev replied dryly:

M. S. GORBACHEV. *The Soviet Union shall act on the basis of the positions it has taken in the UN Security Council. [...]*

S. AL-FEISAL. *[...] We are facing a difficult choice and look at the Soviet Union's historical role with hope. In the Arab world, some present the affairs in such a way as if only the governments existed, and forget about the people. Iraq's population is 18 millions. Ours is 16 millions and all of them to a man are against Saddam Hussein and what he has done. But in Iraq, I am sure, no more than a quarter of the population supports their president.*[182]

Chapter 11.
Enter United Europe

Our long-term strategy is to undermine the American dominance in Europe… Then we will be able to behave less conservatively towards the Third Word.

Prime Minister Michael Rocard of France
on the goals of European integration.
(Transcript of the meeting with Gorbachev, 6 July 1989)

In this diplomatically fertile mid-September, with "hawks" trying to cut their losses and "doves" – to develop their Helsinki success, Kremlin saw yet another interesting visitor. His name was Gianni de Michelis. It was difficult to say whether he was a hawk or a dove, nor even whom he actually represented. On the one hand, he came as the foreign minister of Italy; on the other hand, he represented the whole European Community where Italy held presidency at that moment. Therefore, all the time de Michelis had to underline that he was expressing "the position of Italy which is essentially the position of all West Europeans". At some points his identity crisis would get even worse:

> *…And now I am speaking not as a Foreign Minister, but as a member of the Socialist Party[183]*

It should be mentioned that Europe of that time was not exactly Europe of Mitterrand's dreams. (Neither is today's Europe, by the way). Simply put, it was not as united as it was pictured. Therefore, the position which de Michelis heralded was a bit eclectic, as it always happens with positions based on consensus.

> **M. S. GORBACHEV.** *[...] Though I realize it is not very polite, I would like, before giving the floor to you, to tell you about the Soviet-American meeting in Helsinki. I would like to reveal a bit more to you than, probably, the Americans did.*

> **E. A. SHEVARDNADZE.** *Maybe, the Americans have told you even more, but from the different point of view. (Laughter).*

> **M. S. GORBACHEV.** *Probably so. I must say that I found President Bush in a very uneasy state of mind...*

Gorbachev then gave a full account of the discussion in Helsinki and the resulting secret agreement.

> **G. DE MICHELIS.** *Thank you, Mr. President, for this extremely important information and for such a comprehensive description of your views on these problems.*

Meanwhile, according to de Michelis, United Europeans wasted no time either.

> **G. DE MICHELIS.** *[...] Ten days ago the EC Council of Ministers decided to accept the Soviet proposal and work out a Euro-Soviet joint statement on the Middle East by the end of September.*

> **M. S. GORBACHEV.** *I would appreciate this very much! This would be a real demonstration of cooperation.*

Indeed, there was much in common between Soviet and European views of the situation.

> **G. DE MICHELIS.** *[...] I would like to stress: in spite of the firm solidarity between the EC and the US, Europe has its own political "ego" and acts independently rather than simply supports the United States' choice of political or military solution.*

> **M. S. GORBACHEV.** *If the Americans think strategically, they must understand that the capabilities of the European Community and the Soviet Union meet their own interests. This is an advantage rather than a problem. It allows to search for solutions on a broader front, on the*

basis of understanding of common responsibility for preservation and development of current processes in world politics.

De Michelis also thought that the best way to self-express "Europe's own political ego" was to restrain the Americans from within the coalition.

It is also extremely important for us to keep close links with the United States[, he said]. This makes them see it as their duty to mate their actions with the position of the whole world community.

M. S. GORBACHEV. *[…] Americans have to act jointly both with us and with the Europeans, with United Europe. I am talking about restructuring the machinery of world politics.*

However, unless they could find a peaceful solution of the Gulf crisis, all of this would remain mere words.

G. DE MICHELIS. *[…] Like you, we are for a politico-diplomatic settlement, and not only because the military way presents a very big danger in itself. It would also lead to very negative consequences in the Arab world for a very long perspective.*

Politico-diplomatic way is possible under certain conditions. First, we need the instruments of international cooperation, in the framework of which the fundamental problems of Middle East, of the Arab world, could be solved. This may happen only after Iraq withdraws, or is forced to withdraw, from Kuwait. We cannot agree to anything else. Otherwise, Saddam Hussein can say tomorrow that he captured Kuwait to exchange it for the solution of the Palestinian question.

M. S. GORBACHEV. *I think there are no insuperable obstacles. The question is just how to combine, to link, to pack all these things.*

And here de Michelis revealed the United Europe's own way to "pack" it: they had invented another design for the international conference, which seemed to make it widely acceptable.

Drawing borderlines

G. DE MICHELIS. *It seems to us that we've found a very good solution, which allows to separate the Persian Gulf crisis from all the other problems. We believe that the discussion on the inter-Arab issues, the problems of Mediterranean and Middle East, should be organized in a slightly different way.*

The question of calling an international conference to solve the Palestinian problem is very complicated. A preliminary consent of Israel is necessary there. And there is a danger that we cannot convene the conference if it does not give such a consent.

What we want to do is to reverse the conditions: to call an international conference which would consider the rules and principles of security and cooperation in the region of Mediterranean and Middle East. It would be a conference like the one which Europeans had in Helsinki in the '70s. Naturally, the Palestinian problem can also be considered in this framework. The question of Palestinian representatives participating in the conference shall also arise.

It seems to us that it would be much more difficult for Israel to say "no" to a forum whose task is to set rules and principles for the whole region. Though, theoretically, it is possible to imagine an international conference without Israel's participation, in case it refuses to take part in discussing and establishing the system of rules and principles for the region.

M. S. GORBACHEV. *Do you mean to organize this conference under UN auspices?*

G. DE MICHELIS. *Of course. We mean that the conference shall allow to launch the discussion on not only such important problems as the Palestinian one, but also on stopping the arms race and maybe even on disarmament in this region, development of cultural and religious dialogue. In other words, asserting tolerance as opposed to "holy wars".*

This will make it possible to discuss the most delicate problem – that of the borders. Saddam Hussein, when annexing Kuwait, claimed that all the borders in Middle East are invalid. This is directly opposite to what we have fixed in Helsinki [in 1975] when we determined the rules of peaceful transition period in Europe.

Europeans, Soviet Union and the United States would take part in the discussion together with the Arabs. The Helsinki precedent would serve as a legal basis.

We would like the whole Arab world, not only some part of it which is immediately connected to the Middle East region, to take part in the conference.

The main danger of this situation with Kuwait is that it may result in a split of the Arab world, and not only to 12 and 8, like it happened in the Arab League. Six countries of the Persian Gulf may resort to making a direct agreement with the United States, in order to protect their regimes, their wealth, their oil. Even a name of such an organization has already emerged, METO, by analogy with the NATO. All of this would have serious destabilizing consequences for the Arab world, ones of a long-term nature. The only chance to prevent this is to create an alternative system of security and cooperation.

M. S. GORBACHEV. *During our talks in Helsinki, as well as publicly, President Bush said that the Americans are not going to keep their forces in this region any longer than necessary.*

G. DE MICHELIS. *Baker told me the same. I think the Americans are frank. But how is it possible to do that unless we create an appropriate concept, work out the principles of security and cooperation?*

M. S. GORBACHEV. *As I understood, your idea is to call an international conference which would not directly consider the problems which exist in the Middle East region, but would discuss the rules and principles for the states of that region?*

G. DE MICHELIS. *Absolutely right.*

M. S. GORBACHEV. *There is some flexibility in such an approach. Saddam refers to the Arab-Israeli conflict. But if we consider all the causes and problems from the viewpoint of rules and principles, we can launch the process. However, all of this needs to be thought over.*

G. DE MICHELIS. *There is another advantage of putting the problem in our way. The question of the Palestinians" right to be present at such a forum would be solved. The Europeans recognize the PLO and always invite its representatives to their meetings with the Arab world. The USSR also recognizes the PLO. The USA, at least, has recognized the PLO as a collocutor, though they have suspended the dialogue with it now. So, only Israel does not recognize the PLO. But I think it would be difficult for them to refuse, only because of the Palestinians" presence, to take part in a conference working out the rules effectual for all.*

Gorbachev agreed, although not without reservations, that all of this might help "to enter the process."[184]

In a way, that was not a bad idea. The denunciation of all Middle Eastern borders is the centerpiece of Baathism and other pan-Arabist ideologies. Now the whole world had seen that the reality behind "Arab unity" was expansionism and aggressiveness. Why not use this unique moment to make the Arabs renounce their dangerous ideologies?

Naturally, the 1975 Helsinki Agreement could not serve as a "legal basis", as de Michelis put it, because it was effectual only for its signatories. He probably meant there would be a new agreement for the Middle East, modelled on the CSCE Final Act. Indeed, bearing in mind this precedent, the introduction of "inviolability of frontiers" principle would have very attractive implications. In Europe, this principle practically meant an endorsement of the de facto borders, thus legalizing the Soviet occupation of half the continent, from Estonia to Bulgaria. In the Middle East, therefore, it was bound to remove the legal question mark from Israel's de facto borders, and eliminate the "problem of the occupied Palestinian territories" from international relations whatsoever. Any other interpretation would obviously expose double standards.

But was this the actual plan behind the EC"s proposal?

If it was, why did de Michelis talk so much about PLO representatives at the projected conference and about the discussion of "the Palestinian problem" there? For example, in Helsinki conference there had been neither representatives of Baltic states' governments-in-exile, nor any discussion on, say, "the Moldovan problem".

Was the Palestinian theme just an incentive for the Soviets and the Arabs to commit them to the inviolability of frontiers with all its implications? Was the reasoning that such a conference would help to oust the US out of the Middle East and prevent the split among the Arabs another carrot? Or maybe, on the contrary, the inviolability of frontiers was an incentive for the US and Israel to drag them into negotiations with the PLO?

Probably, different decision-makers in Europe had different ideas on what was the inventive and what was the real goal. Some of them thought about deceiving Soviets and Arabs, some others – about deceiving

Americans and Israelis, and yet some others – about deceiving the both sides. All of them certainly hoped to deceive each other.

Be that as it may, the Soviets swiftly identified and ruled out the dangerous element in this project. The next month, Gorbachev's envoy Yevgeny Primakov discussed it with de Michelis in Rome. Primakov insisted that

> *In the Middle East, the question of the inviolability of frontiers can be raised only after the frontiers themselves are drawn. The main problem here is still the Arab-Israeli conflict.*

According to Primakov, de Michelis agreed with that.[185]

Actually, de Michelis"s idea was implemented, though in a quite different form and much later, in 1995. By that time there was no Soviet Union, so it could not participate in any conference. To preserve the balance, Europeans kept the United States away from the conference, too. In addition, the Arab unity had only deteriorated since 1990, so many Arab countries, including all the Gulf states, did not come either. As a result, the conference was named "Euro-Mediterranean", though it still remained one "on security and cooperation".

Oddly enough, among the participants was Jordan, which had nothing to do either with Europe or with the Mediterranean. The others were all the EU members, all the Mediterranean coastal states (including Israel on one hand, and Syria and Lybia – on the other), and the Palestinian National Authority represented by Yassir Arafat. All of them met in Barcelona, and signed a document known as Barcelona declaration.

Conversely, the Palestinian participation was a direct violation of the 1993 Oslo Accords, which had explicitly forbidden the PNA to be a party to international treaties. The Barcelona conference de facto denounced this condition, thus opening the way for a Euro-Palestinian Association Agreement (no longer a mere declaration) to be signed in a couple of years.

The structure of the Barcelona declaration was, indeed, modelled on the CSCE Final Act. However, "inviolability of frontiers" principle was probably lost somewhere in the middle of re-drafts. Instead, the parties confirmed their commitment to the Middle East peace settlement based on "the principle land for peace, with all that this implies" – something directly opposite to the "inviolability".

As we see, no matter what the original intentions of the EC could have been, the results were worthy of the decades-long Soviet efforts.

This is what happened five years later. But now let us return to September 1990, when de Michelis was outlining some more of EC ideas.

Eurabia solution

As de Michelis explained, that conference on security and cooperation could be held only after the Gulf crisis was solved this way or another. Meanwhile, time was running short.

> **G. DE MICHELIS.** *[...] We have to search for a politico-diplomatic solution in a way which would allow implementing it within the next two months. Otherwise an impression that the only way to solve this conflict is the military one is very much possible.*

> **M. S. GORBACHEV.** *And this will be the crisis of the whole course towards the new peaceful period in international relations.*

> **G. DE MICHELIS.** *Certainly.*

Naturally, the main obstacle to be overcome was Saddam's stubborn refusal to withdraw from Kuwait. Therefore, more pressure had to be put on him:

> **G. DE MICHELIS.** *However, to make Saddam accept those basic conditions, we have to move towards tougher political and economic isolation of Iraq.*

> *By tougher economic isolation I mean that we should persuade or force all the countries to obey the embargo. It should also cover the air traffic, because it is by air that Iraq gets vital spare parts. Without these spare parts, it would be unable to fight.*

> *We should continue to use the power of the Security Council, in particular to take measures to ban air traffic, and to establish sanctions against the countries which violate the embargo.*

> *Naturally, securing everyone's compliance the embargo requires measures of economic support to those countries which suffer losses because of it. The European Community has already taken the first decisions in this respect. For example, to provide aid to Jordan, although its position towards Iraq is hesitant.*

> *[...]*

It is absolutely clear that the complete embargo is impossible. But if Saddam Hussein can say that he is still seen as a collocutor, that presidents and prime ministers keep addressing him, why should he withdraw from Kuwait? He can firmly stay on his positions.

But then, one fine day, the advocates of military solutions will prevail in the United States and some Arab countries. Even now, it is seen in some quarters as the easiest way. And if Europe and the Soviet Union don't want a military solution, we need to significantly increase our pressure on Saddam Hussein. Otherwise we cannot achieve a political solution.

Thus, you received Tariq Aziz and hardly could notice any flexibility in him. But Baghdad could say they are talking to the Soviet Union as equals, have ways to assert their positions, and therefore their positions are right.

M. S. GORBACHEV. *We should not allow Iraq to be left with no choice. We should try to imagine ourselves in their place, bearing in mind, of course, Saddam's character.*

G. DE MICHELIS. *Two more points. First, it is important to demonstrate to the Americans that most of the Arabs are for a political solution. Both Americans and Arabs must value and try to preserve the international solidarity.*

Second, we need to make the embargo more effective. I am convinced that Saddam would not rethink his positions unless the embargo really starts to "bite" him. And this must convince the Americans that joint actions are useful to them. Of course, nobody can give a 100% guarantee that Saddam will start to think because of strengthening embargo. And yet, it is better to increase pressure. In addition, as I've already said, we need a maximum consolidation of the Arab world.

Indeed, the political elements of this strategy were crafted even more carefully, particularly concerning the Arabs:

G. DE MICHELIS. *[...] As for political isolation, the main problem here is the Arab world. To be precise, those eight countries which did not join the Egypt-led majority during the vote in the Arab League. We should vigorously pull them on our side. Saddam Hussein must be shown that there are no countries on whose solidarity he can count unless he leaves Kuwait.*

We have decided to invite all the Arab countries except Iraq to a meeting on ministerial level in Venice on 7-8 October. There we are planning to discuss possible steps in medium-term and long-term perspectives of cooperation in the region of Middle East and Mediterranean. This will also allow the above-mentioned eight countries to join the consensus which is achieved in Europe and European Community. We have invited them all, including Palestinians, Jordan and Algeria, which plays the key role in this region.

This should demonstrate to Iraq that the consensus is not weakening but, on the contrary, getting more solid. And Saddam Hussein has to seriously accept the conditions we've been talking about.

M. S. GORBACHEV. *Is this just an idea? Or is it born as a result of your consultations with Arabs?*

G. DE MICHELIS. *We have sent the official invitations. A document is worked out in the EC, which determined the basic lines of discussion at this meeting. Though I don't know to what extent it fits into what you discussed in Helsinki.*

De Michelis explained that Saddam's influence in the Arab world was often exaggerated. No matter how hard Gorbachev, Mitterrand and Tariq Aziz were trying to intimidate each other, the Arab reaction was rather anti-Iraqi. Even the eight members of the Arab League who declined to vote against Iraq were drifting away from Saddam.

This is also true in the PLO[, said de Michelis]. Now Arafat regrets his initial actions very much. He is facing very big difficulties.

One of the Venice meeting's objectives is precisely to give Arafat and others an opportunity to retreat. Otherwise they risk to get out of the game. Then we would have to deal with different people.

So, 12 EC states and 20 member-states of the Arab League are supposed to take part in this meeting at the level of foreign ministers. This meeting fits into normal practice of Euro-Arab dialogue. The latest meeting of this kind took place in December last year in Paris. Therefore, this is a normal thing. The only departure is the absence of Iraq, which has put itself to the situation of opposition to the countries of the EC, the Arab League and the UN.

M. S. GORBACHEV. *Iraq is usually invited to the meetings of the*

Arab League. In connection with that, is it going to be understood if you don't invite Iraq's administration to this meeting, which takes place in the framework of traditional bilateral contacts between the Europeans and the Arabs? What will be the Arab countries' attitude towards such an exclusion? Would not this rather look as a legal trial against Iraq?

G. DE MICHELIS. *Yes, this is a delicate point.*

M. S. GORBACHEV. *Which Arab countries' participation you can already count on now?*

G. DE MICHELIS. *First of all, those 12 members of the Arab League which we've talked about. Jordan is receiving, without any conditions, economic aid from the EC. So, it will hardly be in a position to refuse. As for the countries of Arab Maghreb alliance, the Community has a permanent dialogue with them. Therefore, a refusal of Algeria or Tunisia is also difficult for me to imagine.*

M. S. GORBACHEV. *The proposals of Tunisia contain a certain element. They believe that any prospects of movement must include the necessity to avoid any attempts to put Saddam Hussein on his knees. They can tell you: invite Iraq. For example, the Tunisian leaders might put the problem like that: invite Iraq, let it refuse, and then we shall feel free to come to this meeting. If you don't invite it, we will find ourselves in a situation when we are opposed to an Arab country. The matter is not Saddam alone. The actions are taken which do not fit in their ideas about norms of relations within the Arab world. They can put the problem to you in this way.*

G. DE MICHELIS. *I've been in Tunisia, and I know the Tunisians' position. I would like to be absolutely clear. We have 15 more days until October 7. If the Tunisians achieve anything by that time, so much the better. Perhaps, [they arrange] an inter-Arab dialogue with participation of Iraq and Saudi Arabia. But I cannot imagine that Saudi Arabia agrees to it without the US consent. Let me repeat myself: if this happens, so much the better. But what if not?*

If we want to avoid a military solution, we need the Arabs to put pressure on Saddam. Otherwise, military solution may become practically inevitable at some point. Both Algeria and Tunisia have to take into account that they get big opportunities if they cooperate with Europe. Saddam's actions, condemned by the UN, are on the agenda. But it is important to them to discuss with the Europeans the Palestinian problem, the Lebanese one, and others. They have to understand that Saddam is the main obstacle for international solidarity now. If they want such solidarity to exist, they must eliminate the problem which Saddam has created.

It must be made absolutely clear that the annexation of Kuwait has jeopardized and delayed the solution of the Palestinian question. And Saddam is not the main opponent of Israel's right-wing government, but effectively the main ally of the Likud cabinet. I talked to [David] Levy, my Israeli colleague, and he was very pleased with the fact that Saddam had helped him to solve a number of problems, including those concerning the PLO. We need to convince the majority that this is the case.

[…]

M. S. GORBACHEV. *First of all, I'd like to say that, in principle, your ideas fit in the mainstream of our own considerations and suggestions on how we should act in this sharp crisis in the Persian Gulf.*

I used to say, both publicly and to President Mitterrand by telephone, that after the Security Council has passed its resolutions, the key to the resolution of this crisis lays in the Arab world, in its positions, in the necessity of its consolidation. It is important to move the Arab factor to a certain condition, so that it could play its role in the political solution of the problem. On the basis of the Security Council's mandate, it could undertake the burden of normalizing the situation in the region.

Your and our approaches are not simply close, they are identical, and I highly appreciate this.

In this respect, the idea of a meeting between EC and Arab League member-states' ministers in Venice is interesting and realistic, though not indisputable. It seems to me that it might become one of important big steps in present situation. Probably, you should think over your arguments even more deeply, in order to provide maximum participation of the Arab world. For if only a half or some part of the Arab League members comes, the split in the Arab world would only aggravate.

I like your idea and we might help with specific preparations for this conference. We shall continue exchange of opinions with you through the foreign ministries. We shall take your considerations into account. We shall also try to help you through our connections with Arabs, in order to make that conference successful.

G. DE MICHELIS. *This is very important to us. All the more so because, ten days ago, it was decided in the Community framework to agree to a joint EC-USSR statement on the Middle East.*

M. S. GORBACHEV. *It is important to analyze how the events are going to develop further. I am very keen to ensure that Europe's role is seen as more positive, more dynamic, more promising. It must not, so to speak, discredit itself and lose its weight in the eyes of world community.*

Therefore, following a maximum participation of the Arabs, it is important to see how you should conclude the meeting. Consolidation has a huge significance. It shall emphasize once again that Saddam's regime has to make a choice and change its policies. But if consolidation is your only goal, it is not enough.

We have to take into account two points. Arabs must see that, after the crisis is solved and eliminated from the Persian Gulf, Arabic machinery will start working, Arabs themselves shall rule their land. It is important for Europe to emphasize this point.

Second. We must think on how to make Saddam understand that he is in isolation and show our determination and firmness in the principal issue. At the same time, we should let Saddam see that liberation of Kuwait would open an opportunity to discuss all the other issues. Iraq and Kuwait have their own disputed issues, including financial ones.

This shall also open an opportunity to discuss the whole complex of Middle East problems. No matter how little it pleases us in moral sense, in politics we have to do something in order to open some chink for Saddam. Otherwise, if he sees he is in a deadlock, he will look for solution in his own way. And all of us know which way it is. As a result, instead of a prologue to a political settlement, we'll still face the same unpredictable actions.

It is important not only to get him into a trap, but also to give him a chance to get out of it. We have to give him something! This thought haunts me.

Arabs would not agree to a complete isolation of Iraq. It represents a very complex and important element of the Arab world. Arabs must feel that the conference's goal is not simply to put Iraq in the pillory, but to open new prospects for the Arab nation, to which we have to show due respect and care. Now it is particularly important to understand this.

G. DE MICHELIS. *I've been talking to Mubarak about this three weeks ago. As soon as we are clear about Kuwait, it will be possible to conduct negotiations with Iraq on the debts, and on the oilfields, and on the coastline in Mkazu area.*

It is very important both for Arabs and Europeans, while keeping the firm position on Kuwait, to show certain flexibility on the other issues. As for the conference after the crisis, Europeans together with Arabs should take an obligation to move towards arranging such a conference on security and cooperation in the region of Middle East and Mediterranean.[186]

Gorbachev kept his promise to try to influence the Arab countries in order to drive them to the Venice meeting. Thus, two days later he raised the issue with the Saudi Foreign Minister.

M. S. GORBACHEV. *Do you know about the European initiative – their proposal to arrange a meeting between the twelve EC members and the Arab countries in Venice? What is you reaction?*

However, al Feisal's reply did not seem enthusiastic:

We are studying this proposal. It is, actually, not an initiative for the settlement of the conflict. It is just a proposal about a joint meeting of representatives of European nations and Arab states, except Iraq, to consider the situation. The Arabs cannot convene on their own.

M. S. GORBACHEV. *That is true. It would be good if all the Arabs convene there…*

But al-Feisal had already returned to his interrupted oratory against Saddam.[187]

If Gorbachev's intercession had any influence on the Saudis, it was directly opposite to what he wanted. Quite reasonably, the Saudis might conclude that if Gorbachev supported the idea, it was better to stay away from it. Anyway, was it due to Saudi position or something else, the Venice meeting never took place, while the "Arab unity" deteriorated even further. In the end of September, the French Ambassador was complaining about that to one of Gorbachev's advisors:

> *Passing on to the Arabs' positions, [Gorbachev's man reported,] the Ambassador emphasized the disastrous nature of the split between them. Saudi Arabia's attempts to "consolidate" the Arab world by pressure (for example, by closing the oil pipeline to Jordan) are doomed to fail, he said. As a result of such attempts, the Arabs shall find themselves in an even more difficult situation.*

The question was whether the Saudis had done that by mistake or deliberately.

The Saudis were not the only ones to upset the French. Actually, Ambassador Meriyon seemed to be displeased with nearly all the parties to the conflict.

> *First of all, Paris is concerned with the US position. They keep talking about peaceful solution, but they also keep actively preparing for war. In fact, they will be ready to "start" within one month, as Saddam Hussein is giving them plenty of excuses to do so.*
>
> *But apparently, the Americans underestimate the difficulties of a war in a desert. Meriyon himself used to serve in Africa. He knows how difficult it is to conduct military operations there, how the weapons fail, how the soldiers suffer, being unaccustomed to the desert conditions. Even now, although it has not come to war yet, the Americans' equipment "goes on strikes" sometimes.*
>
> *Saddam Hussein, in turn, behaves like he is prepared for war. But he is also wrong. He either does not realize what a war against America would be like, or is simply possessed with an idea-fix. The actions he is taking now are irrational. This alone is dangerous in itself.*
>
> *[…]*
>
> *Meriyon admitted that he could not understand the Palestinians' position. They evidently play up to Iraq, thus weakening their positions in the Arab world, though they need all the Arab countries' support more than anybody else.*

No matter how much the French disliked war, particularly in a desert, they were also quite displeased with the current peace.

> *Probably, Meriyon said, there are some forces which are trying to prolong the conflict (without war) for several months, to make the situation "decay". In such a case it will be even more difficult to find a solution. All the more so since the oil prices may well jump up to 100 dollars for a barrel in the meantime. And what then?*

> *The ambassador did not reply to my question what forces he meant.*

By the way, an increase in oil prices was indeed quite refreshing for the Soviet economy at the brink of its ultimate bankruptcy.

When Gorbachev kept saying that "in strategic terms" he had already won the conflict, he was not entirely wrong. Of course, it would be better if he could mediate a peaceful solution. But even without it, the benefits were evident. Oil prices went up, America was getting more and more friendly, Gorbachev's importance and influence in the world were growing.

In addition, the Western public had concentrated its attention on the Gulf – and hence, away from the Soviet Union and Eastern Europe. This was also quite timely. Gorbachev had some controversial plans there for the near future. He did not want them to be examined too closely.

Chapter 12.
Primakov's mission

October 1990 was the month of intensive secret negotiations between Saddam and the US-led coalition. The very fact that such negotiations took place remained secret until now. It was one of those cases where different parties want different things at the time, but all of them are later united by their common interest in a cover up.

As we remember, at the Helsinki summit Gorbachev proposed he would "send someone" to Saddam to "sound him" about the peace plan, and Bush gratefully accepted this. That "someone" was Yevgeny Primakov – a KGB man, one of Gorbachev's top aides, and a personal friend of Saddam Hussein. Throughout October, Primakov was engaged in a long round of shuttle diplomacy: Moscow - Amman - Baghdad - Moscow - Rome - Paris -Washington DC - London - Moscow - Cairo - Baghdad - Riyadh. One would suspect, on the face of it, that Primakov mediated between Saddam and the West. As we shall see below, that was precisely what he did.

However, his mission was played down at the time, in line with the Gorbachev-Bush agreement to keep it secret. Later, very misleading accounts were given in the memoirs of Bush, Scowcroft and Baker. They picture Primakov as an odd Soviet "hard-liner" who had a very different agenda from Gorbachev or Shevardnadze. They portray his trip as little more than a hopeless private initiative of one man, and certainly a bolt from the blue to them. Baker, to leave no doubts at all, even titled the relevant sub-chapter of his memoirs "Primakov's October Surprise", where he tells what a nuisance "Primakov's meddling" was for Baker's happy cooperation with the Soviets. Baker's own meeting with Primakov is described as "essentially a cosmetic affair, a courtesy to Gorbachev to show that we took the Soviets seriously and needed their continued diplomatic cooperation".[188]

Bush and Scowcroft, for their part, confess they had not a slightest idea on what was going on. All they write about Primakov's trip to Baghdad is a couple of paragraphs, every sentence there starting with the word "apparently":

> *October brought new strains on the coalition. It appeared that Soviet internal political problems were beginning to spill over to the crisis. On October 4-5, Primakov visited Baghdad, apparently carrying a message from Gorbachev. We were uneasy about the trip, especially when we learned that a furious Shevardnadze had not known of it ahead of time, nor exactly what message Primakov was supposed to convey. Shevardnadze promised Baker he would let us know the purpose of the mission as soon as he found out.*

The last sentence is supplemented with a tiny-script footnote: "His deputy, Sergei Tarasenko, told us that Primakov was attempting to float a peace proposal of some sort and that Shevardnadze had objected but had been overruled."

> *The Soviets were also reporting potential compromise or conditional offers from the Iraqis, [Bush and Scowcroft continue,] deals we could not possibly accept. The proposals seemed to reflect a growing influence of the pro-Iraqi faction in the Soviet Foreign Ministry.*[189]

These had been, of course, Bush and Scowcroft who talked to Gorbachev in Helsinki about "sending someone" to "sound Saddam out". Baker was in the next room and first to be told. Their pretence of having been confused may be a good pretence or not (my personal view is that the memoirs of Scowcroft and Bush are an extremely well written piece of fiction, unlike Baker's memoirs); but certainly, not a word of what they write about this matter is true.

So, what are they trying to smokescreen by that gibberish?

Helsinki to Baghdad

Admittedly, there are still gaps in the evidence of what actually happened.

Thus, we do not have the verbatim transcripts of Primakov's negotiations in Baghdad and in Washington. But even the few available documents, compared to the open sources and some pieces of indirect evidence, outline a fairly clear general picture.

Certainly, the mysterious "Primakov's plan" was the same plan which Gorbachev proposed, and Bush accepted, in Helsinki - linking Kuwait to the Arab-Israeli conflict. Therefore, it was only logical that Primakov's mission started with a meeting with Yassir Arafat in Jordan on 3 October. What they said to each other is not known, but we do know something of what they both did in the following few weeks.

On 5 October, Primakov moved on to Baghdad. According to his own account of that visit, Saddam listened to the Soviet plan with interest; and it is certain that he reacted by promising to release 1,500 Soviet citizens from Iraq. It was Saddam's strategy to pay for pro-Iraqi initiatives and gestures by releasing so many hostages to the country which made them. Although the 5,000 Russians who happened to be in Iraq in 1990 had not been officially taken hostages, they were not allowed to leave Iraq either, and Baghdad kept hinting that their future fate would depend on the Soviet approach to the crisis. In Saddam's price-list, 1,500 hostages was certainly a lot.

Primakov wrote:

> *[Next] morning, Tariq Aziz and I went to the airport in his car. He told me:*
>
> *"Saddam expects your specific proposals now. We are looking forward to further contacts."*
>
> *"Tariq, would you repeat this at the airport, in the presence of our ambassador?" I asked.*
>
> *"Why?"*
>
> *"Because, after all, we are travelling by plane. Your statement is important. It is better to double it in a coded cable to Moscow, just in case."*
>
> *Tariq agreed, and then fulfilled my request.*[190]

Belonogov, the Soviet Arabist-in-Chief, confirms that the Soviet Foreign Ministry received such a cable, wherefrom he learned that:

> *In the airport, Tariq Aziz informed that Saddam Hussein asked for Soviet written proposals on a possible "package" solution of the Kuwait crisis. (Apparently, Yeavgeny Maximovich [Primakov] had expressed some ideas on this matter. Otherwise, how could the very idea of a Soviet "package" emerge?).*[191]

Primakov came back to Moscow and reported to Gorbachev on October 7. By the next day, he drafted the plan of "package solution". Gorbachev sent it to the Foreign Ministry, asking for the Arabists' advice, but they took the plan very sceptically.

> *We noted that the package had a number of similarities with the scheme proposed by the Soviet side in Helsinki[, Belonogov writes]. However, we drew the Minister's attention to the fact that bringing forward the problem of Arab-Israeli settlement once again, in the same package as the solution of the Kuwaiti crisis, even without a strict temporal linkage with it, would immediately clash us with the Americans. They were prepared neither to unite these issues nor to take such steps, proposed in the package, as resuming their suspended dialogue with the PLO or taking an obligation to influence Israel. [...]*

> *We also noted it was undesirable to associate the USSR with Iraqi claims against Kuwait, particularly on the territorial problem (the package proposed for Iraq to receive preliminary assurances from Kuwait's leadership, guaranteed by Saudi Arabia, that the issues negotiated in Jiddah with Kuwaiti delegation before the August 2 invasion would be resolved positively for Iraq).*[192]

Furthermore, the Arabists suspected that Saddam had asked for a written plan only to lure the Soviets into a trap. If he had it in writing, he could simply leak it, in a further effort to split the coalition.

After receiving this advice, Gorbachev decided it would be better to send Primakov to Washington and other Western capitals first to have "the package" agreed with the West before it is offered to Saddam.[193]

Were the Soviets divided?

In giving their chaotic accounts of that stage of the Gulf crisis, Bush, Scowcroft and Baker focus largely on speculation about the Kremlin's hawks and doves fighting each other under the carpet. They tell us about the courageous reformers Gorbachev and Shevardnadze, with whom the memoirists had been doing business together so nicely; and about the Foreign Ministry Arabists, led by Primakov, who tried to protect their friend Saddam. The memoirists then suggest that the evil Arabists temporarily got the upper hand. While Shevardnadze was away, visiting his friend Baker, the hard-liners put pressure on Gorbachev, who reluctantly authorised Primakov's mission.

All of this is very far from the truth.

To begin with, Primakov had never had anything to do with the Foreign Ministry or its Arabists. He had always been a KGB man, working under cover as a Middle East studies academic. Under Gorbachev, he rose high in the Soviet leadership as Shevardnadze's personal protégé[194] (which was not surprising, bearing in mind Shevardnadze's own KGB background).

It is true that Shevardnadze and Primakov disagreed about Primakov's mission, but certainly not because one was pro-Western and the other pro-Eastern. The mission had been agreed with Bush at the Helsinki summit, so nobody in the Kremlin would see it as an anti-Western move - not those who were privy to the Helsinki secrets. Thus, Anatoly Chernyaev - Gorbachev's pro-Western advisor if ever there was one - thought Shevardnadze was simply jealous about Primakov's role. On 13 October, Chernyaev wrote in a memo to Gorbachev:

Of course, if E. A. Shevardnadze has reservations about the "package", we should take them into account. But, in a matter like this, his jealousy is rather misplaced.[195]

When forwarding Chernyaev's memo to Shevardnadze, Gorbachev cut off the "offensive" paragraph about jealousy.[196]

According to Chernyaev, the objection to Primakov's mission given by Shevardnadze himself was this:

"Do it without me" [*, Shevardnadze said during the discussion in the Kremlin*]. *"I am not going to take part in it. The Americans will never start the war."*[197]

Shevardnadze probably thought the Helsinki summit had already done the trick. The Americans had asked to sound Saddam out and were now waiting for news; fine. No news is a good news. Let them wait until the next elections or some new crisis. Why give them any plan to refuse? And why expose ourselves to Saddam's attempts to split the coalition and undermine the Soviet relations with the West?

The course taken by Gorbachev was, in fact, more honest and more loyal towards his US partners. He had promised them to try and mediate a deal with Saddam, and so he did.

As for the Foreign Ministry Arabists, they had known Saddam for a very long time and had no illusions about him; so they advocated a tough line. Among other things, they advised Gorbachev that anything he says or writes to Iraqis would probably be used against him.[198]

As for the rivalry between Primakov and Shevardnadze, all the evidence suggests that the Foreign Ministry stuff loved Shevardnadze, hated Primakov, and were most sceptical about the "package". Belonogov, in his book, makes many critical points about Gorbachev and Primakov, but not about Shevardnadze, to whom he seems to be very warm. After Shevardnadze resigned two month later, Primakov's name was on the shortlist of his possible successors, accompanied by this reservation: "unacceptable to the Foreign Ministry apparatus"[199]. As likely as not, it was for this reason that Primakov failed to become Foreign Minister in 1990.

So, all the nonsense written by Bush, Scowcroft and Baker about Primakov in the Foreign Ministry, about Arabist resistance to Shevardnadze, about the infighting in the Kremlin and the confusion in the White House - all that is merely a misleading attempt to distance themselves from the secret talks Gorbachev arranged with Saddam on their behalf. But in reality, to all intents and purposes, Primakov's negotiations had been secretly commissioned by the White House.

The modest role of Comrade Arafat

After seeing Primakov in Jordan, Arafat also hurried to Baghdad to see Saddam - he even overtook his Soviet companion at that. Of course, Arafat had every reason to work hard these days, the fate of Gorbachev's peace plan being decided. Since "the package" was pulling the "Palestinian problem" back to the forefront, it was a very right moment to re-direct the world's anger from Iraq to Israel.

On October 8, as Primakov had just finished writing his draft in Moscow, a violent Palestinian riot on the Temple Mount in Jerusalem provoked an exchange of fire. As a result, 21 rioters were killed and about 150 were wounded. At once, the UN Security Council made itself busy condemning Israel.

The chain of coincidences did not finish here. These very days, the UN happened to be debating a draft resolution, introduced by Columbia, Cuba, Malaysia and Yemen, which called for the members to act as decisively against Israel over the "Palestinian problem" as against Iraq over Kuwait.[200]

Now, after the Temple Mount events, the PLO representative demanded the Security Council to pass a resolution condemning Israel's actions as a "criminal act" and set up a special UN mission to investigate the situation in Gaza and the West Bank and recommend ways to protect Palestinians. Bush and Scowcroft write:

We did not want to be put in the position of vetoing the resolution, or to appear uncaring about the loss of life in Jerusalem, reinforcing the perception that we were protecting Israel at the expense of the Arabs. In addition, the Iraqis were making noises about connecting the handling of the incident with resolution of the Gulf crisis...[201]

To cut a long story short, they betrayed Israel once again. The US themselves offered a resolution, essentially similar to the Palestinian draft, condemning Israel (in somewhat softer expressions) and endorsing the UN mission. After some bargaining over the harshness of the language, the resolution was passed on October 12.

Naturally, Israel rebuffed the UN mission. As naturally, the UN condemned it again for not cooperating.[202]

Baghdad to Washington

All of this provided a much more favorable background to continue Primakov's mission. On October 16, he, armed with his "package", was sent to Rome, Paris, Washington and London. His visits to Rome and Paris were necessary just to keep Gorbachev's friends informed, while London was added to this list at the last moment as a mere courtesy.[203] Of course, the actual negotiations took place in Washington.

The *official version* of this visit is narrated in the memoirs of Bush, Scowcroft and Baker in very vague expressions and a grotesquely confusing way. Thus Baker begins telling about 'Primakov's October surprise' from February 1991; then, within one page, he jumps to October 1990, then to January 1991, then back to February 1991 and then back to October 1990. However, the general structure of his account is exactly the same as that of Bush and Scowcroft:

1. In mid-October, Primakov suddenly came to us (vociferous expressions of surprise at seeing Primakov).

2. Primakov was a Soviet hardliner not on very good terms with our great friend Shevardnadze (at least a page of speculations about the Soviet Arabists, their sympathies and influence).

3. He proposed some kind of plan which involved a lot of concessions to save Saddam's face: something about Bubiyan, something about Palestinians, this kind of thing. (Be very brief and vague about the substance of the plan)

4. Of course, this was very far from the unconditional surrender we wanted, so, obviously...

Overall, this leaves a strong impression that they rejected the plan without going deep into detail, although none of them says so in plain English.

Supposing this is true, Primakov's mission was now over.

What they forget to mention is that only a week later Primakov was in Baghdad again.

I am not suggesting that Bush and Baker in fact committed themselves to "Primakov's plan" - they could not possibly do that. As is usual in such situations, a mediator was necessary precisely because the both sides, Washington and Baghdad, were reluctant to commit themselves.

All Bush said to Gorbachev in Helsinki was that plan was interesting and it was a good idea to sound out what Saddam thought about it.

All Saddam said to Primakov in Baghdad was that the plan was interesting and it would be good to know more details and have it in writing.

Whatever Bush and Baker said to Primakov in Washington DC, it was not a commitment, but it certainly encouraged the Soviets to keep negotiating with Saddam.

After all, if they could commit themselves, they would have talked to Saddam directly.

All the Soviets could see was that the both sides seemed prepared, in principle, to make a deal on the basis of linking Kuwait with the Arab-Israeli conflict. The outstanding issues seemed negotiable: how soon Saddam should withdraw from Kuwait, how soon Israel would be made to withdraw from West Bank and Gaza, and how secret the "linkage" should be. Therefore, the Soviets had strong reasons to go ahead with the negotiations.

The immediate reaction of Bush and Baker to Primakov's proposals is merely a matter of speculation. However, after Primakov's visit, Bush sent a message to Gorbachev in writing.

> *I cabled Gorbachev, [Bush writes,] that I felt [Primakov's proposals] violated the basic principles we laid out in Helsinki. "Rather than insisting on Saddam's unconditional withdrawal, this approach would offer him significant "face savers" that he would inevitably present as a "reward".*[204]

However, the Soviet sources suggest that Bush's message was different. Thus, Chernyaev mentions that in this message Bush "thanks [Gorbachev] for sending Primakov to Baghdad, but insists we should not "reward Saddam or save his face""[205]. Gorbachev's own reaction was also remarkably jubilant. "M. G. phoned me as soon as he received Bush's message," Chernyaev writes. "He got it: the US president does need his Michael!"[206]

The next day, Primakov himself returned to Moscow and shared his new impressions:

> *He felt with his skin [Chernyaev writes] that a military attack is imminent. It is a matter of one week. Now he asks me to help him to persuade M. S. [Gorbachev]. He wants to go to Cairo, Ryadh and to Saddam, and tell him: we have done all we could. Unless you agree [to our proposals], you have nobody to blame but yourself.*[207]

Clearly, it was Primakov's view that the success of his mission would now be crucial to prevent the immanent war. Gorbachev agreed, and sent Primakov to Baghdad via Cairo.

Washington to Baghdad

While Primakov was in Cairo, the UN Security Council was busily preparing another resolution against Saddam. This time, it was about Iraq's financial responsibility for the damage, losses and injuries it had inflicted to Kuwait and other countries.

On October 26 the Iraqi Ambassador in Moscow protested against the Soviet participation in preparing this resolution, while in Baghdad Tariq Aziz made a similar protest to the Soviet Ambassador. He added that, if the Soviet Union is really going to support the resolution, there is no point in Primakov's visit to Baghdad the next day.

Meanwhile, the Security Council officially convened to vote on the resolution. Anyone could read a firm determination to vigorously condemn the shameless breaches of international law on the faces of the member-states' representatives. Needless to say, the most determined was the Soviet Ambassador Vorontsov. At that meeting, he made a very strong statement in support of the resolution.

But suddenly, a short man wearing a dirty white collar ran into the room and gave Vorontsov a piece of paper. It was a new instruction from Moscow.

The Soviet Ambassador took the floor again. Now he said that, in view of the newly emerged circumstances, the discussion of the resolution would be rather untimely after all. Actually, there were reasons to expect some good news from Baghdad in the next few days, Vorontsov said. So, he asked the chairman (it was a British representative) to postpone the vote. The chairman complied – and Primakov went to Baghdad.

These very days, Gorbachev himself visited his old friends – the European socialists. While Primakov came to Baghdad, his boss was in Madrid.

F[ELIPE] GONZALES *[Prime Minister of Spain]. You and I have planned to discuss the issue of the Persian Gulf crisis, haven't we?*

M. S. GORBACHEV. *Perhaps, while we are talking here, it is already over?*

(Laughter.)

F. GONZALES. *I am afraid, this may be something even your special* *envoy Mr. Primakov cannot do.*

Gorbachev, however, explained what reasons he had for such self-confidence:

The most recent information from our Ambassador in Baghdad shows that the pressure from the international community, and the failure of all attempts to split the anti-Iraqi front in the UN, are beginning to influence Saddam. If he preferred to express himself in form of ultimatums before, now his tone is changing.

E. A. SHEVARDNADZE. *Indeed, there were signs in the last two days that Saddam is getting more nervous.*

M. S. GORBACHEV. *This means we cannot say that we are losing this conflict. Moreover, as I have told Bush, we can say that we have already won in strategic terms, because we reacted together, in full-scale cooperation, to a very sharp international crisis.*

[…]

Judging by the signals from Iraq, a moment for a significant progress may come soon.

Therefore, the USA should by no means try to put Saddam on his knees now. Nothing except a military conflict can come out of such attempts.

In connection with this, I think a stronger involvement of the Arab factor is necessary.

F. GONZALES. *This is a very right idea.*

M. S. GORBACHEV. *If only we manage to encourage Saddam to go to an all-Arab forum! He would face a very difficult choice there. He would have to think and think again. And if he does not go, he will expose himself in front of his "brothers".*

It looks like the Arabs may agree to arrange such a forum. They might offer something there. Our task is to encourage them to do that, thus helping them to raise themselves in the eyes of the world community. So, everyone would benefit from that.

F. GONZALES. *I absolutely agree with your analysis. This is the only possible way. One must not put one's finger in a fresh wound. The role of the Arabs, of the Arab League, must be central.*

Our main objective is not just an implementation of UN resolutions, but also a balance of armed forces in this zone. This can be achieved in two ways. We can break Iraq's war machine through military conflict, or we can establish the balance by negotiations.

I would like to emphasize that an iron unity of the international community is absolutely necessary for the solution of this conflict. Only if this is ensured, it will be possible to open the way for the Arab factor and achieve the balance of military forces in this zone.

M. S. GORBACHEV. *I absolutely agree with you. Without unity, there is no chance for a political solution. Such is the dialectics.*

Then Gorbachev complained about his recent embarrassment in the UN Security Council, when the Soviets had to give up to Saddam's blackmail and stop the adoption of a resolution. Naturally, Gonzales was appalled with that story. 'But how did the question of this new resolution emerge at all?', he asked angrily.

M. S. GORBACHEV. *It was rather surprising. It looks like it was the initiative of the British, who are chairing the Security Council now. Thatcher is always trying to run two steps ahead. And we have to dash to follow her, like Joan d'Ark, although her and our approaches to the situation are different.*

However, this is not so terrible. Actually, we are prepared to discuss the ways to strengthen the UN sanctions.

F. GONZALES. *Perhaps, Saddam should be given a new deadline?*

E. SHEVADNADZE. *Of course, we can give him another deadline, but with a clear warning that the sanctions are inevitable.*

M. S. GORBACHEV. *This would give us additional ways to put pressure on Saddam.*

F. GONZALES. *Diplomacy of the ultimatum…*

M. S. GORBACHEV. *Obviously, we understand each other very well.*

On October 28 Gorbachev moved to Paris to see Mitterrand. Instead of greetings, the French president asked about Primakov's adventures. Gorbachev replied he was expecting his report the next morning.

Baghdad's final word

October 29, 1990, Rabulliex, France.

F. MITTERRAND. Let me express my delight that I am receiving you in a different place from the Elisee Palace. It will allow you to see France from a slightly different side.

M. S. GORBACHEV. This morning, at 5am, a cable from Y. M. Primakov was received. He reports that this Sunday, October 28, he had talks with practically all the Iraqi leaders, and then a one hour of tête-à-tête conversation with Saddam Hussein.

It is clear from Primakov's talks with the Iraqi leader that Saddam still has some hope that at least a small gap in the united front of the UN Security Council's permanent members might emerge.

Primakov told him it was hardly possible to count on the "package solution" of the situation in the region to be based on the principle of stringent linkage between the settlement of Kuwaiti crisis and the solution of other regional problems.

Saddam says he is firmly committed to the search for a peaceful solution of the current situation. But, interestingly, even at this stage of the Persian Gulf conflict, he firmly states he would not agree to any scenario which includes his capitulation. Furthermore, he firmly rejects any scenario that means his public humiliation in connection with Iraqi forces' withdrawal from Kuwait.

My impression is that Saddam has got sort of "idea fix". He is convinced that there is a conspiracy against Iraq, and among its goals is an elimination of the Iraqi president, his physical death. Saddam believes that the United States, Great Britain and Israel want only one thing – to undermine Iraq, – and that is actually why they insist on unconditional withdrawal of Iraqi forces from Kuwait.

His discourse implies that he sees three acceptable scenarios of further events.

1. *Development and implementation, under control of the Soviet Union or another influential state, of a comprehensive package for the crisis's settlement. Apart from the withdrawal of Iraqi troops, it would include solution of the other problems of the region, solving the issues of Iraq's concern.*

> 2. *A convocation, with no preliminary conditions, of an international conference, to discuss not only the Kuwaiti problem, but the whole complex of Middle East issues.*
>
> 3. *An implementation of an "Arab scenario", meaning the solution of all problems without any pressure from the outside.*
>
> *In general, Primakov's impression from his talks in Baghdad is that the Iraqi president is beginning to move, although very slowly and painfully, towards realizing he must withdraw from Kuwait. But this process is going on very painfully indeed.*

In a word, it was a fiasco. Gone were all Saddam's earlier hints, which had given Primakov some hope of success. Sorry, dear comrades, all of this were your fantasies.

Now Primakov's mission had indeed ended in failure.

The moment this was clear, the tone of Gorbachev-Mitterrand talks changed suddenly and dramatically:

> *F. MITTERRAND. Speaking of the US position on this issue, compared to out approaches, it is necessary to note the difference in tone, style, specific means. But we have no disagreement with the Americans on the essence of the matter. We believe we should preserve this course of actions. Naturally, this does not mean any subordination. As far as our tone and style are concerned, they should be cool-blooded and calm.*
>
> *M. S. GORBACHEV. I should agree with this approach. But this is not to be made public.*
>
> *F. MITTERRAND. Not at all.*
>
> *M. S. GORBACHEV. [...At] today's press-conference [, t]he journalists are surely going to interrogate me in connection with Primakov"s mission. We should stress our commitment to joint actions, according to the collectively adopted UN resolutions concerning the Iraqi aggression.*

Indeed, when asked by journalists about Primakov's mission a few hours later, Gorbachev assured the journalists:

> *It was not any separate branch of the process. And of course, it was not something opposed to our common efforts. On the contrary, it was an integral part of these efforts. There are a lot of such visits, meeting,*

conversations underway. They are undertaken by various sides. Some of them are open and known to the press, others are confidential.[208]

Ten days later, on 8 November, President Bush ordered a deployment of an offensive force to Saudi Arabia in addition to the "Desert Shied" defensive force. The countdown to the "Desert Storm" began.

Meanwhile, Baker went to Moscow to try and persuade Gorbachev to vote for a UN resolution authorising use of force to liberate Kuwait.

M. S. GORBACHEV. *[…] We can see that you are disappointed, and we are also not pleased with the results of the efforts undertaken. However, I would like to assure you: whatever we do, whatever we are yet to do, our agreement with you is still in force. We will take no separate steps behind your back.*

J. BAKER. *Thank you. We are confident of that.*

[…] There has been no shortage of attempts to solve the problem by diplomatic means. The Soviet Union also made such attempts, and we do not criticize you for that. We could not have agreed to a partial settlement, we believe it would be a terrible mistake. Frankly, we can see no difference between "face-saving" and rewarding the aggressor…[209]

Even today, will all these secret documents, we still have to rely largely on circumstantial evidence to figure out what was behind "*Primakov's October surprise*", as Baker puts it. But let us briefly sum up what we know for sure:

- In Helsinki, Gorbachev proposes a peace plan and offers to "send someone to Baghdad" to "sound Saddam out". <u>Bush accepts</u>. In their memoirs, Bush, Scowcroft and Baker deliberately give misleading and confusing accounts of that summit and the agreements reached there.

- Gorbachev sends Primakov to Baghdad. Primakov reports Saddam is interested in the peace plan.

- Soviets work out detailed proposals and send Primakov to

Washington to get Bush's approval. Bush's account of that visit appears confusing and not credible.

- After seeing Primakov, Bush cables Gorbachev. In his memoirs, Bush claims he objected to a continuation of Primakov's mission; the Soviet documents suggest he encouraged it.

- After seeing Bush, Primakov feels everything now depends on Saddam's reply: if he says no, the Americans may attack Iraq as "a matter of one week".

- Primakov on his way to Baghdad, the UN Security Council convenes to pass another resolution. Saddam warns them to stop that nonsense or he won't talk to Primakov. The Security Council complies, despite the embarrassment, with no objections from the Western side.

- Gorbachev, waiting for Primakov's report on his talks with Saddam, tells his friends that the whole crisis may be resolved any moment now.

- Primakov reports Saddam has rejected the peace plan. Ten days later, the US starts preparing for war.

What a chain of coincidences.

Chapter 13.
The Living Shield

While Gorbachev and others were painstakingly searching for a compromise solution, while the White House was meticulously weighing pros and contras of the military action, while the Arab emirs prayed Allah to enlighten the stupid Americans and make them destroy Saddam - Saddam himself was just having fun.

So were all other progressive patriots in Iraq, military and civilian. Entire Kuwait lied before them rich and helpless - nearly all Kuwaitis had fled to Saudi Arabia, only leaving 300,000 Palestinians behind to build, if they so wished, a new and happy socialist life under the leadership of dear Comrade Saddam. So, Iraqi citizens were encouraged to board their squalid cars, drive to Kuwait, grab anything of any value and drive back. This practice greatly raised the morale of all progressive patriots, their confidence in Saddam's wisdom and eventuality of victory.

Saddam, too, was confident he would win the Mother of All Battles. His strategy, military and political, rested on the same single foundation: hostages. If and when the Americans attack, Saddam told his generals, we should capture some of their soldiers and tie them up around Iraqi tanks, because "the Americans will never fire on their own soldiers". The generals listened to him in quiet horror, silently nodded and took notes.[210] Their great field-marshal had hardly learned anything since the time he failed his entry exams at Royal Military College; unsurprisingly, he was still thinking as a terrorist, not a statesman or a military leader.

Thousands of foreign nationals who happened to be in Iraq or in

Kuwait at the moment of the invasion became hostages. Saddam made speeches to them, explaining they were his dear guests performing an important "peace mission". A photograph of a 7-year-old British boy, and Saddam patting his shoulder with a gesture clearly hinting at a threat to break his neck, was released to horrify the world.

Then Saddam invented another entertainment: to invite Western politicians to come shake hands with him, in exchange for releasing some quantity of hostages from their countries (proportionally to the importance of the visitor). In this way, he meant to get out of the international isolation. Many accepted the invitation, including former British PM Edward Heath, former West German Chancellor Willie Brandt, and former Japanese PM Nakasone. During each such handshake, Saddam would tightly grip the eminent visitor's hand, and then abruptly and strongly pull him down. At that moment, a specially trained photographer would take a shot of the distinguished statesman bowing - almost kneeling - before the great leader.

All the peace plans then in circulation - Gorbachev's one being only the most serious attempt among the many - were treated in a similar spirit. Saddam correctly identified the main weakness of his opponents: the cumbersome, diverse and disloyal coalition. However, he never found a right way to use that weakness. All he did was trying to split it: by engaging "doves" into negotiations over their peace plans, and then leaking what they had said behind closed doors; or by inducing them to make divisive statements in exchange for his promises of concessions or releasing some more hostages.

This strategy could not succeed, for many reasons. One was that such experienced international schemers as Gorbachev or Mitterrand could easily see through his primitive traps. At times, they could play into his hands; at times, they could play against him - but either way, they knew what they were doing.

M. S. GORBACHEV. *[...] Primakov has an impression that the Iraqi president, while still emphasizing the Arab factor, now pays more attention to the role of the Soviet Union and France.*

[...] we must not ignore his attempts to win time, to use salami tactics, to split the unity of UN Security Council's permanent members.

[…] Interestingly, he even proposed his draft of a possible Gorbachev-Mitterrand joint statement on the problem of hostages.

F. MITTERRAND (ironically). This is really curious, I have not heard about this.

M. S. GORBACHEV. He suggests that the Soviet and French presidents appeal to the Iraqi president, calling him to cooperate on the issue of hostages. We would confirm our commitment to the political way of settling the crisis in this Persian Gulf zone, as well as of the whole region's other problems. In his opinion, the Soviet and French presidents should support a peaceful solution of all these problems and condemn any use of force or threat of its use.

F. MITTERRAND. Judging from the concluding sentences of this text, Saddam obviously demands too much from us.

He explained that Saddam was simply trying to trap them into publicly ruling out the use of force.

M. S. GORBACHEV. Primakov replied to this proposal that it was hardly possible to expect that the Soviet and French presidents accept such a text. Then, the Iraqi collocutors said: we are prepared to discuss any proposals of the Soviet and French presidents; and we are prepared to act in the spirit of openness.

[…]

Saddam is still trying to use the special relations his country enjoys with the USSR and France, to create a crack, a gap in the united front of UN Security Council permanent members. I don't think this demonstrates his far-sightedness.[211]

One day, Saddam suddenly freed all Bulgarian hostages, because Bulgaria was a good country, he had nothing against it.

On another occasion he went out to praise German Chancellor Helmut Kohl, said that Kohl was making good statements about Middle East, and freed all German hostages. Poor Kohl was very embarrassed, and painstakingly went through his own earlier statements: what had he said wrong?

Such generous gestures were, at first, only made towards countries which played a negligible role in the coalition or no role at all.

More mysterious was the decision to free all French hostages in November 1990. Belonogov writes he heard from certain "Arab sources" that it resulted from secret negotiations between Tariq Aziz and former French foreign minister, former EEC Commissioner Claude Cheysson.[212] If this is true, it is still unclear how they reached a deal, on what conditions.

And then, out of the blue, on 6 December Saddam announced that all hostages, including the Americans and the British, could go. This decision still remains one of the big riddles of the Gulf War.

The Soviet archives suggest one possible – just possible – answer.

But before we come to that, we must look at what happened on the Western side in November.

"Masters of the war"

The wise and fair procedure of the UN Security Council's response to a crisis has been devised by the best minds of the humankind. Nobody can possibly invent anything better than that.

First of all, it is necessary to decide what the crisis is: is it a threat to international peace and security, a breach of them, or perhaps an act of aggression?

The UN Security Council determined: Saddam"s invasion of Kuwait was a breach of international peace. And security.[213]

Next, the Security Council should call upon the parties to stop it.

This done, and ignored, the Security Council should consider the appropriate "measures not involving the use of armed force", such as "complete or partial interruption of economic relations and of rail, sea, air, postal, telegraphic, radio, and other means of communication" or else ordering UN members to break diplomatic relations with the offender.[214]

If none of this helps, the Security Council should consider moving on to the next stage…

In the end of the process, when everything else has been tried and failed, the Security Council may, ultimately, as a last resort, order UN members to use force to ensure compliance with its earlier resolutions.

That is to say, if they ever reach this stage – because any of the five permanent members can use its right of veto to stop the movement towards it at any point.

And then, in the end of that brilliant chapter of UN Charter, Article 51 spoils everything:

Nothing in the present Charter shall impair the inherent right of individual or collective self-defence...

In other words, once Saddam has started a war, it was perfectly legitimate for the United States to come and help Emir of Kuwait to fight back, without disturbing the Security Council and distracting it from more elevated global problems.

This is what is normally done in such cases – but it was a new world order now. Bush and Baker decided to go through the full charade of the Security Council procedure. All along, they had a right just to attack Saddam without anybody's permission except the Emir of Kuwait (it could, of course, have been a different matter if the Emir objected, but he was not likely to).

So the coalition doves remembered this every minute: Article 51 was hanging over their heads like a sword of Damocles. Any moment, the Americans could simply throw them all out of the game.

F. MITTERRAND. [...]Unfortunately, the United States and Great Britain are still not prepared to agree it is necessary to introduce a transitional stage in solving the Kuwaiti question. I have not talked to them about this, though.

They have to co-ordinate their actions with France and the USSR in order to provide unity in the UN Security Council. Therefore we have a certain trump, certain space for manoeuvre. However, an opinion is being expressed in the US that Article 51 of the UN Charter is sufficient to let them use force independently, without asking the Security Council. I note with concern that such statements have become more frequent recently. [...]This would mean that the USA may decide to start the war on their own, without appealing to the UN Security Council. They would become, so to speak, "the masters of the war". In such a case we would lose the trump I've mentioned, which makes the US appeal to the UN Security Council to get consent for their actions.[215]

This scenario had to be avoided at any cost, if at all possible. To be on the safe side, Mitterrand even decided to send a French force to the Gulf. Now, unlike the Soviets, he would still have a say - even if the UN was no longer the "master of the war".

Besides, from the outset, the "doves" made a firm strategic decision. It was important to keep it all peaceful, and it was important to keep it all in the UN. But if they cannot do both, the higher priority was to keep it in the UN – even if that meant backing Americans and authorizing war. It was a global power game with very high stakes; it was no time for any "not in my name" moralistic nonsense.

M. S. GORBACHEV. *We should act strongly, consistently, demonstrate unity, and by all means try to avoid slipping down to the military solution.*

F. MITTERRAND. *It is difficult to rule out such a scenario a priori. We cannot create dangerous illusions. If we cannot overcome Saddam's will, and if Bush and Thatcher don't want to listen to anything, the war is inevitable.*[216]

The 678th final ultimatum

At length, all the peace plans had failed. The UN Security Council had passed ten resolutions on the matter and was at risk of running out of ideas. In fact, even under the UN Charter procedure, it had now reached the point where it was to authorise a military action.

From the military viewpoint, it was seen as axiomatic before the Operation Iraqi Freedom in 2003 that, starting in March, a military action against Iraq becomes impossible due to weather conditions. It is time for actual desert storms, not for military operations of that name.

So, no matter how you look at it, it was time for America to enter the war. The question was only whether that would be done along the "new world order" lines on the orders of the UN Security Council, or under the "right to individual or collective self-defence", if you like the expression from Article 51 of the UN Charter.

Bush Administration decided to stick to "new world order" principles and ask permission from the UN Security Council. Only if that failed would they hit Saddam with all the dreadful power of Article 51.

Baker then came up with this idea: make a finally final ultimatum, UN Resolution number 678, giving Saddam a few weeks to withdraw peacefully, or else… Bush agreed. This re-opened the Pandora Box of Baker's diplomacy: it was now necessary to persuade the Soviets, the French, the Chinese not to veto the resolution, and also to persuade other members of the Security Council to keep it as unanimous as possible. After all, this could become the first war authorised by the UN in forty years, and the second ever (after the Korean War in 1950).

It was agreed that Bush would talk about this to Gorbachev and Mitterrand at the CSCE summit in Paris on 19-21 November 1990. In addition, Baker was sent to give the Soviets an advance warning.

So, on the same day as Bush ordered the offensive force to be sent to Saudi Arabia in addition to the Desert Shield force, Baker came to Moscow to tell Gorbachev that his finally final ultimatum would probably persuade Saddam to withdraw from Kuwait peacefully at the last moment. (Did he realise such a scenario would actually put the United States into a rather silly position, unable to use the vast forces sent to the Gulf or to pull them back?)

J. BAKER. *[…] We still hope for a peaceful, political settlement of this crisis. At the same time, we are convinced that the madman we are dealing with will only withdraw from Kuwait if he can see that we are serious and determined. We are not sure that time is on our side. […]*

M. S. GORBACHEV. *We have noticed that, in this situation, you hold your nerve. Unlike, for example, Mrs. Thatcher who, in my view, is beginning to cross the line from the rational to the emotional.*

J. BAKER. *The reason is, we know who will have to suffer casualties in this conflict. We have thought about that a lot, and it is not with a light heart that I am performing my mission.*

We believe there is some chance for a settlement only if we cooperate to pass a US Security Council resolution which would, in general terms, authorise using all necessary means to ensure the implementation of all earlier UN resolutions. Simultaneously, the US and other forces in the region will be increased. Only this will show clearly to Saddam Hussein that, unless he withdraws, we have the sufficient will to resort to the military option.

[…] We expect that, if such a resolution is passed, Saddam will withdraw his troops and only leave them in the Northern sector and on the Isle of Bubiyan.

Note that, even at this stage, continuing occupation of merely a part of Kuwait was seen as an acceptable compromise - in spite of the whole new world order and the UN"s clear instructions to the contrary.

Baker then explained that, if the operation was to be kept under UN auspices, they could no longer postpone issuing the finally final ultimatum from the Security Council. A threat to use force after 1 February would be an empty threat, because of the weather and Ramadan; and the US forces could not stay in the region till autumn 1991.

We would have to withdraw at least some of them, and then the whole world would see that UN resolutions are not implemented and the aggressor is being rewarded for his aggression.

[…] I must say, there are many people in the US government who tell us: if you continue acting in the UN framework, you will simply drown in the procedural arguments, you will be tied hand and foot. Therefore, they say, we should act on the basis of Article 51 of the UN Charter. We have already had a polemic of this kind in our government, when we discussed how to enforce the sanctions in sea. In those days, I phoned Eduard [Shevardnadze] from Wyoming two to three times every day. The President was under great pressure to act on the basis of Article 51 and not to engage the UN. However, we did not take this path, and the President believes we were right. For the same reason, he has sent me for this trip to find out whether we can further act in the UN framework.

The resolution we propose won't automatically mean use of force. However, I agree with E. A. Shezardnadze's comment that after January 1, unless Saddam withdraws from Kuwait, we have to act or we won't be respected. Therefore, we will continue to increase the US and other forces in the region. We very much want to act in unity with the entire international community. But I would like to inform you that the President is prepared to take responsibility for the dirtiest part of this operation, because we are convinced that an important principle is at stake.

[…]

The resolution will not specifically mention a military action or a use of force, but we will say during the discussion in the Security Council that this is permitted.

M. S. GORBACHEV. *That it does not rule out use of force?*

J. BAKER. Moreover, authorises use of force.

[…] Of course, we do not have much time, because the resolution has to be passed while the US is chairing the Security Council, and we also have two resolutions on [condemning] Israel on the agenda, so we have to agree how we can arrange this from the procedural point of view to have enough time to pass this resolution as well.

[…]

As for the question of how to act – on Article 51 or in the UN Security Council framework – we would prefer to cooperate with you and other members of the Council. This is why I am here.

M. S. GORBACHEV. I support this.

J. BAKER. Had we chosen the Article 51 option, I would not have been here. But on serious and lengthy consideration, we came to a certain conclusion: the most important thing is to send a signal to Saddam Hussein.[217]

This formidable masterpiece of diplomacy was largely wasted; the only thing that mattered to Gorbachev was that, if he says no, the Americans will simply attack Iraq without another UN resolution. The Soviets would be out of the game, so would be the UN, and the whole war would end with a quick and splendid American victory. Perhaps even a downfall of Saddam's regime and a Nuremberg-style tribunal - after all, Bush did mention that idea in such periods when the coalition hawks got the upper hand. And if there was a tribunal, all sorts of things could come out…

So, Gorbachev reached his decision instantly. Or rather, he simply understood the time had come to implement the earlier decision: if and when it comes to the question of a military action, the "new world order" game should be his priority above any hopeless attempts to protect Saddam.

M. S. GORBACHEV. […] We are facing a very serious challenge. Are we or are we not capable of solving the emerging difficult problems on the basis of new approaches, not like we did during the "Cold War", and without being accused of trying to be a global policeman? I would like to stress: we want to be with you in any situation. We want such decisions to be taken which would strengthen, not undermine, the reputation of the United States. Therefore, we need to think very seriously about all that. In all scenarios it is necessary to ensure that the United States are not left in isolation, without support from the UN Security Council, without understanding from everybody.

We have always presumed that the military option does exist. [...] We want the United States and ourselves to stay together, and together we shall be able to solve this crisis. Therefore, we should use the potential of the UN Security Council, and we are going to cooperate with you to do so.

But of course, he would not be Gorbachev if he simply said yes. He kept saying it was all "very serious" and he would need "to think seriously" about Baker's "serious considerations".

He asked three times whether Baker was absolutely sure that his ultimatum was more likely to make Saddam withdraw peacefully than to lead to war. Baker thrice replied that he certainly hoped so.

Then he suggested an upgraded version of Baker's ultimatum: to pass a resolution giving Saddam a few weeks to withdraw, or else – the UN Security Council will convene again – and then...

Baker, to his credit, would not have that.

So, Gorbachev would now "think seriously" and then talk to Bush in Paris. In the end, Baker added:

J. BAKER. *[...] I would like to express another consideration unofficially, as I am not authorized to do that. If the timing is significant to your calculations and January 1 is inconvenient for you, please bear in mind that our final deadline is the period between 15 January and 1 February. If this is more acceptable to you, I could talk to President Bush about such an adjustment of timing.*

Later, in negotiations with Bush, Gorbachev, of course, jumped on it – for no particular reason, just playing for time:

G. BUSH. *[...] How much time do you think we should give in this ultimatum?*

M.S. GORBACHEV. *Let's say, till mid-January.*[218]

This is why the deadline eventually given to Saddam was January 15, not January 1.

I wonder if Baker ever tried to calculate the cost of his smallest concession alone – two extra weeks of the vast American force sitting and waiting in the Saudi desert?

In the next two weeks, between Gorbachev's meetings with Baker on 8 November and with Bush on 19 November, the Soviets thought about a couple of other change coins to ask for.

One Comrade Kovalyov from the Foreign Ministry had the idea to name the period between the ultimatum and the final deadline "the pause of good will".[219] That was accepted – and that is what we find in the final text of Resolution 678. Classic Soviet hypocrisy rapidly contaminated the language of the new world order.

Another condition Soviets came up with was that, before the deadline, the Americans must try direct negotiations with Iraq. Or, alternatively, send the UN General Secretary for such negotiations. That was accepted without question. In event, both these things were later done – obviously, with no result.

Although Gorbachev was clearly prepared to go ahead with the ultimatum, at the meeting in Paris, Bush expressed himself by way of pleading and sobbing:

> **G. BUSH** *[…] I need your help on this issue. […] I do not want to use force. However, I have come to the conclusion that such a resolution is necessary. And, thinking on how we want to build our relations in the long term, I believe that your support would be a bright illustration of our partnership.*
>
> *This is why I am asking you to help me. And even not just me - who knows, someone else may become president in two years. I am asking you to help do the right thing.*
>
> *If you cannot give me your final answer yet, I am prepared to understand you, but please take into account that your answer is extremely important to us.*
>
> *Our two countries used to be opponents, and now we work together. If*

you cannot help me in this case, we are going to cooperate anyway. But I am asking you to help send Saddam this signal. We expect that it will be enough to make Saddam do what is required of him.

I wanted to talk to you about this while we are alone, not in the presence of colleagues, for two reasons: to open my heart to you, and to avoid putting you in a position where you have to give you final answer now.

M. S. GORBACHEV. *I have thought over everything, including our conversation with James Baker, and your letter, Mr. President. This moment is extremely important not only for both of us, but for everything you and I have begun to do in the world. If we cannot prove that now, at this new stage of global development, we are capable of solving such problems, this would mean what we have started is not worth much. If you and we are unable to stop an aggression, an annexation, an outrageous violation of the international law, this would mean we are doing something wrong. No, we must prove otherwise, and therefore, we must find a solution to this problem. This is my first, and most important, point.*

Second point…

On reaching the second point, Gorbachev apparently realized that while Bush sounded sentimental, he himself merely sounded pompous, and this, perhaps, did not make a very good contrast. So he began changing his tone, gradually but rapidly:

Because of the choice we have made in the Soviet Union (and I assume you have made a similar choice in the United States) we do not want the United States and its President to find themselves in a difficult, critical situation. If we part our ways in this situation, this would mean we have achieved little in our relations. Of course, though, we will probably have our differences in the future, and then we should sit at a table and discuss them. But in this case, I am convinced we must be together.

In my heart - and I am sure you feel the same - I very much wish to avoid bloodshed, casualties, deaths of American kids, because a big bloodshed would damage the US President. This would also be very bad for ordinary Arabs. Therefore, we certainly prefer to reach a settlement without bloodshed. And I assume that you also support this. Because if the war begins, it can be worse than Vietnam.

Here is the dilemma we have to solve. On one hand, we should try and avoid the military solution. On the other – we should make another step to increase pressure on Saddam Hussein.

When I talked to Jim in Moscow, I asked him not to use Article 51 of the UN Charter. We should firmly determine that we are going to act within the UN framework. This is very important. [...]

G. BUSH. *[...] I very much appreciate the position you have just outlined. I am very pleased that we are reaching an agreement. We will act tactfully when drafting the resolution, in order to take account of your considerations. [...]*

M.S. GORBACHEV. *[...] I also think we should restrain the travellers of various sorts and make the Iraqis understand they will have to talk only to those who have adapted the UN resolutions.*

[...]

G. BUSH. *Thank you, I am very grateful for your position. [...] I think we can now [...] conclude this meeting with a friendly dinner.[220]*

I guess Gorbachev somewhat overdid it: that stuff about his heart bleeding over the possible deaths of the *American kids*, all because that would *damage the President*, was over the top. But apparently, Bush did not notice.

Mitterrand reacted to the idea in a remarkably similar way to Gorbachev. They could have, of course, allocated roles, but the whole thing was just a child's play. There were not many things they could ask for in the situation - the whole idea of postponing the operation was the best the "doves" could dream of. And anyway, as we have seen above, the Americans were readily making additional concessions on every point raised, just as long as Gorbachev promised them the Soviet vote. What else could the doves wish for?

Mitterrand told about his conversation with Bush in these terms:

I said France won't object if the US propose such a draft resolution. But then I stressed that much will depend on finding the right language, i.e. practically on editorial work, even on style.

The task is to leave Saddam Hussein in no illusion that he can avoid war unless he leaves Kuwait. At the same time, however, he should be given some space for manoeuvre, so that he really can leave.

M. S. GORBACHEV. *Yes, we've discussed that with you before.*

F. MITTERRAND. *Our foreign ministers will have a lengthy exercise in [literary] style to find the balanced expressions (laughs). But Saddam Hussein must under no circumstances have an impression that the future resolution is in an exercise in [literary] style.*[221]

And so the drafting began. Mitterrand demanded that the resolution must be written in such a way as to prohibit the Americans to use force before the deadline – just to rule out the Article 51 scenario.[222] He succeeded in that.

The Soviets, for want of any better demands they could invent, insisted that the resolution must not mention force, or a military action, or anything like that. So, how should we call it? "All necessary means" or "all appropriate means"? Bush confided to Gorbachev that he did not understand the difference.[223]

In the end, they decided to call it "necessary".

And then, of course, it was all named the "pause of good will".

Why did Saddam drop his shield?

As the world leaders were on the way to Paris for their CSCE summit-conference (which was ostensibly about Europe but in reality about the Gulf and issuing Baker"s 678th ultimatum), Saddam publicly made another proposal. He would free all his hostages "in instalments" between now and the end of March, if only he receives guarantees that force will not be used before that moment.

And then, of course, he would be protected by weather conditions.

The proposal was, naturally, rejected.

While the Paris conference was underway, Saddam made another proposal – this time, secretly.

President Bush writes in his memoirs that, during this conference in Paris, on 20 November,

At one point [Gorbachev] hurried over with his interpreter to report that he had just heard from Primakov. Saddam Hussein would agree to withdraw from Kuwait in exchange for access to the Gulf.

When reminded there could be no conditions, Gorbachev appeared disappointed, but optimistic we could still persuade Saddam to leave peacefully.[224]

This small episode fits perfectly well into the general picture drawn in Bush"s memoirs: all sorts of compromise proposals coming time and again from here and there, only to hit his stone wall and bounce back. Naïve, idealistic Gorbachev sometimes gets over-excited, but Bush takes a sober statesmanlike view and calms his young friend down.

However, it seems very odd in the context of what we now know from the Soviet documents: just twelve days before that alleged conversation, it was the US position at Baker-Gorbachev negotiations that Saddam may be permitted to continue occupation of Bubiyan and other "disputed territories", securing his access to the Gulf, if he withdraws from the rest of Kuwait (see above).

On the other hand, except this claim by Bush, there is no evidence that Saddam ever agreed to such a scheme before the Operation Desert Storm actually began.

Furthermore, just after the end of the Desert Storm, *Pravda* serialised a pamphlet by Primakov, *The war that could have not happened,* accusing the damned imperialists of using force needlessly. Primakov tells about all compromise proposals he was involved in, and how they were rejected by stubborn Americans. This one - if it was made - could have become a jewel in his collection. And yet, he does not mention it.

So, did Saddam really make such a big concession at that stage? Did Bush really reject it?

And here is the answer. There was, indeed, a brief conversation between Gorbachev and Bush on 20 November, duly recorded by the interpreter, about a fresh proposal Primakov had brought from Saddam. However, he did not offer to withdraw from Kuwait - he offered to free the hostages. And he did not want Bubiyan (which he held anyway) - he wanted access to **deep-water areas** of the Gulf, that is to say, a lifting of the sea blockade. And Bush did not reject the proposal - he just told the Soviets to go and ask Baker:

Transcript of the conversation between M. S. Gorbachev and US President G. Bush

Paris, 20 November 1990

The conversation took place in the International Conference Centre during the CSCE conference.

M. S. GORBACHEV. *To continue our yesterday's conversation, I would like to let you know that I have received a cable from E. M. Primakov, where he reports another step taken by S[addam] Hussein.*

S[addam] Hussein states he is prepared to cancel his decision to free the Western and Japanese hostages "in instalments" over three months, and free all of them at once. He is also prepared to start any negotiations with G. Bush. The only preliminary condition he sets is for Iraq to be given access to the deep-water areas of the Persian Gulf.

G. BUSH. *This is an interesting report. Obviously, the preliminary condition about the deep-water areas of the Gulf will create difficulties. Our [foreign] ministers [Baker and Shevardnadze] are having a separate meeting now. Do they have this information?*

M. S. GORBACHEV. *No. I will now forward it to them. You and I should have another exchange of views after they discuss this issue.*

G. BUSH. *I agree.*

Intriguingly, neither Bush nor Baker mention this proposal in their memoirs. Nor does Primakov in his *Pravda* pamphlet. There is no record of a further Bush-Gorbachev discussion on the issue in the archive. The only other hint at this proposed deal appears in the transcript of Gorbachev's conversation later the same day with the Dutch Prime Minister, who wanted his views on the draft public statement rejecting Saddam's earlier proposal to free hostages "in instalments". Gorbachev replied:

M. S. GORBACHEV. *I can tell you straightaway that the section about hostages no longer corresponds to the most up-to-date information.*[225]

And then the documentary trail is lost.

16 days later, Saddam suddenly announced all hostages may go home.

Was this a coincidence - or was there a secret deal of some kind after all?

Chapter 14.
The Eleventh Hour

While Bush and Baker still solemnly swore they were eagerly searching for a peaceful solution on the basis of UN resolutions, Gorbachev's confidential sources in Washington were telling him something different.

One such source was Senator Edward Kennedy.

His secret collaboration with Moscow went back a long way. It is known that in 1978 Kennedy "requested the assistance of the KGB to establish a relationship" between Moscow and a firm owned by his friend, ex-Senator John Tunney. The KGB's secret report about this, published in Russia in 1992, recommended to grant that request, because Tunney's firm was already connected to one David Karr, a KGB agent in France.[226]

In 1980, Kennedy again contacted Moscow through Tunney and Egon Bahr, West Germany's top Social Democrat and KGB's secret collaborator, to coordinate plans for undermining President Carter's tough stance over the Soviet invasion of Afghanistan.[227]

In 1983, Tunney conveyed another secret message from Kennedy to the KGB. Now the Senator proposed to work together "in the interests of world peace", against "the militaristic policies of Ronald Reagan." However, the then Soviet leader Andropov declined the offer.

In Gorbachev's times, the Soviets decided to legalise their secret connections with the Senator. In 1986 he was openly received by Gorbachev in Moscow. The arrangements for day-to-day contacts were also changed: the relations with Kennedy were removed from the KGB's remit and assigned to Vadim Zagladin, a high-ranking Comintern veteran who now became an advisor to Gorbachev. At two confidential meetings with Zagladin in February 1986, Kennedy accused President Reagan of abusing the political capital from his recent summit-meeting with Gorbachev, and urged the Soviets to "put more pressure" on Reagan.

> *At the same time, E. Kennedy underlined, there are some issues which slow down the improvement of Soviet-American relations, though these issues are not of such global importance as the problem of disarmament.*
>
> *The first among these issues, according to E. Kennedy, is the problem of terrorism. "I wouldn't like to get involved in an argument on how we should regard the national-liberation movements. But I would like to note", the Senator said, "that there are different kinds of terrorism. I, personally, would consider the Chilean regime, the authorities' actions in South Africa or contras' activity in Nicaragua as terrorism. Of course, there is left-wing terrorism as well, but I don't think we should reduce everything to that.*
>
> *I noticed that the terrorism which the Senator calls left-wing is a manifestation of the sentiment of people who had been driven to despair. Although we are against their terrorist methods, we understand this distinction. The Senator replied: "Sure, we should take into account the fact that terrorism may be different. Nevertheless, our common interest is to eliminate the grounds for any kind of terrorism. And, perhaps, USSR and USA might find mutual understanding on that at least partially."*[228]

Kennedy's go-between was also replaced in Gorbachev''s times: it was now his chief of staff Larry Horowitz - not John Tunney - who would go straight to Moscow to see Zagladin whenever the Senator had anything to say to the Kremlin. Thus, in 1986, Zagladin reported:

> *Kennedy's aide L[arry] Horowitz told me with anger that Reagan had said to the Senator: "I will meet the Russians this summer, but not in August, when my mares are going to be in labor. This is more important for me than any talks with the Russians."*[229]

In December 1989, one month after the fall of the Berlin Wall, Horowitz delivered to Gorbachev Sen. Kennedy's letter on the German question. In addition, Kennedy requested for his envoy to be received by Zagladin. He confided that President Bush was secretly opposed to unification of

Germany, even though he could not say so publicly; and might soon talk about this to the Soviets.

He also revealed the contents of US Ambassador's recent confidential dispatches to Washington concerning the pro-independence movements in Lithuania, Latvia and Estonia, then under Soviet occupation. In response, Horowitz continued, the State Department instructed the Embassy in Moscow to discourage the growth of such movements in occupied Baltic states. He added that President Bush did "not consider separation of Baltic states from the USSR to be desirable. However, he is not going to recognize these republics as a part of the USSR either."[230]

In May 1990, Kennedy again sent a word concerning the unification of Germany. Horowitz told Zagladin that the Senator was lobbying for a reform of the NATO on the understanding that the Soviets would demand that as a condition of their agreement for united Germany's membership in the Alliance. The same view was now held in the National Security Council. "The first steps towards revising [NATO] strategic doctrine are already blueprinted. Probably it would be important if M.S. Gorbachev with absolute clarity indicates the "necessary parameters of change" during his visit to the US. Using this situation, L. Horowitz added, you can achieve much now."[231]

And so it happened again - this time, in connection with the Gulf. On 27 November 1990 Zagladin reported to Gorbachev:

> *On the situation in Persian Gulf. In L. Horowitz"s words, a final decision to solve the crisis in the Gulf by military means has already been taken in the White House. The deadline is spring [1991].*
>
> *[...]*
>
> *In military circles, Horowitz continued, it is believed that Iraq can be "suppressed" promptly. [...]*
>
> *While President Bush, in accordance with the American tradition, is already thinking about the prospects of the next presidential elections, it is important to him to take immediate action to strengthen his prestige in the country. That is why he needs a quick and effective victory over Iraq. It is believed that a prolonged conflict may cause complications with Arabs who, Horowitz said, "strongly dislike Americans". Bearing*

this in mind, he continued, Bush "would be very unhappy if Saddam withdraws from Kuwait peacefully".

After the effective military operation and resolution of the crisis, Bush would be prepared to start solving the other problems of that region, including the Palestinian one, immediately. The matter, Bush believes, is long overdue. The Palestinian problem must be solved in order to "appease" the Arab countries, to extinguish their "anti-American syndrome".[232]

Soviet troops to the Gulf?

As we remember, at the Helsinki summit Bush invited the Soviet troops to join the Americans in the Middle East, much to Scowcroft"s horror.

In November, as the offensive force was about to be deployed to join the defensive one, Baker repeated the invitation:

Of course, I will understand the Soviet Union's position if you come to the conclusion that you cannot take part in our action. You are now carrying out large-scale reforms, and the memories of Afghanistan are still fresh in your mind. And yet, I am haunted by the thought that, if we have to use force, the picture of Americans and Russians fighting side by side (even if your participation is limited to a small subdivision) would make a very strong impression.

[…]

I hope you can join us. We fought side by side in the World War II. We won that war, but then we lost the peace. If we have to fight again, we are going to win this war. This is necessary to make a just order triumph in the world. We cannot allow this dictator to defy ten resolutions of the Security Council, most of them unanimous… [etc., etc.][233]

Gorbachev simply did not react.

Then, suddenly, he received an astonishing proposal from two former Japanese Prime Ministers. A member of his Politburo, Vadim Medvedev, was on a visit to South Korea with a routine mission to borrow some money for the salvation of the bankrupt Soviet Union. In a picturesque cloak-and-dagger fashion, he was approached by a mysterious messenger who claimed Japan could loan to the Soviets 20 to 30 billion dollars if

Gorbachev sends 50,000 to 100,000 Soviet troops to the Middle East. To launder the money in the public eye, the Soviets would also have to return the four Japanese islands they had been occupying since the Second World War.

The first signal came from South Korean billionaire tycoon Chung Ju-yung - the founder of Hyundai Group and the chairman of the Korean-Soviet Economic Association, who was rapidly developing business links with the Soviet Union in that period:[234]

24 November 1990
President of the USSR

Comrade M. S. GORBACHEV.

Dear Mikhail Sergeyevich,

This is to inform you of the proposals by Nakasone and Takeshita on the Middle East, linked with Soviet-Japanese relations, addressed to you and conveyed to me confidentially during my stay in Seoul.

Korean businessman Chung Ju-yung, who is known to you, strongly recommended me to meet Shin Kyuk-Ho, the owner of a major international corporation, Lotte. According to Chung Ju-yung, Shin Kyuk-Ho is one of the most influential tycoons and is among the top ten richest people in the world. The meeting took place.

Shin Kyuk-Ho said he lives and works in Tokyo most of his time, and keeps closely in touch with Japan's leading businessmen and politicians. He is a personal friend of Nakasone.

He asked to convey the following from Nakasone and Takeshita to you. Bearing in mind the difficult state of the Soviet economy and the fact that the countries of the West, except Japan, are unable to offer large-scale loans to the USSR, the Japanese side would be prepared to arrange for financial aid of 20 to 30 billion dollars to be given to the Soviet Union.

It emerged from the collocutor's further discourse that such a loan would be linked with the Soviet Union's actions for a resolution of the Middle East crisis and the development of Soviet-Japanese relations.

In Shin Kyuk-Ho's view, the situation in the Middle East has reached a dead-end. The present status-quo can continue till March at the latest, and then it may be ended with disastrous consequences. Such a development, in his opinion, can only be prevented with some help from the Soviet Union. A deployment of 50,000 to 100,000 Soviet troops to the Middle East, accompanied with a statement that the Soviet Union can no longer tolerate Iraq's rough violations of the international law, could become crucial.

This does not mean that they would have to be involved in a military action. But the very fact of a deployment of Soviet troops would demonstrate that the USSR not only condemns Saddam Hussein's actions, but takes real measures to restore the international order. This would invalidate any grounds for the theory that Saddam Hussein counts on USSR's non-intervention, or even secretly hopes for its support. It would remove the suspicions widespread in some quarters that the USSR is almost interested in prolonging the present situation, e. g. because of the high oil prices.

Publicly, this massive financial aid to the Soviet Union should be linked not with the Middle East situation, but with solving the problem of the four South Kuril islands. Returning the islands to Japan, the collocutor said, would not be a big loss to the USSR. However, this will allow Japan to establish close links with the Soviet Union. Otherwise, financial aid to the Soviet Union would be unacceptable to big sections of the Japanese public.

Shin Kyuk-Ho said that, unlike many others, he believes the Soviet Union has a legitimate right to these islands. However, he also thinks that a stabilisation of the Soviet economy would be much more important than keeping those four islands. He particularly stressed this idea, and added that Japan could become more active in helping the development of bilateral links in economy and technological cooperation.

He remarked that Nakasone or Takeshita could come to the Soviet Union to discuss these proposals.

I told the collocutor that I would convey this information to M. S.

Gorbachev. At the same time, I made some preliminary comments on the issues raised.

Soviet Union now really needs commodity credits and financial aid, and we already have such arrangements with a number of countries in West Europe. The leading circles of South Korea are also expressing a favourable view of that idea. Naturally, we would welcome Japan's participation in this process. That would be its contribution to the development of Perestroika in the Soviet Union and to the cause of mutually beneficial economic cooperation between the USSR and Japan. However, economic problems should be solved primarily on the basis of their own logic. Tying them into a tight knot with the so-called territorial problem and, on the top of it, with the Middle East problem hardly helps progress.

I reminded the collocutor about our principled stance on the Middle East conflict, which involves using all the potential for its political resolution; and about our policies of not using Soviet troops outside the Soviet Union and their gradual withdrawal from abroad, reflecting the will and the interests of our people.

As for his reference to Japanese public opinion regarding the Northern territories, we cannot ignore the public opinion in the Soviet Union, where the question of the border is acute and sensitive. So, the four islands are not just an insignificant problem for the USSR.

I remarked that meetings with Nakasone, Takeshita, or other figures are not ruled out in our preparations for the Soviet President's visit to Japan. But it seems to me that the proposals should be more realistic.

An answer to Nakasone's and Takeshita's proposals conveyed through Shin Kyuk-Ho could be given through the Soviet embassy in Tokyo.[235]

There is no evidence, however, that the Soviets pursued this line any further, and it is certain that, in the end of the day, the offer was not accepted.

Nor could it possibly ever be. For it was something directly opposite to Gorbachev's strategy: to increase the Soviet presence around the Gulf without anybody noticing it until it was too late. Here, the invitation was to cause worldwide panic with the TV pictures of Soviet troops near the Gulf without really achieving anything. The idea of sending a small subdivision was simply ridiculous; but the idea of sending a 100,000 army was not much better. In propaganda terms, it would have been a disaster. In practical terms, so long as it was together with the Americans, all it could do was help teach Saddam a lesson and then go back home to celebrate.

Gorbachev badly needed 20 to 30 billion dollars. But there was no way those cunning capitalist sharks in Japan and South Korea could bribe him to undermine the cause of the World Revolution.

Finally final

Bush kept his promise to Gorbachev to arrange for direct US-Iraqi negotiations during *the pause of good will*. On 9 January, Baker and Tariq Aziz spent six hours at negotiations in Geneva.

Obviously, in diplomatic terms, the meeting was pointless. The negotiations between US and Iraq had already taken place - and failed - in secret. Now, it was just necessary to arrange the *official version* laundering performance for the press and the public: we did sit and talk, but alas... So, the only result expected from that meeting was the photograph of the handshake. Presumably, the both sides prepared for that at endless, exhausting rehearsals and dry runs.

Aziz won by using a modified version of the famous Saddam's handshake. At the world-famous picture, the two ministers shake hands across the wide table, Baker standing, half-bowing to the Iraqi delegation, his Good Friday face turned to the camera, his hand extended at about two thirds of the distance towards Aziz. Aziz, sitting and lazily leaning at the table, holds Baker"s hand in a gesture of mild contempt. A scornful smile can be guessed hidden under his moustaches.

Otherwise, the two guys just had very boring six hours - until, free at last, they could go and give separate press-conferences. They made all sorts of inventions to kill time. Baker read out UN resolutions from his memory; Aziz entertained him by reciting Saddam's "peace initiatives". Approximately by the end of the first hour, they exhausted that material and proceeded to make vociferous threats against each other. Six hour were, indeed, a very long period, but it was thought that anything else would not be seen as a failure of sufficient magnitude to justify war. After all, the real - secret - negotiations had taken much more time before they failed.

But then, even this was not enough. This was not to be a US-Iraqi war, this was a war for the new world order. Respectively, the UN General Secretary was sent to Baghdad to give Saddam a finally final ultimatum.

The day before the deadline, on 14 January, the General Secretary solemnly reported to the Security Council that all peace efforts had failed. Meanwhile, the Iraqi "parliament" solemnly authorised Comrade Saddam to defend Iraq's sovereignty over Kuwait by all necessary means.

Minutes before the deadline, in the evening of 15 January, the UN General Secretary made a dramatic public appeal to Saddam on behalf of the permanent members of the Security Council: just *begin* withdrawing forces from Kuwait now and, we promise, you won't be attacked!

Baghdad ignored that.

The French, who were secretly in touch with Saddam until that point, asked even less. As the French foreign minister later told Gorbachev:

R. DUMAS. *[…] We were in touch with him until the evening of 15 January, when I talked to him on the phone. I told him: "Say just one word on the withdrawal of troops from Kuwait, and then something can be done." But he would never say that one word.*[236]

Now it was 16 January. The deadline had passed. The performance was over.

"Dictatorship is forthcoming"

There was yet another reason why it had been necessary to keep the world's attention fixed on that performance.

The Soviets had invented "Perestroika" to fake democratic reforms and trick the West into financing and supporting its greatest enemy. But even a fake democracy tends to get out of control.

The Party assigned Comrade Gorbachev to an important mission, which had something subtly Arabian about it: to free the powerful genie imprisoned in the jar of the Soviet system, and make him serve the cause of the global victory of communism.

Gorby opened the bottle and made three wishes:
- to be universally seen as a young, charming reformer;

- to get massive loans from the West;

- to become the most powerful man on the world stage.

The efreet duly fulfilled all three.

Then, he got out of control.

It turned out that, in those 70 years that they were imprisoned in that bottle, the peoples of the Soviet Union had developed vehement hatred of socialism. Once the dissent was no longer contained by the threat of terror (under Gorbachev, some limited "pluralism" of opinion was even encouraged) the peoples of his vast empire suddenly began to speak in their own voices. Opposition factions gradually consolidated in his puppet parliament. Even members of his own government, confident of impunity, would now suddenly resign and pursue a new-style political career as Gorbachev's critics. Above all, the local rulers in the outskirts of the empire suddenly recalled that, constitutionally, they were supposed to be leaders of sovereign republics.

It was necessary to bottle the genie again until it became too late. But how to do that without undermining the whole game?

As the East and the West were now bound together in a cordial alliance, marching into an important war, as the world's attention was totally focused on the Persian Gulf - the Soviets realised there was no time like the present. The preparations to stop all that nonsense began.

Of course, they would not just dissolve their ostensibly democratic government and resurrect their old Politburo (now defunct). Not overnight, anyway. Yet, one by one, the more liberal-minded figures in Gorbachev's government were replaced with the old-style, brutal apparatchiks and siloviki*.viWhen the time would come for the actual coup, they were expected to stand firm amidst the bloodshed.

On 20 December 1990, Baker's friend, Foreign Minister Shevardnadze, was due to address the "Congress of People's Deputies"

---

* Russian term for veterans of "power ministries" - KGB, the Interior, the Army

about the situation in the Gulf. The address was prepared by Baker's fantasy enemies, the Foreign Ministry Arabists, and naturally reaffirmed Moscow's commitment to the alliance with the West and determination to put a stop to Saddam aggression.

But Shevardnadze never made that address.

Instead, he dramatically announced his resignation. He revealed that the Kremlin was preparing an anti-democratic coup, that Gorbachev was in league with the siloviki, Shevardnadze himself had been aggressively pushed to the margins because he was labelled pro-Western (what a smear!), and he could no longer share responsibility for the actions of Gorbachev's government. He concluded the speech by declaring: "A dictatorship is now forthcoming."

The motives of the future dictator of Georgia for doing that are a matter of some dispute. But undoubtedly, Shevardnadze's resignation speech was addressed to the West at least as much as to the public at home. It was on the world stage that his reputation became formidable at the time - second, perhaps, only to Gorbachev's. It was also in the West alone where his parliamentary statement on the Gulf was anticipated with interest. Shevardnadze hoped the free world would do something to stop Gorbachev's junta before it was too late.

That was precisely how he was understood by the Western media and by the White House.[237]

The West did nothing. All the Bush Administration was worried about was whether or not "Primakov", "Arabists" and "conservatives" could now make Gorby defect to Saddam's side.[238] To keep them in suspense, Gorbachev would not appoint a new foreign minister for almost a month after Shevardnadze's resignation - until the mid-January deadline given to Saddam. Speculation grew that there was a furious struggle under the carpet between soft-liners and hard-liners, the latter lobbying for "pro-Arab" Primakov.

Meanwhile, the preparations for the coup continued. The first stage of the plan was to suppress the independence movements and restore the full Soviet rule in the USSR's own chronic Kuwaits - the occupied Baltic states Latvia, Estonia, and especially Lithuania. After these local "dress rehearsal" coups, the experience gained there would be used to prepare a similar coup in Moscow.

It was reassuring to know from Ted Kennedy that President Bush was secretly opposed to the independence of the Baltic states, and that the US Embassy in Moscow had been instructed to discourage the pro-independence movements. To that, Kennedy's envoy added:

> *In America, many serious people are surprised: why force is not being used in the USSR to enforce the triumph of law? In the US, for example, if some state takes actions which contradict federal laws, the president sends the National Guards there, and nobody sees that as an anti-democratic gesture.*

Such prompting, coupled with the importance of the anti-Saddam alliance, made Kremlin hope there would be no significant reprisals from the West. A UN resolution at the most.

So, on 11 January 1991 - four days before Saddam's deadline - Gorbachev finally fulfilled his threat of the past few months[239]: to replace the democratic government of Lithuania with an appointed one. A Moscow-backed "salvation committee of Lithuania" announced that the democratic government was now deposed, and assumed power. Simultaneously, Soviet airborne troops arrived and captured key strategic positions in the capital by force.

Thousands and thousands of pro-independence protestors went to the streets...

Transcript of the telephone conversation between M. S. Gorbachev and US President G. Bush[240]

11 January 1991, 16.00-16.40

M. S. GORBACHEV. *Decided to call you, George. Both you and we are having stormy days.*

G. BUSH. *Very much so. Of course, I am very interested to know how are you doing, what is happening. We are very busy here with the Gulf matters.*

M. S. GORBACHEV. *What we have here is this: finally, we have passed the budget. We had to work hard for it, work out an economic agreement first. That was not easy, but now we have it.*

G. BUSH. *Good.*

M. S. GORBACHEV. *The budget is being voted item by item, and 20 items have already been approved. The Supreme Soviet has reduced the military expenditure for 2 billion from what was originally planned. So I can tell you that we are disarming.*

G. BUSH. *Very interesting.*

M. S. GORBACHEV. *We have subjected the entire budget to a serious critical analysis. I have been working hard over the past month to take control of the finances, to achieve a real breakthrough in that area.*

G. BUSH. *I see.*

M. S. GORBACHEV. *In addition to the market developments which we have put in motion, we have to resort to extraordinary measures to preserve the economic links. So, there are conflicting processes. But now we have an economic agreement and a food supplies agreement between the republics.*

Tomorrow, I will chair a meeting of the Soviet of the Federation and nominate candidates for the position of the new Prime Minister and his deputies. We shall also discuss the issue of continuing work over the Union Treaty and how it can be accelerated. We have serious problems in Baltic republics, especially Lithuania, in Georgia and in Nagorny Karabakh. I am trying to do everything possible to avoid sharp turns. But this is not easy.

I would like to talk to you, obviously, bearing in mind this is an open line, about the Persian Gulf. But before that, perhaps, you want to tell me anything?

G. BUSH. *Your internal problems worry me, even pain me. I would like to hope that you find it possible to avoid using force to solve them. The US position on that is clear. I appreciate the fact that you have told me about your difficulties. As an outsider, I can only say that if you can avoid using force, that will be good for your relations with us, and not only with us. I think you understand that.*

M. S. GORBACHEV. *That is precisely what we want. We will only intervene if there is bloodshed or if there is such a disorder that threatens not only our constitution, but people's lives as well.*

The Supreme Soviet and I are now under colossal pressure to introduce the presidential rule in Lithuania. I still hold on, but frankly, the Supreme Soviet of Lithuania and [its pro-independence chairman] Landsbergis seem to be incapable of any constructive moves.

In response to the pressure I am under, yesterday I appealed to the Supreme Soviet of Lithuania to restore the operation of the [Soviet] Constitution themselves. But even today, the situation is developing in an undesirable way. There are industrial strikes in Lithuania, and difficulties are escalating.

You know my style. It is essentially similar to yours. I will try to exhaust all the potential of a political settlement and will only resort to any tough steps if there is a very serious threat.

G. BUSH. *I appreciate this. You know, we have our own view of the Baltic republics, but that's only due to historic reasons. I appreciate your explanations.*

M. S. GORBACHEV. *We are going to act responsibly, but not everything depends on us. There was shooting there today, already.*

G. BUSH. *This is bad.*

M. S. GORBACHEV. *I will do everything I can to ensure that the developments do not lead to extremities. But of course, if there is a serious threat, certain steps will become necessary.*

G. BUSH. *Let's talk about the Gulf.*

M. S. GORBACHEV. *I have a question to you.*

Saddam Hussein's letter in response to my letter reveals preparedness to listen to Moscow's view. It is written in discreet, even polite language. Basically, he is asking for our advice.

Obviously, before doing anything, I wanted to talk to you. I know that Eduard, on my instructions, is closely in touch with Jim. If you don't mind, we could take certain additional steps, for example, send my personal envoy there. We have some ideas. If you think this could be useful, I can ask Ambassador Bessmerthykh to give them to you.

G. BUSH. *I have a reservation on this concerning the January 15 deadline.*

I spoke to [UN Secretary-General] Perez de Cuellar shortly before his trip to Baghdad. I stressed it would be very bad if Saddam Hussein wins time till after January 15. This is really the deadline. Saddam Hussein will try to imitate flexibility in various ways in order to undermine that deadline. If we are talking about sending your personal envoy there, what might cause our concern would be the timescale, not the idea itself.

M. S. GORBACHEV. *You could see our ideas even today, [Ambassador] Bessmertnykh has them. If you agree with us, I could send my man there as early as tonight, that is to say, before 15 January.*

G. BUSH. *Fine. I would be glad to see Bessmertnykh today. He can call Scowcroft, or Scowcroft will call him…*

So Gorby made him agree to yet another secret mission to Baghdad. It is interesting that, five days before the beginning of the Desert Storm, US President and National Security Advisor still had time for a flurry of calls and meetings with the Soviets just because they came up with another compromise proposal. Furthermore, later, on the second day of the military action itself, Gorbachev told other coalition doves that "George" was now chasing him about Saddams reply to Gorbachev's last-minute pre-war epistle.[241]

In event, Gorbachev did not even bother to send anyone to Baghdad this time. The idea, it turned out, was only to involve the Bush Administration more deeply into the secretive Soviet peace schemes. Or, to be more precise - to remind them how deeply involved they already were.

The man behind this weird phone call from Gorbachev was Chernyaev. Two days later, he wrote in his diary:

On Friday, I persuaded Gorbachev to call Bush about the Persian Gulf, on the eve of Day X. The conversation was "friendly". On Lithuania, however, M. S. [Gorbachev] told him bullshit, promised to avoid use of force.

Indeed, on the day this entry was made, 13 January - two days before Saddam's deadline - the Soviet troops in Lithuania fired into the crowd, killing 15 protestors and wounding hundreds. By Lithuanian proportions, this was comparable to the Tiananmen massacre.

Chernyaev commented:

I've never thought that everything Gorbachev had started in such an inspiring way would end so gracelessly. [...] I am fed up with his [...] inclination to trust "his own" and, in the end of the day, to seek support from precisely them - the Communist Party of the Soviet Union!

All this has led to "spontaneous" actions by paratroopers and tanks in the Baltic states, and ended in blood. [...]

The Lithuanian affair has ultimately destroyed Gorbachev's reputation and, possibly, his position [as the Soviet leader]. Yes... This is so, in spite of his contempt for the "alarmists". [...]

I predict that tomorrow, in the Supreme Soviet, the bullshitting will begin.

While Chernyaev boiled with anger, the whole world froze in horror. One last, desperate hope in some quarters was this: perhaps, Gorbachev will now condemn the massacre, dissociate himself from it? After all, even Comrade Stalin, after his collectivisation campaign had killed 10 million peasants, blamed it all on local comrades' excessive zeal and "dizziness from success". Perhaps, Gorbachev will also deny responsibility? In that case, whether we believe him or not, at least we can give him another benefit of the doubt, blame the hardliners who had gone out of his control...

But Moscow was silent.

Even the Supreme Soviet bullshitting would not begin.

And then, Bush and Baker realised they had to act, if only the words freedom and democracy meant anything to them. But, Baker writes,

On the other hand, there was no doubt Gorbachev was under growing pressure from the enemies of reform. Coming down too hard might embolden his critics and weaken his standing, which obviously was contrary to American strategic interests. Moreover, we didn't want to be so harsh that Gorbachev might be tempted, as the President said, to bail out on us. The President and I agreed that our response must be measured, but with sufficient vigour so that all parties understood our seriousness...[242]

So, Baker continues, he successfully "*struck that delicate balance*" by taking serious and well-measured steps.

First, he made a public statement praising Gorbachev for the perestroika. In the end of it, he referred to Lithuania and firmly declared:

"Peaceful dialogue, not force, is the only path to long-term legitimacy and stability."

Second, he summoned the Soviet charge d'affairs and expressed concern.

That was it. The incident was now over.

Meanwhile in Moscow, Gorbachev's associates - Primakov, Yakovlev, Ignatenko - tried to persuade their boss at least to go to Lithuania and express regrets. He still had a chance to receive and exploit the benefit of the doubt. Gorbachev declined. "Ignatenko concluded that, contrary to what many think, M. S. [Gorbachev] is not "misinformed"; he is fulfilling his plan of intimidating the Baltic peoples", Chjernyaev reveals.[243]

Instead of any conciliatory gestures towards Lithuania, the Soviets began a similar campaign of violence in Latvia.

It was now 15 January - the deadline for war.

But the Desert Storm would not yet begin.

On 16 January, "hardliner" Primakov saw Gorbachev to tender his resignation in protest against violence in Baltic states. To that, the dictator replied:

"It is for me, not yourself, to decide what you do."[244]

Primakov accepted that. But at least, he and other high-ranking apparatchiks who resigned (or tried to resign) in those days showed firmer commitment to democracy than Bush and Baker.

On the same day, 16 January, Gorbachev proposed to the Supreme Soviet to re-introduce censorship of the media.

He also, at last, appointed a new Foreign Minister. Naturally, that was Bessmertnykh, hitherto his ambassador in the US. All the rumours on "pro-Arab" Primakov were as false as the January 11 "peace plan".

And it would only be on January 17 that Chernyaev recorded in his diary:

The war in Perisan Gulf has started. I've never doubted it would.

They woke me up at 4 am. Went to the Kremlin. Went to see Primakov and found Dzasokhov and Falin with him. So, we began drafting Gorbachev's statement.

At about 7 am Gorbachev gathered in the Walnut Room... when I saw - whom - my jaw dropped agape... Politburo members, Secretaries of the Central Committee...

Everything back to its circles, I thought. This is a symptom.

Of course, [Defence Minister Marshal Dmitry] Yazov was there, too. He put a map over the table and showed what and how was going to happen. [A later-day addition by Chernyaev:] (By the way, he turned out to be correct)

[...] Gorbachev asked Yazov "When did you notice it?" (i.e. when did the military intelligence find out that the American attack had began).

"Heard, not noticed", he replied. ""One hour after the beginning". They overheard a conversation between a B-52 and a "Miluoki" carrier.

[...]

Ignatenko was sitting next to one of the Central Committee secretaries. When the ships were mentioned during the discussion, the secretary bent aside to Ignatenko and asked: "Why ships? Is that near the sea?"" Well, I don't know whether it's true or Ignatenko made it up...

Chapter 15.
Caught in the Desert Storm

The greatest (though open) secret of the Operation Desert Storm is that it failed to achieve its objectives.

On 15 January 1991, President Bush signed National Security Directive 54 authorising the military action against Iraq. The goals of the operation were (in summary) to liberate Kuwait, destroy Iraq's WMDs, destroy the Republican Guards as a fighting force, and a rather open-ended one to "*promote the security and the stability of the Persian Gulf*".

The directive in its point 10 also envisaged a more robust Plan B:

10. Should Iraq resort to using chemical, biological, or nuclear weapons, be found supporting terrorist acts against US or coalition partners anywhere in the world, or destroy Kuwait's oil fields, it shall become an explicit objective of the United States to replace the current leadership of Iraq…

In that war, Saddam did not resort to using WMDs or to terrorist attacks. However, on February 22, he ordered the Iraqi troops to leave scorched earth in place of Kuwait's oilfields. Fire was set at about 700 oil wells.

From that moment, it became an explicit objective of the operation to overthrow Saddam's regime. Or at least, it should have.

Why were the objectives of the Desert Storm achieved no sooner than 12 years afterwards?

◆ ◆ ◆

The "H hour" - the exact time when the Desert Storm would begin - was a closely guarded military secret.

However, there were so many countries in the coalition that even Baker had lost count. Obviously, all allies had to be informed.

So, the National Security Council made up a timetable.

The British Prime Minister would be told first, 12 hours in advance.

Most others - such as Gorbachev, Mitterrand, the Saudi King, the Israeli Prime Minister, etc., would be given about one hour's notice. Less trusted allies, such as Mubarak, would only be told precisely at the H hour.

The H hour was, in fact, 19.10, Washington time, on 16 January 1991.

At 18.11, Baker telephoned his Soviet opposite number Bessmertnykh and told him the operation would start very soon. Bessmertnykh demanded to know the exact time. Baker told him.

At 18.38, Bessmertnykh phoned back and said that Gorbachev was asking for a personal favour from President Bush: postpone the whole thing for 24 hours, to let him have another word with Saddam. Baker said it was unfortunately too late. It was impossible to call back an operation of such a scale at half an hour's notice.

In his TV statement next day, Gorbachev said:

Having received, about one hour before the start of the military action, a notice from US State Secretary Baker about the decision taken, I immediately addressed President Bush with a proposal to take additional steps - through a direct contact with Saddam Hussein - to secure his immediate announcement on a withdrawal of troops from Kuwait. Simultaneously, I instructed our ambassador in Baghdad to contact the President of Iraq, inform him about my appeal to George Bush, and...

What?!

So, once Gorbachev knew the secret of the H hour, he immediately contacted Saddam to talk about it? Baker blabbed the secret to Bessmertnykh, Bessmertnuykh reported to Gorbachev at half past six or so, and then, while Bessmertnykh kept Baker busy by requesting impossible favours, someone else contacted Baghdad and revealed what the H hour was?

Belonogov, who was made the Soviet spokesman on the matter, writes:

Fortunately, we managed to dispel these suspicions by showing that the phone line to Baghdad was no longer operational by that time. Gorbachev's instructions only reached the Soviet embassy in Baghdad long after the bombing began, and were implemented only the next day.[245]

It was, of course, a great relief to know that Gorbachev's betrayal was thwarted by a technical breakdown.

A lot of questions, however, remained unanswered. For example, is it certain that Gorbachev had no other urgent channel of communication with Saddam?

It is incredible that the Bush Administration chose to risk the lives of US servicemen by giving an advance notice of the operation to the Soviets - for no good reason, just for the sake of good relations.

But, anyway, the rumour was killed.

Doves in the storm

The objectives of the Desert Storm were not agreed with - or shared by - the coalition. Indeed, the "doves" faction was determined to limit those objectives, so that the Americans could not go an inch further than just enforcing the UN resolutions.

The next morning after the start, at 10.05 Paris time on 18 January 1991, Mitterrand phoned Gorbachev to tell him:

As far as France is concerned, we are fulfilling our allied obligations with the only objective: to start the process of peace restoration in the region after Kuwait is liberated.

[...]

In my view, as soon as Kuwait is liberated, it would make sense for you and I to intervene in the events in some way in order to limit their scope. But we have not reached this stage yet, because Kuwait is not yet liberated.[246]

Mitterrand felt, however, that any attempts to stop the war in the first few days would be untimely. Saddam had just begun throwing his Scuds at innocent civilians in Israel, so - Mitterrand calculated - for the next few days, the whole world would still be outraged. In addition, he complained:

We simply don't feel comfortable asking the United States to weaken their military effort in a situation when the American pilots risk their lives.

Therefore, Mitterrand concluded:

We won't be able to propose any peace initiative in the nearest few days. That won't be possible before the middle of the next week. In such a case, I will contact you immediately.

Gorbachev disagreed. He said he was making efforts to stop the Desert Storm right now - the next day after it started. As for Saddam's missile strikes at Israel, it all depended on how you call them. If you call them an example of a spread, or internationalization, of the conflict, it can be an argument for stopping the military action:

First, everything must be done to stop the military action and reach the solution of the problem. Second, it is necessary to prevent expansion of the conflict. You've mentioned the last night's events involving Israel. The Turkish medjlis spent yesterday discussing the problems connected to the crisis and agreed to provide Turkish airbases for American aircrafts. It has also authorised Turkish president to use armed forces abroad. All of this shows the extremely dangerous trend towards an expansion of the conflict. Heads of many states and governments, particularly Arab ones, have paid special attention to this very fact - the danger of expansion. I have cabled them about this.

Now, Mr. President, I'd like to look at the situation from the other side. In my view, the events have reached a different stage now. Yesterday, Saddam's regime kept demonstrating its ambitions, stubbornness, threatened everyone, and especially Americans. Today it has suffered a political defeat. A huge damage to its defence potential and even industrial potential has been done. Iraq is now different from what it was.

At the first stage Iraq was shown its place. Yes, this was done in a tough way, and I hope you understand our feelings. Yet, this has been done.

Now the conflict is entering its second stage. Further bombings would mean targeting the troops, i. e. the people. The ground forces would come into contact, which would mean a bloodbath for US and other soldiers, especially the Arabs.

F. MITTERRAND. *Yes.*

M. S. GORBACHEV. *It may develop in such a way that it comes to the annihilation of the people, the country. The situation would become absurd. We will come into conflict with our broader objectives.*

At present, the following question is being asked to Saddam Hussein on my behalf through the Soviet Ambassador in Baghdad: "If there is a pause in military action, are you prepared to declare you are going to withdraw from Kuwait?"

F. MITTERRAND. *This idea has a critical significance.*[247]

Fluttering wings

There was no reply from Baghdad when the morning of January 19 came to Washington. Nonetheless, Gorbachev telephoned Bush:

At first, the conversation was cold[, Chernyaev writes]. M. S. [Gorbachev] did not find it necessary to praise Bush for taking responsibility for the war on behalf of all. No condolences for the kids who have been killed there already. He went straight to his theory of two stages...[248]

The whole theory was, of course, the usual Gorbachev propaganda. Two key arguments were these:

1. Saddam's military power is already destroyed. He is no longer dangerous; leave him alone.

2. Saddam still has significant military power. If the war goes on, he will be able to inflict significant casualties to American troops. The battles will be long, hard and bloody. Do you really want to go through that?

18 January 1991, 17.15-18.35 [Moscow time]

M. S. GORBACHEV. *Greetings, George. These are difficult times.*

G. BUSH. *Yes, it is really very difficult.*

M. S. GORBACHEV. *Naturally, I would like to discuss the situation in Persian Gulf.*

G. BUSH. *I will be glad to share our information with you, or I am prepared to listen to you.*

M. S. GORBACHEV. *First. Your and our doubts about Saddam Hussein have been confirmed. As a result, use of force became necessary - of course, with full understanding of the burden of responsibility to the nations of the world which we all bear. Also, I do realise that casualties are now inevitable.*

But, so to speak, everything is underway now. So the question arises: what now?

G. BUSH. *Indeed. And I hope we are all in agreement that a complete implementation of relevant UN resolutions must follow.*

M. S. GORBACHEV. *I have issued a statement where I confirmed our firm position, called the aggression an aggression, put all the blame and responsibility for the fact that the war became inevitable on Saddam Hussein, and stated that he must withdraw from Kuwait and obey the UN resolutions.*

G. BUSH. *That was an excellent statement.*

M. S. GORBACHEV. *The military action has now begun. Now, first of all, we must think on how to limit it, how to prevent its expansion. For there is such a tendency.*

G. Bush. *This worries me a lot, too. I suppose, when Saddam Hussein deliberately targeted his missiles on Israel, his intention was just to expand the conflict.*

M. S. GORBACHEV. *Yes. And your position, your timely advice to the Israeli government [not to strike back] were absolutely right.*

G. BUSH. *Right now we are trying to estimate what Israel might do in this situation. We hope it won't take any actions which may result in expansion of the conflict and an involvement of more countries.*

M. S. GORBACHEV. *This is what Saddam Hussein would very much want.*

G. BUSH. *We are also very worried about the Jordanian corner. Perhaps you have some ideas about this?*

M. S. GORBACHEV. *Right now, I would like to share my considerations about possible further steps.*

G. BUSH. *I will be glad to listen to you.*

M. S. GORBACHEV. *After two days of a powerful military action, the situation has entered another stage. Previously, Saddam Hussein made threats, demonstrated ambitions and contempt for the USA, the USSR, the whole community of nations. Now he has suffered a political defeat.*

Secondly, Iraq's military and industrial potential has suffered huge, hardly recoverable, damage. It no longer has a sufficient material base for its ambition to dictate its will in the region. This is an important, critical victory. It is important both for you at home and for the future of the world. The aggressor has been taught a lesson.

Therefore, it is time to think: what is the point of going on with the military action? If you go on with air strikes and bombing, and especially if you start massive use of ground forces, this would result in great casualties of American troops, big casualties of Arabs, civilians. I know you don't want this. In your appeal to the nation, you said it was necessary to minimize casualties not only among American troops, but among civilian population as well.

G. BUSH. *Yes, this is my deep conviction.*

M. S. GORBACHEV. *And this is very important. So, what now? New strikes at Iraq's territory, casualties among its population? In such a case, this action will change its nature. Besides, I don't want to underestimate the fact that Saddam Hussein still has some potential, especially in ground forces.*

Then Gorbachev told about the instructions he had sent to Soviet Ambassador in Baghdad while Bush slept. Then he asked:

If, unlikely as it is, he says he agrees, are you prepared to pause the military action? [...]

I know you were worried that, if Saddam simply withdraws, he would still have significant potential and therefore play a destabilising role. This is no longer relevant.

Besides, then we would be able to continue our cooperation in the UN Security Council framework to implement the idea we discussed: to create new security structures in the Middle East, to solve the numerous problems of that region.

G. BUSH. *Let me give you quite a detailed answer. First, we have no reasons to believe he will agree to your proposal. Second, it is not correct that the military potential which has enabled him to behave so insolently in the region no longer exists. A substantial part of his military potential is still there, and this would enable him to go on threatening his neighbours. The question of the right time to stop the military action should be considered carefully. Wouldn't that make him look like a hero in the Middle East? Is it the right time now, when he has just attacked Israel, when he continues using Scud missiles, and his Republican Guard is still at his disposal? It seems to me that a cease-fire in the present situation would let him emerge victorious from under the ruins of defeat.*

One more point causes concern. At present, the coalition troops, including its Arab members, are highly motivated. However, if we stop the military action now, they will see it as Saddam's victory. In such a case, they would find themselves in a great disadvantage.

So, it seems to me, we cannot agree to a compromise while Saddam still preserves a significant part of his military potential, even if it is weakened. I am worried that such a step would be premature.

I would like to add one more personal comment. I am very concerned about the problem of casualties, which you raised. So far, we have been very fortunate in this sense. We are succeeding in striking the targets with high precision, and we do everything possible to keep our strikes different from Saddam's strikes at Israel. We never bomb mosques, hospitals, schools, large residential areas. The analysis reveals that we are successful in that.

May I stress: nobody likes war, and I feel no joy in connection with the events. I think we are capable of solving this problem. But I am deeply convinced we must not turn back until it becomes absolutely clear that the task is accomplished. That is to say, until Saddam Hussein withdraws from Kuwait, unilaterally, without concessions or appeasement.

Obviously, we would be very interested to know how he replies to your ambassador. But we certainly don't want to give Saddam any hope that the coalition may be satisfied by just a statement, just a promise to hold talks.

His yesterday's actions - the strike at Israel's residential areas with powerful and very imprecise missiles - complicate the matter even more. If we stop now, he would say that the military action has been stopped precisely because of that. He would claim victory: like, I attacked Israel, and the war is over. Rather than being seen as a fanfaron and aggressor, he would be seen as a victor, even in such countries as Egypt which now oppose him. This would be a challenge to the new order which we both want.

[...]

I would like to give you assurances on one more point. None of us wants to see a vacuum in place if Iraq, to see that country so weak and impotent that it becomes a destabilising factor as a possible victim of aggression by its neighbours. I would like you and others to be confident that we do not want a liquidation of Iraq.

M. S. GORBACHEV. *Have you finished? Then I would like to say a few words.*

G. BUSH. *Yes, finished. I only want to thank you for your efforts. [...]*

M. S. GORBACHEV. *[...] I would like to draw your attention to the central point of my considerations once again. The first stage of the military action was justified. It achieved important practical and strategic results. Just a week ago, you and I were in agreement that if Saddam Hussein leaves Kuwait, we can start negotiations. If he could be allowed to withdraw a week ago, he certainly should be now, when he is weakened and incapacitated for years ahead. A lesson has been taught. The UN has shown that an aggressor cannot go unpunished.*

It is, of course, a different matter if there is a task to continue the military action using all forces. That would have meant a new stage of escalation with much greater casualties than now. It would become much more difficult to find a way out. We should also think about long-term consequences, especially political ones. It is important not to miss the opportunity - important for you, for us, and for everybody.

In the end, they just agreed to keep in touch as ever, to let Bush know if there is any reply from Baghdad, and then they'd see. Bush invited Gorbachev to call him any time, day or night.

Yet, there was nothing to call about. Saddam never replied to the message.

Doves regroup

This was only the first in a series of attempts by Gorbachev to stop the war before too much damage was done to Saddam. In doing that, he would sometimes start a dangerous game of being publicly disloyal to the coalition. But of course, Mitterrand supported him secretly, and the Americans would soon forgive him like they always did.

In February, Gorbachev again discussed the issue with the French:

R. DUMAS. [...] Saddam Hussein certainly does not help you with his actions.

M. S. GORBACHEV. And we, like you, helped him in this war. But he would not listen to us. [...] His actions are irrational, he is simply paranoid.

R. DUMAS. Precisely.

M. S. GORBACHEV. But we do not weaken our efforts. An illustration of that is E. M. Primakov's trip to Baghdad. At present, he is awaiting a reception in the Presidential Palace.

R. DUMAS. I think nothing will come out of this mission. But you are right: one must act to the end. We are also trying to act in the same way.

M. S. GORBACHEV. Efforts should be taken now to make the conflict change its character, because the circumstances have changed.

R. DUMAS. I agree. And we should keep in touch and discuss this problem.

M. S. GORBACHEV. Yes.

R. DUMAS. We are talking not only about a test of the new international order, but also how far we can solve the crises in other regions and other problems of this region. We cannot do that on our own, nor can you.

M. S. GORBACHEV. We take a responsible and firm stance towards the crisis in the Gulf. We strictly follow the UN resolutions. By this alone, we are making a very big favour to those who have undertaken the burden of military action, especially the Americans. The US should now show responsibility and not exceed the mandate of the UN Security Council, which authorises liberation of Kuwait but not annihilation of Iraq. Americans should be reminded about that.

R. DUMAS. *Yes, we should remind them about this, and repeat this more often. As for France, our position is somewhat different because we are directly involved in the coalition. However, we emphasis that our actions are strictly limited by the UN mandate, i. e. the mission of liberating Kuwait. By the way, this position creates certain difficulties for us. I hope we will yet have another opportunity to discuss this problem, because it is necessary to solve it.*

M. S. GORBACHEV. *I would like to ask you a question which I also would like to be conveyed to President Mitterrand. If Saddam Hussein undertakes to withdraw his forces from Kuwait immediately after a cease-fire, within 10 to 12 days or 2 weeks, how should all of us react to such a new situation?*

R. DUMAS. *We have already discussed this possibility with F. Mitterrand. Indeed, the situation in such a case would be entirely new. There will be sufficient conditions to call a meeting of the Security Council. We would be able immediately to start creating the machinery in order to solve the problems of security and disarmament in the region, and also to verify that Saddam Hussein would really leave Kuwait within a reasonable time. Naturally, the questions related to verification of actual actions of the troops in the field will be difficult to solve. But in any case, such a statement would be a strong enough fact in itself to create a new trend in the world public opinion. Then nobody would be able to take responsibility for missing a chance of achieving a peaceful solution of this conflict at last.*

M. S. GORBACHEV. *Looking at the whole spectrum of the existing opinions, I come to a conclusion that such a solution would satisfy all parties, probably with one exception. The trouble is, such a development would unsettle the Americans to some extent, because all their earlier actions would, to some extent, become pointless. But we should impress upon them that no such statement could have been made without their earlier actions (assuming, of course, that such a statement will be made).*

R. DUMAS. *But there are other approaches as well. Some forces want Saddam's regime to be eliminated, so as to deprive it of any ability to harm anyone. I am not talking about the Bush Administration, but about certain forces in America, and also about Israel. The same is true about Kuwait, Bahrain, Saudi Arabia.*

M. S. GORBACHEV. *I think Assad would not mind seeing Saddam removed.*

R. DUMAS. *You are right. In general, there will be a clash between different viewpoints, but it is clear that an announcement of a decision you have mentioned would be sufficient to create a new situation. It would be very good if you could secure such a statement.*[249]

A few days later, Gorbachev also gave his secret views to his recently found Iranian allies - who, in this conflict, also openly sided with Iraq.

M. S. GORBACHEV. *If we find a way out of this crisis now, Iraq will preserve a potential for reconstruction and a quick rise. [...] If Saddam Hussein firmly states that he will withdraw troops from Kuwait in the next 2 to 3 weeks, without any preliminary conditions, Iran, we, others will find it easier to support him, to talk about some guarantees of that process. Then we could call a meeting of the Security Council. Please convey my considerations to President Rafsanjani. I hope we have mutual understanding here, and shall keep each other informed. Severe losses can be avoided if we stop the confrontation, even at this critical point.*

And another confidential consideration. If the force becomes the crucial factor in solving the Persian Gulf crisis, that would encourage the opponents of improvements in international relations, both in the US and in the world. I think that the "war party" in the US would receive powerful arguments to make its case. When we are talking about a country like the US, with its powerful military forces, this is all very serious! If it is solved by force, the questions of the region's security will be solved on a different basis and with the [leading] role of different states. This is the most important point to be conveyed to Iran's president.

A. A. VELAYATI. *Our understanding is: if it is solved by force, thereby the role of militaristic states in the solution of regional security problems will grow.*

M. S. GORBACHEV. *There will be a re-grouping of forces, not in favour of the countries of the region, but in favour of other states.*

But the consequences of such a development won't have a limited, regional character. You see, the whole emphasis on political approaches to the solution of international problems would be discredited. Than an issue would arise again about changing the attitude to the problems of arms control and disarmament. The role of the UN, which has been on the rise recently, would also be questioned.

[...]

***A. A. VELAYATI.** [...] Iran is also very concerned about the developments in the region. In our view, the true goals pursued by the West in this situation are fundamentally different from what they state openly.*

***M. S. GORBACHEV.** This is a very precise formula.[250]*

Even Chernyaev was a little taken aback by Gorby's hypocrisy:

15 February 1991

Yesterday, Gorbachev received Kuwait's foreign minister. Lots of "Sabahs" in his name. A very cunning Arab. [...]

Today, it was Iran's foreign minister Velayati - clever, discreet intellectual - but what a Persian! Stayed silent almost for the whole meeting. He only asked a couple of "clarifying" questions in the end. Recorded every word.

Gorbachev charmed him, too, by showing trust and sharing his concern that the Americans may make arrangements in the region as they please if they crash Saddam with military force and the political factor is not involved in time. And of course, he discovered a "mutual anti-American understanding" with the collocutor.

And to the Arab yesterday, he convincingly and firmly spoke about inviolable unity with the US against the aggression, the USSR's loyalty to the UN Security Council resolutions, etc.

Chapter 16.
The Double Crossing

··

There are reassuring signs. Primakov
(A coded cable from Baghdad)

··

In late January, the KGB proposed a plan to spread disinformation that the US were about to use nuclear weapons against Iraq. They even arranged for a statement of protest to be drafted in the Soviet Foreign Ministry. Chernyaev writes in his diary:

I asked to send it to me, added a scornful memo from myself, and forwarded it to Gorbachev. He returned it to me with his own resolution note: "Await a special occasion".

Indeed, our departments are full of wankers! They cannot even do an elementary thing, like distinguishing between big politics and tactical propaganda games.[251]

Chernyaev clearly believed that Gorbachev was also being scornful about the idea. Hardly did he realise at first that Gorby's resolution note was serious. He really meant a special occasion, which came in less than two weeks - on 9 February.

On that day, Gorbachev officially defected the Coalition (nobody ever kept this against him, though). He made a statement declaring that the Desert Storm, if continued, would go beyond the mandate given to the Allied forces by the UN Security Council and therefore become illegitimate. He protested against those mythical plans to use nuclear weapons against Saddam, and concluded by stating it was not too late to solve the conflict through diplomacy.

The draft statement was prepared by the Foreign Ministry and then edited by Chernyaev. On 9 February, he wrote in the diary:

Gorbachev was a bit fussy about the text of the statement. Made wicked jokes: Chernyaev has not done enough sucking up to the Americans in his corrections to the Foreign Ministry draft. But then he strengthened the text precisely in this direction: he added that we confirm our support of the UN Security Council resolution.

However, the criticism of the fighting members of the coalition for their conduct of the operation stayed.

Simultaneously, Gorbachev sent Primakov to Baghdad once more. This time, the Soviet attempts to stop the Desert Storm were taken jointly with Iran - one of the few regimes who openly helped Saddam in that war. Primakov flied to Tehran, and from there, he was driven to the Iraqi border. There, he was met by a high-ranking Iraqi Foreign Ministry official, with a convoy of cars which drove Primakov to Baghdad, where he arrived by the late evening of 12 February. Next day, he was received by Saddam. Primakov writes:

I said I wanted to be left alone with Saddam. When that was done, I clearly stated: the Americans are determined to begin a wide-scale ground action, which would crash the Iraqi forces in Kuwait. Do you understand - you will be crashed. I told him that politics was the art of achieving the possible. On behalf of the President of the USSR, I proposed this: announce a withdrawal of troops from Kuwait, and determine a very brief time limit for that withdrawal in the same statement. And the withdrawal must be complete and unconditional.

And here, for the first time, I could see a real breakthrough. Saddam Hussein began to ask questions on the substance: are there guarantees that [the Allied forces] won't "shoot his troops in the back as they are leaving Kuwait"? Will the strikes at Iraq be stopped after the withdrawal of his troops? Will the sanctions against Iraq, introduced by UN resolutions after his refusal to leave Kuwait, be cancelled after the withdrawal? At the same time, Saddam began to sound me about the possibility of changing the regime in Kuwait. I said clearly that we are taking about restoring the situation which had existed prior to 2 August.

Saddam promised to send Tariq Aziz to Moscow to deliver his answer.

Two days later, on 15 February, Iraq's Revolutionary Command Council issued a 7-page statement. The first five pages consisted entirely of colourful curses of the vile schemes of Zionism and American imperialism, their Arab accomplices and puppets, the godless alliance of treacherous, evil and cunning forces waging a dirty and cowardly aggressive war against great Iraq and its great leader. In the final two pages, the Revolutionary Command Council declared they would withdraw in accordance with UN resolution 660, on the following conditions:

- Full and final cease-fire;

- All other UN resolutions and sanctions against Iraq to be cancelled;

- The withdrawal of all Allied forces from the region within one month;

- The Allies to pay for the damage done to Iraq during the war;

- All Iraq's debts to be written off;

- Regime change in Kuwait;

- "Full preservation of Iraq's historic territorial and sea rights in their comprehensive scope";

- Israel's withdrawal from all "occupied territories".[252]

Basically, it was just another propaganda "peace initiative", very similar to all the earlier ones.

Of course, the White House rejected it straightaway. To that, President Bush added the words which later became infamous:

But there is another way for the bloodshed to stop, and that is for the Iraqi military and the Iraqi people to take matters into their own hands, to force Saddam Hussein, the dictator, to step aside and to comply with the UN resolutions.[253]

The US rejection was echoed by London, Paris, and other Allied capitals.

In stark contrast to that, the Soviets officially welcomed the statement. They said it meant Iraq was prepared to withdraw and the war could end very soon. Tariq Aziz would now come to Moscow, and they would arrange everything.

Gorbachev's Plan

Aziz came to Moscow in the evening of 17 February, and the next day, Gorbachev had the following "tough conversation" with him (as he later described it to Western leaders[254]):

18 February 1991

M.S. GORBACHEV [...] What have you brought for me?

T. AZIZ. Thank you for your words of welcome. May I convey to you cordial regards from President Saddam Hussein and all members of the Iraqi leadership.

Just a few days ago, we received our great friend Primakov in Baghdad. He had a very serious and significant conversation with President Saddam Hussein. It is important that, in the present conditions, we could confirm the great significance of the Soviet-Iraqi relations. In our view, those relations are, as ever, based on mutual trust and friendship.

President Saddam Hussein, all our leadership have highly appreciated your decision to send a special envoy to Iraq. We have shown a serious attitude and interest to the ideas which E. M. Ptrimakov brought to us. On this basis, we have decided to continue our contacts with you.

Then Aziz went on to declare, several times in a row, that Iraq would never capitulate or accept the American conditions, but would want to make an "honourable peace", if at all possible. The idea of the RCC statement, he said, was *"to help the USSR participation in the process of achieving an honourable peace in our region".*

As I already told Comrade A.A. Bessmertnykh, the first step should be a stop of the US aggression. Without that, it is practically impossible to facilitate contacts and carry out the dialogue. The political process cannot go on under fire. I am talking not just about the moral and psychological climate which is necessary for the political dialogue, but also purely practical considerations. So far, even while E. M. Primakov was in Baghdad, the Americans continued to drop bombs and missiles at all areas of our capital. There was even a bombing raid on the Palace of Congresses, as one of the possible places of Soviet-Iraqi talks.

However, Gorbachev realised full well that the West would never openly agree to the Iraqi conditions. It was the same old question of face-saving: conditions could be made, but could not be called "conditions", could not be demanded by Iraq, and at any rate - not publicly.

M. S. GORBACHEV. *It is particularly important to know whether the set of issues raised in the RCC statement is a preliminary condition for solving the Kuwait crisis. It is one thing if you make this a condition, and a different matter if it is just a reminder to everyone that we cannot just solve one problem in the region without considering the other problems of the Middle East. It would be right if you could distinguish the most significant points of your statement connected to Kuwait crisis. But if you are talking about dealing with the whole complex of issues at once, this would be unrealistic.*

I am asking this question directly because there is a real threat of the conflict developing in such a way which is not in the interests of Iraq, the Arabs, all of us. We have no greater task today than to stop the escalation of military action, to save the people and the country, to help you raise again so that you can play your role in the region and in the world once more.

T. AZIZ. *[...] Our statement outlines an agenda.*

M. S. GORBACHEV. *So it is an agenda, not a condition?*

T. AZIZ. *You have vast diplomatic experience. If you express some ideas, some demands, you struggle for these demands to be put into practice. Meanwhile you are trying to get support in the world, to influence your opponents, to find a basis for negotiations. But we have no reason to capitulate.*

M. S. GORBACHEV. *This is why I asked what you brought for me. I know what the strategy and tactics of negotiations are. But we are friends, so we must know what each other really means.*

The agenda includes the Middle East problem, the Palestinian problem, the return of the Arab lands - all this is clear to us. But our present task is to find a way to stop the war, and to arrange for the security in the region to be provided by Arab forces plus UN forces, not anything else.

If the events develop in the same way as before, and the Americans get very deeply involved in the military action, including on the ground, it will not be so easy to take a course in the interests of Arabs and the world community. There can be very different scenarios.

On the question of honourable peace, Gorbachev again recalled his favourite story about Lenin's "obscene peace" with the Germans in 1918:

You are talking about honourable peace for Iraq. And I am thinking about the "obscene" peace in Brest which the Soviet state had to make with Germans in 1918. At the first stage of negotiations, the Soviet delegation was headed by Trotsky. He believed that our revolution should rather perish than agree to the Germans' hard conditions. As a result, the negotiations were in deadlock and Lenin had to stand a grand battle, categorically demanding that the party agrees to that very peace he himself called "obscene".

Likewise, now it was better to surrender Kuwait and save the Iraqi regime than to lose both if a US ground offensive begins.

If we stop the war and start political settlement, is it not an honourable peace for Iraq? Yes, it is honourable. Iraq has at least three indisputable reasons to make its resolute choice in favour of political settlement:

- You've withstood such a storm, you haven't let them crush you. You have something to say about this.

- The military action has not yet resulted in any irrecoverable damage to the country. Iraq can quickly raise again, with the help from Arabs and the world community. In spite of this severe confrontation, the main mass of the population has been saved.

- This is an honourable peace because, if the military action is stopped today, all the parties will participate in the subsequent settlement and the opponent won't be able to impose their approaches. Of course, there won't be any orchestra, and we don't need it. But this would be a strong position. It would give us a right to say that Iraq has made an honourable peace.

T. AZIZ. *This is practically what we say in our statement. We are really* *resolute in our intentions on the settlement. Our plan does not include simply winning time. In the present conditions, winning time would be useless to us.*

President Saddam Hussein's instructions to S. Hammadi and me are based on the notion that the process of political settlement is complicated and cannot go on under constant missile strikes at Iraq. We have been instructed to discuss with you how we could work together to achieve an honourable peace.

The point is that the present conflict is not formally a US-Iraq war. The military action is supposed to be conducted on behalf of the UN, because the Security Council has authorised use of force. That is why we believe that the Soviet Union, as a permanent member of the Security Council, can put an end to the military action.

M. S. GORBACHEV. *Fine. My understanding is: the statement of the Iraqi leadership is made on the basis of stopping the military action at the beginning of the process. But that includes the understanding that positions will be fixed in the Security Council, opening a new stage in Middle East settlement taking account of the whole complex of the region's problems.*

But I must say it won't be acceptable or realistic if you stringently link the problems of ceasefire and liberation of Kuwait to the problem of Middle East settlement. The opponents of [peaceful] settlement will use this to reject your plan and start the next stage of military action. Then we would be in a situation when you get obscene peace rather than honourable one. This will result in huge difficulties for Iraq, the Arabs, and all of us.

On this basis, I propose the following plan:

- Iraq must unreservedly state it is prepared to withdraw its troops from Kuwait.

- The withdrawal begins on the second day after the ceasefire, which is necessary for practical conduct of such a withdrawal.

- It must be clearly determined how much time you need for the withdrawal.

- The Security Council must provide full guarantees of your safe withdrawal from Kuwait.

If Iraq puts forward such a plan in development of the statement, that would give us and other like-minded countries the grounds for an immediate convocation of the Security Council for a comprehensive discussion of the current situation. It would accept the whole complex of Middle East settlement problems for consideration, and deal with them.

This way, you "agenda" would also come into operation. Its first part would be implemented by Iraq, and also its opponents in the coalition. As for its second part - the Middle East settlement, other regional problems, establishment of the security structures, - that is a prerogative of the Security Council, especially those of its members who fully understand the significance of these problems. We know for sure that there are such forces in the Security Council.

We allocate roles, so to speak. You announce a withdrawal and demand guarantees of that withdrawal both from the USA and from the Security Council. Meanwhile, we and others in the Security Council not only insist on immediate end of the war, but also on the settlement of all the other problems of the region.

A.A. BESSMERTNYKH. *I suppose this is a very clear recommendation. If the Iraqi side accepts it, it will become a guarantee of starting a peaceful settlement.*

E.M. PRIMAKOV. *In this connection, I would like to emphasise the importance of the time factor. With Mikhail Sergeevich[Gorbachev]'s permission, I can inform you that on the eve of your arrival, the Soviet President specifically appealed to President Bush to persuade him not to begin the ground offensive during these days. However, there are forces in the US who want to break this agreement.*

M. S. GORBACHEV. *This is correct. Indeed, Iraq must not lose time. The Americans believe the military solution is better for them than a political one. They say that Saddam, allegedly, should not be trusted. All he is interested in is winning time. Therefore we must do everything now to achieve an honourable peace before the ground war begins.*

T. AZIZ. *We have already stated we are prepared to withdraw in the Statement of February 15.*

M.S. GORBACHEV. *Kuwait is not mentioned in the statement.*

T. AZIZ. *This is something that goes without saying.*

M. S. GORBACHEV. *If so, why did not you mention it?*

Secondly, I am not asking you to retract your statement. The idea is to make it more specific, directly declare your preparedness to withdraw troops, and fix all four points we have discussed. This is sort of an implementation plan for your statement. Leave the further steps to us. Together with France and China, I am sure, we can raise all the regional issues outlined by Iraq in the Security Council. I am not saying it will be easy. Once we raise the issues of Middle East settlement, the Americans will suspect us of an attempt to link the Middle East problems with each other. Nevertheless, it is possible to work in that direction.

[...] Obviously, we will raise these problems on our own, so the US won't be able to accuse Iraq of trying to link them with each other.

This can be done in the form of an initiative concerning the future security structure in the Middle East, settlement of the Palestinian problem and other Middle East problems. We have certain understanding on this matter with France and Italy. Moreover, I am sure that, in the light of recent events, the United States now also have better understanding that an establishment of a system of collective security in the region is necessary.

T. AZIZ. *And what will happen with the whole series of the Security Council resolutions which establish a complete blockade of Iraq, deprive us of our ability to receive the necessary goods from abroad, including food and medicines, to export oil?*

M. S. GORBACHEV. *This issue must be considered in the Security Council after the withdrawal of Iraqi troops. I cannot promise those resolutions will be cancelled, as that would create an impression they had been illegitimate and void. However, their operation can be stopped. We are prepared to make such a proposal. In any case, once we agree on the principal points, all these things can be thought over - what should come first and what second.*

T. AZIZ. *What do you think about the presence of US troops in our regions?*

M. S. GORBACHEV. *I think they should not be there. The Americans* *must leave as soon as the conflict is over. Inter-Arab forces, or UN blue helmets from the neutral states, can be stationed in the region. Raising this now would be unrealistic, but this can be done.*

T. AZIZ. *Our statement mentions Iraq's historic rights on the land and in sea.*

What is your opinion on that?

M. S. GORBACHEV. *When it comes to the settlement, raising any issues is legitimate. This is a question for an inter-Arab agreement. Whatever the Arabs can agree upon will be accepted by the world community. The process will be complicated, difficult and lengthy. Before the war started, as I remember, the Americans stated that Iraq and Kuwait can reach an agreement on access to the sea on their own, but then they abandoned that proposal. In principle this is, of course, primarily a matter between Iraq and Kuwait.*

I suggest we make a small break in out meeting.

x x x

M. S. GORBACHEV. *I have just had a telephone conversation with Chancellor Kohl. Apart from other things, he was interested in the progress of our meeting here. We have a constructive dialogue with the Germans, as well as with the French and the Italians.*

T. AZIZ. *Recently, Kohl made a very negative statement about us. I don't know what made him to.*

M. S. GORBACHEV. *So, to sum up the first part of our conversation. Our friendly appeal and recommendations are these: new steps should be made following your statement. You make [another] statement on withdrawal of troops from Kuwait, and specify that the withdrawal will start on the second day after the termination of military action and that it will be completed within a certain time period - as short as possible. You also raise the question of guarantees that the military action won't be resumed under any circumstances.*

We, for our part, will raise the issue of convening the Security Council, get in touch with all parties to the process, and propose that the operation of UN resolutions on the blockade of Iraq should stop when the withdrawal of troops is completed.

This would open the way for the resolution of other problems. There are, of course, many details: on the government of Kuwait, on the regional security, the resolution of the Palestinian problem, the return of the Arab lands, demilitarisation of the region. I am confident that both the Americans and the Security Council cannot avoid solving all these problems if you begin the withdrawal of your forces. In this case, no other demands to you should be made. Here you have two parts of the same process.

T. AZIZ. *Obviously, the Soviet Union is not a party immediately involved in the Iraq-Kuwait disputes. But it would be important to know to what extent, in your view, the legitimate claims of Iraq can be satisfied.*

M. S. GORBACHEV. *In our view, these problems merit consideration. The best way would be to achieve an agreement in the pan-Arab framework. However, now it is important to stress that we are talking about a complete withdrawal of Iraqi forces from Kuwait. You should not raise this issue in the statement on the withdrawal of your forces.*

Gorbachev then expressed his confidence that *"you and I are not playing any political games here"* and assured him that everything he said was motivated by *"friendly feelings"*. He reminded about his earlier calls for the Iraqis to withdraw from Kuwait, and pointed out they would have been far better off now had they listened to him in the first place.

T. AZIZ. *I would like to assure you that we have never had any doubts or suspicions about the position of the Soviet Union.*

[...]

M. S. GORBACHEV. *If this plan is accepted, this would mean that Iraq has demonstrated its strength, its ability to resist, and then has decided to leave Kuwait on its own, even though you could have fought for it. The issues will be discussed, and decisions taken, in connection with the new situation. The process of the settlement of the whole complex of Middle East problems would begin. This is all very serious.*

And what is the alternative [...]: to fight? How would it end? Iraq would be ruined and suffer huge losses. Even if the Americans suffer some damage, it won't be comparable. Let's put it on the scales. And what about your responsibility before your conscience, God, the people? The first option is better.

T. AZIZ. *The criminal actions taken by the US against Iraq demonstrate a deep moral fall of the US administration. Wouldn't this fact influence the progress towards a new world order, which is being discussed at the international stage?*

Gorbachev could not give any sensible answer to this excellent question.

T. AZIZ. *S. Hammadi will go to China tomorrow. I will go to Tehran tonight, see President Rafsanjani tomorrow morning, and return to Baghdad in the second half of the day. I will give a detailed report of our meeting to President [Saddam] Hussein. I am sure that it will be thoroughly analysed by the Iraqi leadership, and we will give you an immediate answer on the substance of the matters raised.*

M. S. GORBACHEV. *What can we tell to the world about the results of today's meeting?*

[…] I propose the following release. We should note we had a long and substantial exchange of views on the situation in the Persian Gulf and the whole complex of problems. In view of the present situation, which requires urgent steps to prevent an escalation of military action, and in view of the RCC statement, President Gorbachev proposed a specific action plan to resolve the conflict by political means. Following the exchange of views, Iraq's foreign minister departed to report to President [Saddam] Hussein and the Revolutionary Command Council. President Gorbachev expressed hopes for a speedy response to his proposals.

T. AZIZ. *This suits us completely.*[255]

Chernyaev commented in his diary:

Gorbachev carried out a masterful operation. He set out his plan of Iraq's withdrawal from Kuwait. Aziz did not squeak anything this time. Gorbachev hinted that Bush is extremely reluctant to appease Saddam. He wants to destroy him completely (both for moral and practical reasons).

Gorbachev is trying to outplay Bush on humanism which, from the American point of view, does not cost him anything. Let's see whether Saddam agrees to his plan.

But won't the Americans attack precisely during these days, in order to wreck this plan?[256]

From the press statement alone, the media correctly figured out that Gorbachev's plan was actually a new disguise of Saddam's plan announced three days before.

The confidential Soviet messages to Western leaders were more detailed. The response from the White House included many thanks[257], but was not very enthusiastic. On 19 February, Chernyaev wrote in the diary:

> *It follows from the answers to the Aziz information, which we've sent to Bush, Mitterrand, Kohl etc., that Gorbachev's plan is not good enough at least for Bush. He wants to destroy Saddam.*

According to Bush's and Scowcroft's memoirs, in their reply, they made the following corrections to the plan:

> *No cease-fire until the withdrawal was complete, no more launching of Scuds, no use of chemical weapons, and an immediate swap of POWs.[258]*

It also seems from subsequent negotiations (see below) that the US advocated a 4 days time limit for the withdrawal of Iraqi troops.

Mitterrand"s advice

Yet, the ground offensive was apparently put on stand-by pending the results of Gorbachev-Aziz negotiations. It was only three days later that, at last, the news came that Aziz was on his way to Moscow. To save some hours and minutes, Gorbachev sent a Soviet plane to collect him from Tehran.

Meanwhile, he immediately informed Bush and then called Mitterrand:

21 February 1991, 11.05-11.20 [Moscow time]

[...]

F. MITTERRAND. As you know, your role in this matter is crucial, at the present critical stage of the events. It is this stage which will determine: will there be peace or will the military action escalate? What is particularly important now is the factor of time, and also that Saddam Hussein makes no new conditions. It is necessary for them in Baghdad to understand: this time tomorrow, unless we receive Saddam's absolutely unequivocal answer to a single question, nothing, probably, can stop a wide-scale offensive of the ground forces. It is important for him to understand the extreme urgency of solving this question, especially because there are individuals and countries who would want to continue the conflict even if Saddam gives a positive answer. I would go so far as saying that now the final, crucial quarter of an hour has come.

M. S. GORBACHEV. *I am doing everything in my power.*

F. MITTERRAND. *I know you are doing everything in your power. Now it all depends on one man alone.*

M. S. GORBACHEV. *Your deep relations with the United States could play their role here.*

F. MITTERRAND. *I have already sent a letter to President Bush and spoke to him on the phone yesterday. It is very important to inform him immediately if Saddam Hussein agrees to accept the proposed conditions.*

[…] Iraq must understand: something still can be done tonight, but then it will be too late. Especially if you bear in mind the time difference: when Aziz arrives to Moscow, it will be 9 pm there, 7 pm in Paris, and 1 pm in Washington.

M. S. GORBACHEV. *As soon as Tariq Aziz arrives here, even if it is in the middle of the night, I will see him immediately and then inform you of the results.*

F. MITTERRAND. *Thank you.*

Saddam's response

Aziz arrived about midnight, a cigar in his mouth, calm as an Olympian god. He would not hide his surprise when he was told that he must immediately rush to see Gorbachev in the Kremlin. What is the matter comrades, have you got any crisis here, or what? You can't leave these Soviets to their own devices even for three days, without them having another crisis…

The heavily panting welcoming committee put him before Gorbachev a few minutes past midnight.

"*What have you brought to us this time?*" - Gorby exclaimed impatiently.

Aziz cast a regretful look at all that turmoil, took an appropriate pose, and announced:

T. AZIZ. *I am here on a very important mission. Having returned to Baghdad, I conveyed to the President and all our leadership everything you had said, word for word. We discussed your ideas very carefully and thoroughly. We agree that the principal urgent task is to stop the aggression and prevent the Americans and their allies from achieving the goals they pursue.*

In the interests of fulfilling this task, in the interests of saving Iraq and its potential, which is very significant for the future of our entire region, the Iraqi leadership, the Revolutionary Command Council, has taken a fundamental decision. I am instructed to inform you of this decision, which is the response to your ideas and the acknowledgement of your key role in this situation.

The substance of Baghdad's counter-offer was this:

1. Cease-fire;

2. Immediately after the cease fire, the withdrawal of Iraqi forces from Kuwait over a fixed period of time (time limit to be agreed separately);

3. All relevant UN resolutions (sanctions, reparations, restoration of the Emir, etc.) except the one on withdrawal (660) to be cancelled immediately;

4. Cease-fire to be monitored by Soviet observers.

T. AZIZ. *Yes, Soviet observers. That is what we wish. If anyone else is involved, the Americans will get in.*

All those points were to be fixed in a new UN resolution.

The Soviets tried to persuade him to drop point 3, as it was obviously another preliminary condition - but to no avail:

M. S. GORBACHEV. *[...] In principle, Iraq's request to stop the operation of all those resolutions is legitimate. But this is a separate issue, which should be considered just after your withdrawal from Kuwait. We are convinced that it cannot be linked with the first two* *points, or those who want to start the ground operations will see it as a preliminary condition. It can be used as an excuse to begin a ground offensive. The issue of stopping the operation of the resolutions should follow immediately after the first stage. Then the US can hardly find an excuse to continue the war.*

E. M. PRIMAKOV. *It is clear that Iraq wants the operation of the resolutions to stop because, first of all, you are interested in the cancellation of economic sanctions and of the demands for reparations. We should not draw attention to that at the moment, because the Americans will certainly jump on this issue. These problems would best be solved in the Pan-Arab framework at the further stages of the settlement of the crisis.*

M. S. GORBACHEV. *May I again draw your attention to an important fact. There is only one reason why we still restrain Bush: because we have a plan which includes the known elements and can be a basis for a political settlement. We must not give the Americans any additional condition as an excuse to reject that plan. It is important to keep the formula of Iraq declaring a withdrawal, than there is a cease-fire and a withdrawal itself. However, there is an understanding that as soon as the implementation of this plan begins, the question of the settlement of the crisis will be considered in the Security Council. As a result, the operation of the other resolutions will stop.*

T. AZIZ. *What are the guarantees that the Security Council will take such a decision?*

M. S. GORBACHEV. *The guarantee is that we are gong to make this proposal ourselves. We will seek understanding with the US and others that such resolutions must be cancelled as a result of the withdrawal of your forces.*

[…]

T. AZIZ. *[…] Of course, we understand that the Americans will seek any, even most bogus excuses to continue their aggression. However, we expect that the Soviet Union will support us and take a firm stance here. We do not consider the USSR as a mediator or an intermediary between us and the Americans. We see you as an active force with its own firm positions.*

M. S. GORBACHEV. *Your assessment of our role is correct. Some* expect that the Soviet Union may give in to pressure, abandon its principles because of the internal difficulties. But this is not going to happen.

T. AZIZ. Your actions in the recent days concerning the crisis in the Persian Gulf have provided the Soviet Union with a high authority at the international stage. As for the Americans, we do not trust them at all. If the anti-Iraqi resolutions are not cancelled, the Americans will go on stifling us economically, chase us for reparations, block our assets abroad, etc. In that case, we'd rather die in battle than be stifled in a blockade.

M. S. GORBACHEV. We don't need to be persuaded that Iraq has good grounds for its demand of lifting the blockade once there is an unconditional withdrawal from Kuwait. The problem is that the Americans cannot be persuaded of that at this stage. It would be more realistic to raise this issue at some stage of the implementation of Resolution 660 - for example, one week or ten days after the withdrawal begins.

E. M. PRIMAKOV. It is important to understand that the Americans calculate time limits from 2 August 1990. They cannot wait any longer. Their forces are poised to attack, and they cannot remain on stand-by for a long time. They have either to attack or to cancel the stand-by.

M. S. GORBACHEV. On the American side, it is now a matter of hours, not even days. I can tell you that we have reliable intelligence from three sources that the ground offensive should have started already. It was only our intervention that delayed it. If we are in agreement about the essence of the matter, we should immediately adapt the plan of settlement and say so. The announcement on the agreed plan must not include points which can be read as preliminary conditions. We should trust each other that the agreements reached will be mutually implemented. I think France and China will also support such a plan.

[...]

T. AZIZ. Be that as it may, the need to cancel the economic sanctions and relevant resolutions should be fixed in the plan. I have clear instructions about that from the leadership.

Then they discussed the time limits for withdrawal. Aziz wanted six weeks; Gorbachev said the Americans insisted on 4 days. However, he thought that was only a bargaining position, and they could push it up a bit.

In haste, Gorbachev then compiled the following statement:

"On the instructions of the President of Iraq and the Revolutionary Command Council, T. Aziz presented the proposals which were essentially positive and far-reaching. After a thorough discussion and exchange of views, a scheme has emerged, including the following points".

Then we should list the points proposed by E. M. Primakov.

"- Iraq declares a full and unconditional withdrawal of its forces from Kuwait.

- The withdrawal of troops begins next day after the termination of military action.

- The troops will be withdrawn within a certain time limit.

- It is understood that after the time limit for the withdrawal of two thirds of troops from Kuwait expires, the economic sanctions against Iraq will be lifted.

- After the withdrawal of Iraqi forces from Kuwait is completed, the reasons for the Security Council resolutions will be removed, and the resolutions will lose force.

- Immediately after the cease-fire, all POWs from both sides will be freed.

- The control over the withdrawal of troops will be carried out by observers from countries which do not participate in the conflict, on a mandate from the Security Council.

The work on precise formulae and specific details shall continue. The final results of that work will be reported today, 22 February, to the members of the Security Council and the UN Secretary-General."

Your request for the Soviet Union to send observers should not be mentioned in the release, because that would cause strong jealousy from the other side. We also should not say more than that the troops should be withdrawn within a certain time limit. However, I think, realistically, we can start talking to the Americans from the period no longer than 20 to 24 days.[259]

Bush's amendments

At four in the morning of 22 February 1991 (still the evening of 21 February in Washington), Gorbachev rushed to call Bush and tell him the news. Of course, he did insert some lies into it:

We are talking about a withdrawal of Iraqi forces from Kuwait's territory without any reservations. We fought off their attempts to link the resolution of the conflict with other problems. We firmly, in the spirit of your position, raised the issue of the POWs and arrived at recognising the necessity of returning the legitimate government of Kuwait into the country. [...] The question of returning the legitimate government of Kuwait into the country was very difficult.

In reality, the Emir is not mentioned in the Gorbachev-Aziz transcript. The closest they came to that issue was the discussion on cancelling the UN resolutions, one of which required a restoration of the Emir; and both sides agreed that the resolutions should be cancelled.

In response, Bush raised the issues of Iraq's WMDs, questioned the point on cancelling the UN resolutions and sanctions (especially regarding the reparations), and pointed out that six weeks was obviously a very long time limit. Then he promised to think about all this.

In their memoirs, Bush and Scowcroft claim that their minds in the subsequent hours focused on figuring out a way to refuse politely. Be that as it may, as a result they only worked out their own more detailed plan on the basis of Gorbachev's plan:

- A large-scale withdrawal from Kuwait begins at 12 pm (New York time), 23 February;

- Withdrawal to be completed within one week, including the withdrawal from Iraq's border with Saudi Arabia and Kuwait, Bubiyan, Wasra, and Rumaila;

- Withdrawal from the capital city El Kuwait to be completed within two days;

- The legitimate government to return as soon as practicable;

- The Coalition forces will not attack the withdrawing Iraqi troops if these conditions are satisfied and if Iraq does not attack any other country;

- Iraq stops flights of military planes in the air space of Iraq and Kuwait, except transport planes removing the troops;

- Coalition forces have exclusive right of controlling the air space of Kuwait;

- No more destruction of Kuwait's or its citizens' property

- All detained Kuwaitis to be freed.

- Iraq's conditions, e.g. on cancelling the UN resolutions, are not acceptable.

- All POWs and civilians forcefully detained to be freed within 2 days;

- All the bodies of killed coalition troops to be returned within 2 days;

- Iraq removes all land mines and explosive devices, including those around Kuwait's oil installations;

- Iraq discloses full information on the location and characteristics of land and sea mines;

- Iraq assigns respective liaison officers to make it all work.[260]

Judge for yourself whether it looks more like a polite refusal or an attempt to work out a face-saving detailed agreement on the basis of Gorbachev's plan.

In the morning of 22 February, Bush phoned Mitterrand to discuss that. Mitterrand proposed some minor changes.

As they spoke, however, the latest news from Kuwait changed absolutely everything. Bush was handed a report that Iraqi forces were blowing up Kuwait's oil fields.

It was now Plan B from his National Security Directive 54. It was now a war for a removal of Saddam from power.

Any peace deal with Saddam, good or bad, was now out of the question...

Or was it?

Chapter 17.
At the gates of Baghdad

Perhaps Allah has contrived these events to rid us of Saddam.
King Fahd of Saudi Arabia

As we remember, the UN Resolution 678 was meant to be the final ultimatum.

In event, however, it was anything but final.

On 9 January 1991 in Geneva, Baker gave Tariq Aziz another ultimatum: a personal letter from Bush to Saddam. Aziz glanced at it, said the tone and style were unacceptable, and threw it at the negotiations table, where it was left for good. That was the finally final ultimatum rejected.

On 11 January, the UN Secretary-General went to Baghdad to deliver yet another - finally, finally final - ultimatum to Saddam.

On 14 January, one more ultimatum (let's mark it "F.F.F.+1") was publicly made by the UN Secretary-General on behalf of all permanent members of the UN Security Council. Here, the demands to Saddam were dramatically reduced: from "unconditional withdrawal" by midnight 15 January to just making a statement that Iraq is prepared to withdraw.

Quite apart from that, individual members of the coalition were also writing one letter to Saddam after another, arguing, convincing, imploring, promising, threatening and appealing: withdraw from Kuwait until it is too late!

After Saddam ignored all that, it was thought permissible to start bombing Iraq. However, when it came to a ground action, President Bush thought (or perhaps, someone else thought so for him) it was necessary to issue another ultimatum and give Saddam 24 hours more.

Meanwhile, the Kuwaiti oil wells, refineries, sea terminals, the entire industry, were in flames. However, because the news came during a phone call to Mitterrand, or for some other reason, the officially approved objectives of the Operation Desert Storm did not seem to have any bearing on his decision. His plan, as amended by Mitterrand, was announced publicly on 22 February, and Saddam given 24 hours to accept it.

The last hoax

The American plan gave Saddam one week to withdraw. After all, it had taken him just a couple of days to occupy the whole territory of Kuwait. Surely, he did not need more than a week to move the same army to the same distance, though in the opposite direction?

But Saddam, as we remember, wanted six weeks.

What followed at the Soviet-Iraqi talks in Moscow was a typical debate of the kind you can hear thousands of times, every day, on every bazaar in the Middle East.

M. S. GORBACHEV. Then, maybe, you can manage in 10 days? It might be possible to try and persuade the Americans that such a term is necessary.

10 days! And what about our equipment?! What about our stores of ammunition and food?! May Allah be our witness… etc., etc. Well, perhaps we could just manage in four to five weeks, but that is an absolute minimum…

So it continued for many hours, and eventually came to these terms: four days to withdraw from Kuwait City, three weeks to withdraw from the whole country. The agreement was cabled to Saddam in Baghdad, who cabled back his approval, and Tariq Aziz announced in Moscow: we accept the Soviet plan, three weeks it is, and that is also our response to the American ultimatum.

Three weeks would expire in the second half of March - at the beginning of the Ramadan, the beginning of the heat, the beginning of the sand storms.

The whole thing had been simply another time-winning hoax.

And everyone who could count understood that.

However, Gorbachev spent the final hours before the ultimatum expired trying to prevent the ground offensive. For the whole day of 23 February, he was phoning the Western leaders, one by one, trying to persuade them to keep searching for compromise. Having enlisted another leader, Gorby told him to go and lobby Bush, and would start dialling the next leader. In the end of the process, Bush would be besieged by a crowd of allies, all giving him the views of the world community, and then, Gorby would finally call him directly and hammer the final nail.

But it did not go quite as planned.

British PM John Major, who was the first on his list, thanked Gorby for his efforts but said that the ultimatum was an agreed position of the whole coalition, its finally final word, and it was not negotiable.[261]

He had more luck with his next call, to the Italian PM Julio Andreotti:

M. S. GORBACHEV. *[...] My idea is this. We should stay united, as before, and use this window of opportunity to avoid moving on to a tragic phase of the war. We should raise this issue in the Security Council as soon as possible. There, we can discuss the plan of settlement proposed now, compare it with the American plan, and reach some integrated solution. [...]*

This is what I wanted to tell you, Julio, as usual, in a sincere and friendly way. The only conclusion is – we should act. We must help George keep calm, persuade him a great victory has been achieved.

J. ANDREOTTI. *Thank you. May I take the liberty to comment briefly. What has been done is already a lot. Just a few days ago we could hardly hope that such a thing can be done. [...] The remaining differences are not so big. The most important condition which should be implemented is to return freedom to Kuwait. Many fear that Saddam would remain with his 500,000 army. But all that can be discussed later, not now, which also fits in the UN plan.*

M. S. GORBACHEV. *I agree with you.*

J. ANDREOTTI. *For my part, I will try to influence G. Bush in this direction. The positions are very close and it would be absurd not to achieve a constructive solution.*

M. S. GORBACHEV. *I very much welcome your words, Julio.*

J. ANDREOTTI. *I shall also contact F. Mitterrand. I think he will agree with us. As far as I know, he has a similar approach. You should talk to him personally unless, of course, you have already done so.*

M. S. GORBACHEV. *I am going to talk to F. Mitterrand.*

J. ANDREOTTI. *Thank you for calling. We shall keep in touch. All of us will have a lot of work these days.*[262]

But Andreotti did not quite realise who Mitterrand was: the only Western left-winger in history who entered a "united front" with communists and survived. Not only had he emerged from the "united front" alive (almost a unique achievement in itself), but outplayed the communists and stayed in power. That was unprecedented and contrary to all the laws of history. Mitterrand had achieved that miracle through a combination of qualities which hardly included naïve idealism or an ability to hope against hope...

So, before Gorbachev even finished his discourse, he said:

F. MITTERRAND. *May I interrupt you. Our difficulties are not connected with the information received from Tariq Aziz. I can see there are specific disagreements. Apparently, Iraq does not agree to the proposals put forward in the joint statement [the ultimatum] of the United States, France and other countries. As I understand it, the principal disagreements are about the time limits. The 21-day period expires in the end of March, when the period of great heat and sand storms begins in that region. If Iraq shows no good will, our troops would hardly be able to resist in a military action in such conditions. The ground offensive would have to be postponed for half a year, which would have created exceptionally big difficulties for our troops.*

I can tell you directly that we do not trust Saddam Hussein. [...] The question of time is very important to us. We insist on the 7-days limit. Iraq proposes too long a period. Soon it will be March with its extremely disadvantageous weather conditions. If it was January or December now, this could have been acceptable. We have reasons to believe that Saddam Hussein wants to create a delay until the end of the acceptable period. This is a risk we cannot take.

Such is our position. Such is, if you wish, my position.

However, I very highly appreciate your efforts. The 8 points proposals which emerged as a result of your meetings with Tariq Aziz made us change our position, too. As you have noticed, there is not a word about Iraq in our statement [ultimatum]. It only discusses Kuwait.[263]

As we remember, that had been Mitterrand's objective from day 1 of the Desert Storm: to limit the operation to a liberation of Kuwait. Gorbachev's plan had helped to achieve that. Mitterrand could see no point in raising the stakes in this game beyond that.

The reaction of another leading "dove", Mubarak, was roughly the same. Indeed, he seemed more concerned with Gorbachev's standing in Washington than with saving Saddam Hussein from an American offensive:

M. S. GORBACHEV. *Good afternoon, dear Hosni.*

H. MUBARAK. *(Speaks in Russian). Good afternoon, Comrade Gorbachev. How are you?*

After Gorbachev told about his plan to convene the UN Security Council and create a hybrid peace plan, Mubarak replied:

H. MUBARAK. *The problem is that nobody believes the Iraqi leaders. They want to win time, and that is why they need a meeting of the Security Council. None of the Arabs believe Saddam Hussein.*

I have a request to you. You are my friend, and the Soviet Union is a friend of all Arabs. We very much want the USSR to enjoy high prestige in the Arab world. We very much want you to have good relations with Bush. Contact him and talk to him. Maybe, you can jointly present conditions of peaceful settlement to Saddam. There are just a few hours left. It is very important for you to agree with Bush.

The main problem is that nobody, neither Americans nor Arabs, believe Saddam. I don't believe him. He has deceived us too many times.

Please, contact Bush.

[…]

I can talk to Bush, but please, you contact him as well.

M. S. GORBACHEV. *Dear Hosni, have not I told you that I have talked to George for an hour and a half already?*

H. MUBARAK. *I know this, but you should talk to him again.*

M. S. GORBACHEV. *Okay, I will probably try to do that. And you talk to King Fahd.*[264]

Perhaps, it was the reaction of his principal allies within the coalition that made Gorbachev hold his horses, too. Of course, he continued his phone calls – to his friends Assad and Rafsanjani, to Japanese Prime Minister Kaifu, to German Chancellor Kohl, and finally to Bush – and kept telling them it was absolutely necessary to convene the UN Security Council urgently. However, while that was quite easy to do for the Soviet Union as its permanent member, Gorbachev would not order his man in the UN to make a move. He just kept making his phone calls.

Eventually, the evening came, and the ultimatum expired. At the dawn of 24 February, the ground offensive began.

The Desert Sabre

The military history of the ground offensive – the Operation Desert Sabre – is well-known. In two days, by the morning of 26 February, the Republican Guard and all Saddam's combat troops were reliably encircled in Kuwait. The road to Baghdad and beyond lied completely open before the US forces.

That night, Tariq Aziz walked into the Soviet embassy in Baghdad and brought a letter from Saddam Hussein. Saddam wrote he was now prepared to withdraw from Kuwait – this time, for real – and asked the Soviet Union to help him achieve a cease-fire.[265]

The same night, the Soviets raised this in the UN Security Council. It was agreed that Iraq must officially address the Security Council and declare it is prepared to implement all its resolutions on the matter.[266]

In the morning of 26 February, Saddam made a speech on Radio Baghdad about the withdrawal from Kuwait:

Oh valiant men of Iraq! Oh glorious women of Iraq! Kuwait is a part of your country, torn apart from it in the past. The circumstances today command that Kuwait will stay in the state it will be in after the withdrawal of our fighting forces... [But] Iraqis will remember and never forget that on 8 August 1990 Kuwait became a part of Iraq legally, constitutionally, and factually... Everyone must remember that it was not from the first attempt that the gates of Constantinople opened before the storming Muslims...[267]

This was not very helpful in terms of persuading the UN Security Council declare a ceasefire.

Next night, however, the Soviets passed to the UN Secretary-General and the Chairman of the Security Council the following letter from Tariq Aziz: "as a sign of respect to the Soviet Union", Iraq would comply with resolutions 660, 662 and 674, but only if the Security Council cancels resolutions 661, 665 and 670...

Of course, that was also rejected.[268]

It was only next night that Iraq finally declared it was prepared to comply with all 12 relevant resolutions. That letter was officially filed in the Security Council. The White House immediately announced that the military action would be terminated the next morning, at 8 am, Iraqi time, 28 February 1991.

Later, Andreotti and Gorbachev would praise Bush for his "new world order" obedience to the UN Security Council:

J. ANDREOTTI. [...] During the Iraq-Kuwait crisis you said the main problem was to achieve restoration of Kuwait's independence but not go beyond that. Some began polemics with that at once. They would say that was a "limitation" thesis. But in fact, that was a question of respect for the UN decision. And eventually, President Bush also agreed with that approach, even though he was criticised for not going further than he did.[269]

Indeed, it had always been a "new world order" war, with the UN Security Council as "the master of the war". The way the coalition had been framed by Bush and Baker, they could not make decisions on their own. As soon as Iraq agreed to obey UN resolutions, the causes of war were removed, and the war itself was over.

Later, the detailed terms of the ease-fire were also spelt out the longest UN resolution in its history, "the mother of all resolutions", following lengthy discussions and bargaining with the Soviets, the French, Ecuador, and other great powers.

The Mother of All Battles ended as it began: no defeat, no victory, only the endless bureaucratic farce in the UN.

The final betrayal

The Cold War was fought, all over the world, throughout the 20th century, between the socialist totalitarian regimes and the people enslaved by them. The socialists had tank armadas and weapons of mass destruction. The people never had that. All they could hope for was some sympathy and support from the free world.

That was why the crucial question, the question of life or death for millions of people caught in that war, the question of life and death for Russia and Vietnam, China and Poland, Lithuania and Israel, was this: if we dare fight, will the West offer us at least some support?

Undoubtedly, this was also a question asked by Iraqi Shiites, Kurds and Sunnis for all those years under the yoke of Saddam's regime.

And now, at last, the President of the United States had publicly given a clear answer: yes, we are seriously at war with Saddam Hussein, and the Iraqi people are welcome to join us.

In a couple of weeks, Iraq was in a nationwide rebellion. By the middle of March, the rebels controlled Basra and other cities of the Shiite heartland in Southern Iraq, entire Iraqi Kurdistan in the North, and the disorders spread to Baghdad itself. At times, it was thought that the regime was finished, while Saddam was nowhere to be found. While celebrating his 60th birthday on 2 March, Gorbachev asked Comrade Primakov:

"So, how's your friend Saddam? Fled already, or still swaggering?"[270]

A couple of days later, German Chancellor Kohl called Gorby with a similar question:

H. KOHL. *Do you happen to know where Saddam Hussein is?*

M. S. GORBACHEV. *I don't know exactly, but my impression is that he is still there. [...]*

H. KOHL. *Aren't you hiding Saddam somewhere in Crimea?*

M. S. GORBACHEV. *Well, he'd better hide somewhere in North Germany.*

H. KOHL. *That's about the last thing we need. We have enough* *madmen there without him.[271]*

But Saddam did not think of fleeing or hiding. He resolved to try and crush the uprising through indiscriminate cruelty, mass executions, and above all, by taking advantage of government forces superiority in artillery and aircraft. The cruelty of that suppression, where whole cities were levelled to the ground, became legendary even by the Baathist standards.

The only trouble was that, by the terms of his cease-fire with the Allies, Saddam could not use aircraft for combat operations - only for transportation of troops. He had to break this condition, massacring rebels and firing at cities from helicopters.

So, it was not only a moral duty, but a legal duty of the Western powers to re-enter the war and enforce the terms of the cease-fire, as well as to help the uprisings which President Bush had personally incited. Furthermore, that was clearly necessary from the practical point of view, too: the Western troops could not be just withdrawn from the region, leaving Iraq in such a mess. Contrary to a widespread myth, all pro-Western regimes in the region insisted Saddam's regime must be finished off first.

From Gorbachev's talks with Turgut Ozal, President of Turkey:

11 March 1991

[...]

T. OZAL. *[...] So long as Saddam's regime is seeking to prolong its existence, the havoc in Iraq shall go on, and this may increase the likelihood of the country's collapse. I believe it is necessary to encourage removal of Saddam now. Otherwise, the bloodbath in Iraq will cost many more human lives.*

The Iraqi people now understand the real state of affairs - they see what is happening in the country. As this process is gaining momentum, the struggle in Iraq will escalate. Stability in the region would not be possible without such an important element as stability within Iraq.

Our goal - or, rather, our wish - is for a democratic regime to be established in Iraq, which would provide decent life to all citizens of that country. Saddam should not be replaced by another dictator. It should really become a free country.

Syria is doing some work in that direction. A meeting between representatives of Iraqi opposition groups is taking place in Beirut today. We have also had contacts with Iraqi Kurds and Turkmen. We may try to find out the real positions and views of other forces opposing Saddam's regime.

I would like to stress again: we should urgently ensure the internal stability in Iraq, which is only possible after a regime change in that country. Without that, we fear, Iraqi people will suffer more casualties.

M. S. GORBACHEV. *Yes, this is a difficult task.*

T. OZAL. *Probably, the most difficult one.*

M. S. GORBACHEV. *We can side with such forces who support a renewal of Iraq, its organic inclusion in the world economic system and international politics. Such a renewal is always connected to internal processes, and that corresponds to our understanding. But, on the other hand, we firmly support the principle which forms the basis of new thinking, namely: people's right to a freedom of choice with no intervention from outside. Any renewed society has to go through its own "perestroika" of some kind.*

The following consideration is, in my view, fundamentally important. If the countries of the region and the countries represented in the Security Council enter a competition for influence over forces supported by one or the other side, that would have led to opposite results [sic]. Saddam's supporters may consolidate and say: the plans of Iraq's dismemberment are now put into operation. And then, even without Saddam Hussein, another "saviour of the nation" may emerge. This is a very delicate matter. Arabs should play the key role in this sense. They can resort to using such forms and methods which would be unacceptable for you and I.

T. OZAL. *That is precisely what Syria and Saudi Arabia are doing.*

We believe that the internal problems of Iraq can only be solved if the rights of all citizens of that country are provided for, including Kurds, Turkmen, and other ethic and religious minorities which have suffered persecution and cruel repression under Saddam. Such a treatment should be excluded in the future.[272]

At the same time, Saudis, Kuwaitis, and other Gulf states were very apprehensive of the idea that the US troops would be withdrawn while

Saddam was still around. James A. Baker III tried to explain to them that their security would now be kept by Egyptian and Syrian "Arab forces" as well as UN blue helmets. Kings and Emirs did not find that very reassuring.[273]

So the moral, legal and political case for intervening to help the rebels seemed overwhelming.

But it was now the new world order. The Soviets and the French did not like the idea. The UN Security Council would only authorize a very limited and purely humanitarian operation under the auspices of the UN and the International Red Cross, to save Kurds (but not Shiites or other rebels) from starvation and massacres in certain "safe heavens" - and not, God forbid, help then overthrow Saddam.

Without hesitation, Bush placed the new world order above everything else. The rebels were massacred, Saddam's regime survived, US forces withdrew.

Was not this what King Fahd meant half a year before, when he demanded from Bush to swear that the deployment of US forces would not be like all other American deployments?

It was only twelve years later that the US forces came to finish the job - and faced a well-prepared guerrilla network, trained and organized to resist occupation, and the population deeply distrustful towards Americans.

Experts in the State Department concluded: what a surprise, Saddam's regime was rather popular after all. Other experts blamed the invisible hand of Al Qaeda. Yet another school emphasized the lack of democratic traditions in the history of the Islamic World in general and Iraq in particular.

But if you repeat this experiment in any other country, the result will be exactly the same. Tell citizens to rise against tyranny, promise them support from the US forces, and when the massacre begins, withdraw quietly. Come back 12 years later and see for yourself, whether the locals would be in a pro-American or anti-American mood.

The argument about the "new world order" or "global policeman", about asking for the UN permission or not, about going to war alone or in a huge coalition - this argument has now been resolved completely.

Bush and Baker went to war with UN permission and under the new world order banners. Their coalition was the greatest in human history. It brought them a splendid victory, but for some reason, it soon became necessary to start the whole thing all over again (and then again, and again).

Twelve years later, however, the United States were not blessed with a State Secretary of such a caliber as James A. Baker III. In spite of all efforts, his successors failed to create a global coalition or to secure a permission for the war from the UN. In the end of the day, the US troops had to do the job as a "global policemen" and not apostles of the new world order.

And only then, it worked.

It could have been done twelve years before, without nearly as much effort, cost or sacrifice; without millions of lives lost or enormous damage done to the international reputation of the United States. It could have been done when Saddam's regime hang on the balance, and a ready-made democratic opposition only needed a little help to replace him. It could have been done when the population was still prepared to greet US forces with flowers – not after the Baath Party and its KGB had spent years and years preparing for a full-scale guerrilla war. Very little was required of the then leaders of the West to achieve that: just forget for a moment about the chimera of the new world order, and follow common sense, decency, national interest...

It took twenty years and many thousands of lives to correct that error and complete that war.

However, the full price of the new world order has not yet been paid.

Chapter 18.
The Pyrrhic Victory

The Western victory in the Gulf War should have put the socialist camp in the worst possible position to achieve their goals in the Middle East.

The Red Arabs were more divided than ever.

The greatest military power in their camp, Socialist Iraq, lied in ruins, the regime of Comrade Saddam desperately fought for survival, and was no longer in a position to contribute to the common pressure on the Zionist enemy.

Furthermore, the Gulf War had ruined the fundamental propaganda myth about the existence of Israel and the "Palestinian problem" being the central problems of the Middle East, the ultimate cause of all conflict in the region. It suddenly turned out that the Red Arab dictators happily invaded their neighbors even if Israel was in no way involved. It emerged that they were not simply overreacting to the "Palestinian problem", but were possessed by an aggressive ideology, which encouraged conquest of the whole region in any case, not just on the way to Jerusalem.

It suddenly became evident that Israel was not an aggressor, but a victim. Saddam"s daily launching of Scud missiles at Israel throughout the war, to which Israel did not respond to help the Americans preserve their Arab coalition, had provoked a worldwide wave of sympathy to the Jewish state.

At the same time, Comrade Arafat with his PLO were utterly discredited by their enthusiastic support for Saddam.

Emir of Kuwait would not miss the God-given opportunity. First thing after returning to the throne of his ancestors, he deported all Palestinians in Kuwait, all 300,000 of them, away from the Emirate as collaborationists.

This made a good contrast to Israel's treatment of its own Palestinians and destroyed several further myths.

And on the top of it, the Soviet Union was now collapsing, it only had a few months left, and was not in a position to back its Red Arab allies.

So, one would expect 1990s to become a good decade for Israel and other pro-Western forces in the region, with the Red Arabs fighting for their survival.

But in fact, changes of a different kind occurred:

- In 1980s and before, the Arab-Israeli peace talks were sponsored and supervised by a pro-Israeli power: the United States. In 1990s, a "Middle East Quartet" emerged, wherein three anti-Israeli members received an equal status: Russia, EU and UN.

- In 1980s, trading "land for peace" was a provocative slogan of defeatists and pacifists. In 1990s, it became a universally accepted principle of "peace process".

- In 1980s, the idea of establishing a Palestinian state was a wild fantasy, questioned as unrealistic even at Politburo meetings (see above). In 1990s, the "two state solution" became universally accepted by the mainstream.

- In 1980s, Israel refused to negotiate over the future of Jerusalem. Jerusalem was the eternal and indivisible capital of the Jewish state. By the end of 1990s, the future of Jerusalem became a negotiation point.

- In 1980s, it was hoped that more moderate Palestinian forces than Yassir Arafat and Fatah would emerge to participate in the peace process. In event, only more radical forces emerged in the 1990s, leaving Fatah at the moderate end of the spectrum.

- In 1980s, Israel and the West refused to negotiate with the PLO as a terrorist organization. In 1990s, the PLO and its successors

(Fatah, Hamas) were firmly established as representing the Palestinian side.

Such a monumental shift in favor of the Red Arabs seemed unthinkable amidst the triumph of the Western victory over Saddam. And yet, it became a reality.

How could that happen? After all, had not the West won the Gulf War? Had not the West won the Cold War?

"Peace process" hidden agenda

As we remember, what happened in 1991 was not a victory, but a face-saving way out of the crisis. That was the deal made by Bush and Baker with their coalition allies: Kuwait would be freed, but in exchange, the Arab-Israeli conflict would be solved in the Soviet way. The "linkage" would be never made public, but the deal remained a deal.

So, at the time when the victorious United States should have been congratulating the Iraqi freedom-fighters for their common victory over Saddam, making arrangements for a Nuremberg-style trial of his regime, and the subsequent de-Baathisation of Iraq - instead of all that, Bush and Baker had to pay a different bill.

The Soviet solution had been known for years: an international conference on the basis of UN resolutions. But there was a problem. Of course, it was helpful that USSR and US were now on the same side; but what was the guarantee that Israel would accept their agreed conditions? Especially in the present climate, after the Gulf War has shifted the world public opinion to the Israeli side and against treacherous Comrade Arafat?

So, it was hardly possible just to impose the Soviet conditions of the settlement overnight. It was necessary, for a start, to involve Israel into the process - on any terms. Further concessions could be extorted later, especially if and when a more convenient Israeli government came to power.

At length, the following terms were agreed:

- The peace conference would take place in Madrid in October 1991.

- It would be a conference under Soviet-American auspices, not UN auspices.

- The Palestinians would not be represented by the PLO. Instead, there would be a joint Jordanian-Palestinian delegation, including some moderate Palestinians from the West Bank (but not from Jerusalem).

- The conference would not determine the exact conditions of the settlement; it would merely agree the basic parameters, and begin a series of bilateral and multilateral talks between the parties.

- The future of Jerusalem was not subject to negotiations in any case.

Such was a solemn promise of the Bush Administration to its Israeli allies.

However, all of that was a cynical smokescreen over a very different agenda.

Novo-Ogaryovo [near Moscow], 31 July 1991

[...]

G. BUSH. *I would like to know your opinion about Arafat. We believe he has damaged himself a lot after the Iraqi aggression by staking at the wrong horse. Nevertheless, we note that he still remains the spokesman for Palestinians in the Arab world. What is your view: will his positions strengthen or weaken?*

A. A. BESSMERTNYKH. *On President[Gorbachev]'s instructions, after my trip to the Middle East, I saw Arafat in Geneva. We also maintain permanent contacts with the PLO. We are aware that there are significant disagreements in the PLO Executive. Arafat's positions have somewhat weakened. However, it is a fact that no decisions are taken in the PLO without him. Therefore, it is necessary to work with him.*

[...]

J. BAKER. *[...] Our task is to bring Israel to the negotiations table. It is very important to have a shared understanding that, at the first stage,* *while the transitional mechanisms are negotiated, there are no people from East Jerusalem at the Palestinian side of the table. Otherwise, there will be no peace process.*

Israel's position is a refusal to negotiate with the PLO. Therefore, we should make arrangements for the delegation to include only Palestinians from the territories, but the PLO leadership in Tunisia would be able to command its people behind the stages.

We are working out a rather sophisticated system of connections, which would enable us to persuade the Palestinians they are not abandoning their claims to East Jerusalem. However, if this issue is brought to the forefront, there will be no peace process, there will never be any peace. East Jerusalem must become the last issue at the negotiations.

When I am asked about the representation of Palestinians, I refuse to comment, just make a statement that the issue should be settled to the satisfaction of all parties.

[...]

G. BUSH. *A very big problem are the Israeli settlements on occupied territories. We are categorically against them. The US Jews used to support the policy of Peres - no new settlements; but now their position has changed under Shamir"s influence. However, I think that American Jews are increasingly beginning to understand that the policy of building settlements is disastrous. We will try to persuade Israel, but that is very difficult.*

M. S. GORBACHEV. *We are also strongly criticised by the Arabs. They demand that we put a stop to emigration to Israel. When Mubarak was here, he warned me he would make a public statement about this, and so he did at his press-conference.*

J. BAKER. *We will give the Palestinians a number of points, like the four points we gave to Assad concerning the UN role. As a result, the Palestinians will be able to say they are not abandoning their position on East Jerusalem, and will have an opportunity to raise this issue at the negotiations on the final status.*

Palestinians will be better off if they make sufficient concessions to us, enabling us to bring Israel to the negotiations table. Between ourselves, we think Israel would prefer this not to happen. Our strategy is to make sure that the Arabs are the first to say yes, and then it would be almost impossible for Israel to say no. However, who knows.

G. BUSH. *In the US, the administration is often criticised for not supporting Israel enough, for not supporting Israel automatically. We support Israel"s legitimate concerns, but we cannot support all its positions. We cannot support Israeli radicalism. I think we shall sustain this criticism. Many Jews in the US feel the settlements are a mistake.*

In general, what the papers write does not damage us in the end of the day. It even allows Jim to talk to Israel more firmly. But we cannot promise that Israel will obey us.

M. S. GORBACHEV. *I accept what you have said.*

J. BAKER. *I would like to stress again, Palestinians must not give Israel an excuse to decline to participate. Raising the issue of East Jerusalem would have given Israel a perfect excuse. We have never recognised the annexation of East Jerusalem. But we cannot ignore the fact that 98 per cent of Israelis support it. Therefore, this issue should be excluded from the public debates.*

Indeed, it was in those very months that the US put strong economic pressure on Israel, demanding to "freeze" all the settlements on "occupied territories". This was the beginning of this endless "freezing" saga, which still dominates the relations between Israel and the West even today. In essence, the "freezing" amounts simply to ousting Israel from those territories. Nowhere in the world can any town be "frozen": it either develops or dies. A demand to "freeze" the settlements is simply a demand to eliminate the settlements. It is just that diplomacy always speaks in a misleading language.

The Secret Quartet

Like exclusion of the PLO or rejection of Palestinian claims to East Jerusalem, another concession to Israel - the conference co-sponsored by the US and USSR, rather than under UN auspices - was also a fake. The "new world order" Quartet of the US, Russia, Europe and UN was already working secretly, long before it openly began to sponsor the "peace process".

M. S. GORBACHEV. *[...] First, we work on the understanding that European countries and the UN must take part in the negotiations at the settlement stage. We support international, not regional peace conference. An agreement on that has been reached at the meeting between A. A. Bessmertnykh and J. Baker in Kislovodsk. The Americans agreed to our proposal that it should be the peace conference on Middle East settlement. Naturally, Europeans will make a contribution in one form or another - this depends on the mechanism - and so will the UN. This is fundamentally important.*
[...]

F. MITTERRAND. *[...] Now, following a quick conclusion of the [Gulf] war, France wants this victory to have a beneficial influence on the process of Middle East settlement as a whole, and have critical significance to demonstrate the role of the UN. In that case, the understanding of the principal role of the UN and its Security Council in the cause of protecting peace would become one of the consequences of the Persian Gulf crisis. This would be in the interest of our two countries. As permanent members of the UN Security Council, we could be confident that no decision could be taken in that framework without our agreement.*

Yes, some think differently, but the world as a whole shows interest in such a new role for the UN. Nobody, including the US, is in a position to oppose that openly. We should play on that. Certain attempts have already been made to deviate from that principle while searching for a solution to the Arab-Israeli conflict. However, we maintain that the UN resolutions, 242 and others, should be implemented. I insist that any conference on the Middle East should be based on UN resolutions and be devoted to the task of their implementation. Whatever this conference, it must be accountable to the UN.

So far, Israel and the US are not prepared to accept this idea. However, it has a rigid outline, and they will have to agree to it sooner or later.

You and I have already made statements in favor of an international conference. An uninitiated observer would find it difficult to see the difference between an international conference which we support and a regional conference proposed by Shamir and approved by Baker. Shamir and Baker propose for the interested countries – Israel and the Arab states – to take part in the conference under USSR and US auspices. Rejecting this idea of a regional conference would mean demanding participation of Great Britain, France and China, i. e. permanent members of the Security Council.

I discussed this problem with Shamir in London. He asked me directly: "Is France offended that it has not been invited?" I replied: "France is never offended if it is not invited to conferences which are doomed to fail". Because, judging by the way in which the so-called regional conference under US and USSR supervision is being prepared, it is doomed to fail. The problem is not that France will not take part in it, but that Israel has too many demands. Apart from the demands on the conference format, they are against PLO participation, against the establishment of a Palestinian state, against PLO representatives in the Palestinian delegation, against negotiating the question of Jerusalem, etc. These demands are unacceptable for the Arabs. In some sense, I would prefer others, not us, to participate in such a conference, and would even wish you every success.

M. S. GORBACHEV. *It is important to stress that our analysis, our approaches are identical. We still support the idea of an international conference on Middle East, we are still committed to it in the new conditions after the Persian Gulf crisis. When the idea of a regional conference co-sponsored by the USSR emerged, we saw it as an opportunity to launch the whole negotiations process leading to a peace conference on Middle East, with compulsory participation of Europe and the UN. This is on the basis of the new role of the UN and the new level of our cooperation in recent period. We consider the peace conference on Middle East with participation of Europe and the UN as a stage on the way to a full-scale international conference dealing with the whole complex of Middle East settlement problems.*

However, all of these are just plans, considerations. The Conference itself can be blocked because of Israel's position. At least, so it seems from the information we have. Therefore we must, if I may use a non-diplomatic expression, keep a united front towards this situation in the Middle East.

[...]

F. MITTERRAND. *In what spirit should we speak at the press-conference?*

M. S. GORBACHEV. As a host, I shall take the liberty to begin the press-conference by saying just a few words on our talks today. As for the problems of the Middle East and Persian Gulf, I think that our discussion was very confidential in nature. Therefore, we hardly should mention the details of our exchanges at the press-conference.

F. MITTERRAND. I agree with you.

Mitterrand was not the only one to whom the hidden agenda was revealed. Later the same month, Gorbachev told the same secrets to Italian Prime Minister Andreotti, the shrewd investigator of the Jewish conspiracy secretly running the US:

I see some concern in the US in connection with the European processes, with Europe moving towards closer cooperation, greater collaboration. We firmly told our partners in Washington that, during the settlement of the consequences of the Persian Gulf conflict, both Europe and the UN should continue to play the same role as during the crisis itself. It was necessary to emphasize that. I think this was correctly understood.

In other words, we have really gone through a difficult trial in connection with the Persian Gulf. And if we cooperate at this stage, too, in solving the problems of settlement of the situation in the Middle East, including the consequences of the Gulf crisis, we may demonstrate for the first time that we are able to be adequate to the present development of the world situation.[274]

Back to 1947

Indeed, both Mitterrand and Andreotti – as founding fathers of the EU and of the UN-based new world order – had their own ideas on achieving peace between Israel and Arabs. Needless to say, their peace would be based on UN resolutions; but the whole trick was in choosing the right resolution. They wanted to go back to the very beginning: the original 1947 partition plan, not simply ousting Israel from the "territories", but from much of the undisputedly Israeli land, including entire Jerusalem; and making the very existence of the Jewish state conditional on the existence of the Arab state alongside it.

Back in 1947, Arabs had refused to accept the partition plan, and began a war to destroy the Jewish state in Palestine – the war which became known as Israel's war of independence. The 1948 armistice lines became Israel's new borders with Jordan and Egypt, occupying, respectively, the West Bank and Gaza Strip. Since the 1967 Six Day War, those territories also came under Israel's control. Now, however, the European demigods felt it was time to go back to where it had all started:

> *F. MITTERRAND. [...] We want Resolution 242 to be implemented, but its interpretation is a matter of dispute. However, there is a resolution which is not being questioned. I am talking about the resolution which has led to the establishment of State of Israel. The same resolution included an establishment of a Palestinian state. If you question the provisions on the Palestinian state, the part about Israel would also be questioned.*[275]

Andreotti's mind was also seeking a solution back in 1947:

> *J. ANDREOTTI. [...] There are some objective difficulties in the Middle East. The first is the Jews' state of mind, fear of persecution, or extermination, which they feel everywhere, even when they are in Israel. Of course, there feelings are not justified, because it was Hitler, not Palestinians, who wanted to destroy them. Secondly, we are talking about the Arab nation, but we must not forget that there are effectively different countries with each leader seeing himself as the leader of the whole Arab world. Therefore, there is no agreement between them.*
>
> *[...]*
>
> *In 1948 [sic], the UN decision included not only the establishment of Israel, but also an Arab state in Palestine. It was a dramatic mistake that that decision has not been implemented.*
>
> *M. S. GORBACHEV. I agree.*[276]

In the subsequent "peace process", the idea of coming back to the 1947 partition plan has never yet come to the forefront; but it is not yet the end. We have seen few documents on the matter, but what we have seen is enough to understand that the hidden agenda of the "peace process" has always been very different from the open agenda. Undoubtedly, this UN resolution, like many others, is still kept up the sleeves of the Quartet diplomats supervising the "peace process". One day, it will be put on the table; most likely, when it will be too late.

We cannot go through the entire subsequent history of the Arab-Israeli "peace process" in this book: that is a long and tragic story in itself, which is still far from its conclusion even today. We have only taken a look at some secrets of its beginning; and that alone is sufficient to make several important conclusions:

1. The "peace process" was started by the US State Department as a reward to its anti-Israeli Gulf War allies;

2. The "Quartet" of the global co-sponsors – the US, Russia, EU and UN – was secretly established as a part of the same agreement;

3. From the outset, the "peace process" was dominated by an anti-Israeli hidden agenda, secretly agreed by the "Big Four" behind the backs of the parties involved.

The *official version* given to the public was that this was a long and complicated conflict, finding a solution would not be easy, but if you *seat and talk* long enough, if you are prepared to make concessions, it is possible to overcome the hard legacy of the past and reach a mutually satisfactory solution. Such was the version fed to the Arab sheiks, Jewish collective farmers, and all people of good will. The problem with this version is not just that it is nonsense. The problem is that it is lies.

In the dark world which simple mortals cannot enter, in the world of secret deals and secret archives, diplomats and statesmen keep a different version. Certain debts have been made while constructing the new world order; and these debts now have to be paid. There can be different views on whether it is better to pay honestly, or to try and hoodwink the debtor, or to re-negotiate the payments Mubarak-style. Indeed, schools of thought have multiplied advocating different solutions. But all of them know that the official version is false. They know it is the legacy of the Cold War, not the legacy of the British Empire, that has created this problem. They know the PLO and its successors are not legitimate representatives of the Palestinian people, but gangsters hired to extort that old debt. They know that Israel is totally blameless for the problem, but has been made into a change coin in global games of great powers.

The truth is that, like other regions of the world, Middle East has served as a battlefield to the most devastating conflict in human history:

the Cold War. Like other regions, it is full of unexploded shells, and gangs of marauders are still lurking in its deserts. The fog of war has not yet cleared; nor have the enemy armies even been fully disarmed. Any real attempt to achieve peace in the region should have started from a recognition that there had been a war; and then proceed, step by step, on the basis of removing its consequences. Even that would no longer be easy: like in the unfinished Gulf War, the time lost in the unfinished Cold War cost dearly. But at least, that could have been a start.

Alas! We are now too busy covering up the mistakes of the past to think about the future. The Middle East problems cannot be solved in this way: the difference between the official version and the secret version is too great. The statesmen and experts are too busy keeping their secrets and emanating the smokescreen of official versions. Again and again, as if all these decades have never happened, they give us all this nonsense about the legacy of colonialism, about the centrality of the Palestinian problem, about national and religious intolerance raising tensions, and about the need to seat and talk. Meanwhile, the secret version is locked in secret archives and the Middle East is left to its own devices.

Peace in the Middle East is possible. It had been possible all along. It would have been established long ago if not for experts with their official versions and their hidden agendas, if not for politicians with their secret deals and their new world order...

One day, the last gang of Red Arabs will be rounded up, a great bonfire of the UN resolutions assembled, and the last roadmap to peace and stability confined to the ash heap of history. Then we will see a new Middle East, a Middle East of freedom and democracy, with grey hills of Israel crowned by white Jerusalem – the ancient and eternal city of peace. This is easier to achieve than we are told by the experts. All you need is a policy based on common sense, decency, and national interest. But this can only ever happen after the matter is taken away from the narrow circle of liars.

Endnotes

1   Transcript of the meeting between M.S. Gorbachev and M. Thatcher, Paris, 20 November 1990

2   *Chernyaev's Diary, 27 March 1982*

3   Ibid

4   GF Archive, f.1, inv.1, Transcript of the meeting between M. S. Gorbachev and A. H. Haddam (May 28, 1986)

5   Chernyaev's Diary, 4 November 1973

6   Chernyaev's diary, 12 November 1976

7   Transcript of the meeting between M.S. Gorbachev and A.H.Haddam, 28 May 1986

8   Transcript of the meeting between M. S. Gorbachev and A. S. al Beid, General Secretary of the Yemeni Socialist Party, 10 February 1987

9   Ion Mihai Pacepa. Russian Footprints. National Review, 24 August 2006

10   Chernyaev's Diary, 15 July 1972

11   Chernyaev's Diary, 22 October 1973

12   Chernyaev's diary, 1 December 1973

13   Chernyaev's Diary, 31 December 1973

14   Ion Mihai Pacepa. Russian Footprints. National Review, 24 August 2006

15   See, for example: Vladimir Boukovsky. *Jugement a Moscou. Un dissident dans les archivus du Kremlin.* Editions Robert Laffont, S. A.,

Paris, 1995.; Christopher Andrew and Vasili Mitrokhin. *The World Was Going Our Way. The KGB and the battle for the Third World.* Basic Books, New York 2005.

16   Andrew and Mitrokhin. *The World Was Going Our Way.* P. 250

17   Andrew and Mitrokhin, P. 254

18   Ion Mihai Pacepa. Russian Footprints. National Review, 24 August 2006

19   Ibid

20   Transcript of the meeting between M.S. Gorbachev and A.H.Haddam, 28 May 1986

21   Transcript of the meeting between M.S. Gorbachev and Y. Arafat. 9 April 1988

22   Ibid

23   Transcript of the meeting between M.S. Gorbachev and former US President J. Carter, 1 July 1987

24   Christopher Andrew and Vasili Mitrokhin. *The world was going our way. The KGB and the battle for the Third World.* Basic Books, New York 2005. P. 167

25   Chernyaev's diary, 16 December 1978

26   Christopher Andrew and Vasili Mitrokhin. *The world was going our way. The KGB and the battle for the Third World.* Basic Books, New York 2005. P.p. 169-174

27   Ibid, p.181

28   Tony Benn. *Conflicts of Interest. Diaries 1977-1980.* Hutchinson, 1990, p.339, 14 September 1978

29   GF Archive, f.1, inv.1, Transcript of the meeting between M. S. Gorbachev and President of Syria H. Assad (15 April 1988)

30   as quoted by president Assad of Syria to Gorbachev. See: Archive of the GF, f.1, inv.1, ranscript of the meeting between M. S. Gorbachev and President H. Assad of Syria (April 15, 1988)

31 Record captured during Operation Iraqi Freedom in 2003; U.S. Defence Intelligence Agency Harmony Database, media file ISGP-2003-10151758. Quoting from: Kevin M. Woods. *The Mother of All Battles. Saddam Hussein's strategic plan for the Persian Gulf War.* Official U.S. Joint Forces Command Report. Naval Institute Press, 2008.

32 Coughlin, p. 176

33 The Economist. 19-25 September 1987

34 GF Archive, f.1, inv.1, Transcript of the meeting between M. S. Gorbachev and A. H. Haddam (May 28, 1986)

35 Politburo meeting, 30 April 1987, On the results of the visit by President Assad of Syria

36 GF Archive, f.2, inv.1. Memo by A. S. Chernyaev, 8 August 1987

37 Transcript of the meeting between M.S. Gorbachev and US State Secretary George Schulz, 23 October 1987. Transcript of the meeting between M.S. Gorbachev and US State Secretary George Schulz, 22 February 1988

38 Transcript of the meeting between M. S. Gorbachev and UN Secretary-General Javier Perez de Cuellar, 19 June 1987

39 Transcript of the meeting between M.S. Gorbachev with the PLO Chairman Y. Arafat, 9 1988

40 Politburo meeting, 24 January 1989, Chernyaev's notes (mistakenly dated 13 February 1990)

41 Ibid.; Medvedev's notes

42 Politburo meeting, 24 January 1989, Chernyaev's notes

43 Transcript of the meeting between M.S. Gorbachev and Ayatollah Javadi Amoli, the personal envoy of Imam Knomeini, 4 January 1989

44 Ibid

45 Transcript of the meeting between M.S. Gorbachev and Ayatollah Akbar Hashemi Rafsanjani, Chairman of the Islamic Council

Session, acting Commander-in-Chief of the Islamic Republic of Iran, 20 June 1989

46 Ibid

47 Transcript of the meeting between M.S. Gorbachev and Ayatollah Akbar Hashemi Rafsanjani, Chairman of the Islamic Council Session, acting Commander-in-Chief of the Islamic Republic of Iran, 21 June 1989

48 Transcript of the meeting between M.S. Gorbachev and Iran's Foreign Minister Ali Akbar Velayati, 31 March 1989

49 Transcript of the meeting between M.S. Gorbachev and M. Thatcher, Prime Minister of Great Britain, 6 April 1989

50 Transcript of the meeting between M.S. Gorbachev and Iran's Foreign Minister Ali Akbar Velayati, 31 March 1989

51 Chernyaev's notes

52 Transcript of the meeting between M.S. Gorbachev and Iran's Foreign Minister Ali Akbar Velayati, 31 March 1989

53 Transcripts of two meetings between M.S. Gorbachev and Ayatollah Akbar Hashemi Rafsanjani, Chairman of the Islamic Council Session, acting Commander-in-Chief of the Islamic Republic of Iran, 20-21 June 1989

54 Archive of the GF. F. 1, inv.1, Transcript of the meeting between M. S. Gorbachev and president H. Mubarak of Egypt (May 15, 1990)

55 Ibid

56 Ibid

57 Ibid

58 Ibid

59 Archive of the GF. F. 1, inv.1, Transcript of the meeting between M. S. Gorbachev and president H. Mubarak of Egypt (September 27, 1991)

60 Ibid

61 Transcript of the negotiations between M. S. Gorbachev and M. Thatcher, 30 March 1987

62 E.g.: '*We should go on with everything we've been doing. We have no reason to review our policies, our approaches*' - Transcript of the meeting between M.S. Gorbachev and A.H.Haddam, 28 May 1986. See also: Transcript of the meeting between M.S. Gorbachev and Y. Arafat

63 Transcript of the meeting between M.S. Gorbachev and A.H.Haddam, 28 May 1986

64 Transcript of the meeting between M.S. Gorbachev and A.H.Haddam, 28 May 1986

65 Transcript of the meeting between M.S. Gorbachev and former US president J. Carter, 1 July 1987. See also: Transcript of the meeting between M.S. Gorbachev and US State secretary G. Schulz, 22 February 1988; et al.

66 Ibid, Politburo meeting of April 30, 1987, p.4, About the results of Syrian President Assad's visit to Moscow

67 Ibid, Politburo meeting of June 11, 1987, p.5, About further steps preparing the international conference on Middle East

68 Archive of the GF, f.1, inv.1, transcript of the meeting between M. S. Gorbachev and President H. Assad of Syria (April 28, 1990); transcript of the meeting between M. S. Gorbachev and President H. Assad of Syria (April 15, 1988)

69 Archive of the GF, f.1, inv.1, transcript of the meeting between M. S. Gorbachev and President H. Assad of Syria (April 28, 1990)

70 Archive of the GF, f.1, inv.1, Transcript of the meeting between M. S. Gorbachev and President H. Assad of Syria (April 24, 1987)

71 http://www.bloomberg.com/apps/news?pid=20601103&sid=asdtPeIfTReg&refer=us

72 Memo by Anatoly Chernyev, 14 April 1986

73 GF Archive, f.2, inv.2. Notes of the Politburo meeting 29 May 1986

74 Politburo meeting, 15 April 1986

75 Transcript of the meeting between M.S. Gorbachev and A.H.Haddam, 28 May 1986

76 Transcript of the meeting between M.S. Gorbachev and A.H.Haddam, 28 May 1986

77 Transcript of the meeting between M.S. Gorbachev and A.H.Haddam, 28 May 1986; Politburo meeting, 29 May 1986

78 Politburo meeting, 29 May 1986

79 Transcript of the meeting between M.S. Gorbachev and A.H.Haddam, 28 May 1986

80 Archive of the GF, f.1, inv.1, Transcript of the meeting between M. S. Gorbachev and President H. Assad of Syria (April 24, 1987)

81 Archive of the GF, f.1, inv.1, Transcript of the meeting between M. S. Gorbachev and President H. Assad of Syria (April 24, 1987)

82 In 1986, Soviet Chief of General Staff Marshal Akhromeyev noted the Soviet-Syrian military cooperation was not confined to arms supplies but embraced the command of troops and technical upgrades - Transcript of the meeting between M.S. Gorbachev and A.H.Haddam, 28 May 1986

83 Ibid, per Gen Shehabi, the Syrian Chief of General Staff

84 In 1986 Syrian Foreign Minister Haddam informed Gorbachev of such a decision – Ibid.

85 Archive of the GF, f.1, inv.1, transcript of the meeting between M. S. Gorbachev and President H. Assad of Syria (April 15, 1988)

86 Transcript of the meeting between M.S. Gorbachev and President of Syria (within delegations), 28 April 1990

87 Archive of the GF, f.1, inv.1, transcript of the meeting between M. S. Gorbachev and President H. Assad of Syria (April 28, 1990)

88 Archive of the GF, f.1, inv.1, Transcript of the meeting between M. S. Gorbachev and A. H. Haddam (May 28, 1986)

89 Archive of the GF, f.1, inv.1, Transcript of the meeting between M. S. Gorbachev and President H. Assad of Syria (April 24, 1987)

90 Archive of the GF, f.1, inv.1, Transcript of the meeting between M. S. Gorbachev and A. H. Haddam (May 28, 1986)

91 Archive of the GF, f.1, inv.1, Transcript of the meeting between M. S. Gorbachev and President H. Assad of Syria (April 24, 1987)

92 Archive of the GF, f.1, inv.1, Transcript of the meeting between M. S. Gorbachev and A. H. Haddam (May 28, 1986)

93 Archive of the GF, f.1, inv.1, Transcript of the meeting between M. S. Gorbachev and Y. Arafat, Chairman of the Palestinian Liberation Organization's Executive Committee (April 9, 1988)

94 Archive of the GF, f.1, inv.1, transcript of the meeting between M. S. Gorbachev and President H. Assad of Syria (April 15, 1988)

95 Transcript of the meeting between M.S. Gorbachev and US President G. Bush (extended composition), 3 December 1989

96 GF Archive, f.1, inv.1, Transcript of the meeting between M. S. Gorbachev and A. H. Haddam (May 28, 1986)

97 GF Archive, f.1, inv.1, Transcript of the Soviet-French negotiations (9 July 1986)

98 GF Archive, f.1, inv.1, Transcript of the meeting between M. S. Gorbachev and J. Andreotti (27 February 1987)

99 Archive of the GF, f.1, inv.1, transcript of the meeting between M. S. Gorbachev and President H. Assad of Syria (April 28, 1990)

100 Archive of the GF, f.2, inv.3, Politburo meeting of February 12, 1987, p.7

101 Archive of the GF, f.2, inv.3, Politburo meeting of February 12, 1987, p.7

102 Archive of the GF, f.1, inv.1, transcript of the meeting between M. S. Gorbachev and President H. Assad of Syria (April 28, 1990)

103 www.gwu.edu/~nsarchiv/NSAEBB/NSAEBB80/wmd02.pdf

104 Archive of the GF, f.1, inv.1, transcript of the meeting between M. S. Gorbachev and President H. Assad of Syria (April 28, 1990)

105 Transcript of the meeting between M.S. Gorbachev and A.H.Haddam, 28 May 1986

106 Belonogov, p.192

107 Archive of the GF, f.1, inv.1, Transcript of the meeting between M. S. Gorbachev and Tariq Aziz, Foreign Minister and Deputy Prime Minister of Iraqi Republic (September 5, 1990)

108 Brian Shellum. A Chronology of Defense Intelligence in the Gulf War: A Research Aid for Analysis. DIA History Office, Defense Intelligence Agency, Washington DC, 1997. P.5

109 Quoting from: James A. Baker, III. *The Politics of Diplomacy. Revolution, War & Peace, 1989-1992.* G. P. Putnam's Sons, New York, 1995. P. 271

110 *The New York Times.* September 23, 1990. The transcript of this meeting was published in Iraq shortly after the invasion of Kuwait.

111 Bush and Scowcroft, p. 310

112 Baker, p.260

113 Bush and Scowcroft, p. 310

114 Shellum, p.10

115 Baker, p.5

116 Bush and Scowcroft, p.p. 302-303

117 Archive of the GF, f.1, inv.1. Transcript of the meeting between M. S. Gorbachev and J. Andreotti, Prime Minister of Italy (July 26, 1990)

118 Archive of the GF, f.1, inv.1. Transcript of the meeting between M. S. Gorbachev and J. Andreotti, Prime Minister of Italy (on the way to the airport), Milan, 1 December 1989

119 Archive of the GF, f.1, inv.1. Transcript of the meeting between M. S. Gorbachev and J. Andreotti, Prime Minister of Italy (July 26, 1990)

120 Archive of the GF, f.1, inv.1. Transcript of the meeting between M. S. Gorbachev and J. Andreotti, Prime Minister of Italy (on the way to the airport), Milan, 1 December 1989

121 Bush and Scowcroft, p.p. 318-319. The further account of Mubarak's role at the initial stage of the conflict is derived from: Ibid, p.p. 318-320, 335-340; Archive of the GF, f.1, inv.1, Transcript of the meeting between M. S. Gorbachev and Tariq Aziz, Foreign Minister and Deputy Prime Minister of Iraqi Republic (September 5, 1990)

122 Transcript of the meeting between Mikhail Gorbachev and Felipe Gonzales, Prime Minister of Spain (With foreign ministers), Madrid, 27 October 1990

123 National Security Directive 45, 20 August 1990

124 Baker, p.p. 1-16

125 GF Archive, F. 2, op.1, Memo by A. Chernyaev (2 August 1990)

126 Chernyaev's Diary, August 21, 1990

127 Archive of the GF, f.1, inv.1, Transcript of the telephone conversation between M. S. Gorbachev and President T. Ozal of Turkey (August 25, 1990)

128 Archive of the GF, f.1, inv.1, Transcript of the meeting between M. S. Gorbachev and J. Baker, the US State Secretary (September 13, 1990)

129 Baker, P. 316

130 Transcript of the meeting between M.S. Gorbachev and G. Bush (Paris, 19 November 1990)

131 Archive of the GF, f.1, inv.1, Transcript of the meeting between M. S. Gorbachev and Egypt's Foreign Minister and Deputy Prime Minister I. Abdel Meguid (August 27, 1990)

132 Archive of the GF, f.1, inv.1, Transcript of the meeting between M.S. Gorbachev and A. Okketto, General secretary of the Italian communist party (November 15, 1990)

133 UN SC Resolution 660

134 Archive of the GF, f.1, inv.1, Transcript of the meeting between M. S. Gorbachev and J. Baker, the US State Secretary (September 13, 1990)

135 GF Archive, inv. 1-1, Transcript of the meeting between M. S. Gorbachev and A. Okketto, general Secretary of the Italian Communist Party. 28 February 1989

136 GF Archive, inv. 1-1, transcript of the meeting between M. S. Gorbachev and C. Menem (25 October 1990)

137 Archive of the GF, f.1, inv.1, Transcript of the meeting between M.S. Gorbachev and R. Dumas (25 August 1990)

138 Archive of the GF, f.1, inv.1, Transcript of the meeting between M. S. Gorbachev and J. Baker (November 8, 1990)

139 Archive of the GF, f.1, inv.1, Transcript of the meeting between M. S. Gorbachev and F. Gonzales, President of the government of Spain (October 27, 1990)

140 Archive of the GF, f.1, inv.1, Transcript of the meeting between M.S. Gorbachev and R. Dumas (25 August 1990)

141 Archive of the GF, f.1, inv.1, Transcript of the meeting between M. S. Gorbachev and Egypt's Foreign Minister and Deputy Prime Minister I. Abdel Meguid (August 27, 1990)

142 Archive of the GF, f.1, inv.1, Transcripts of M.S. Gorbachev's talks during his visit to France: to President F. Mitterrand of France (July 4, 1989)

143 Baker, p.300

144 Chernyaev's diary. Entry of September 2, 1990

145 Archive of the GF, f.1, inv.1, Transcript of the meeting between M. S. Gorbachev and Tariq Aziz, Foreign Minister and Deputy Prime Minister of Iraqi Republic (September 5, 1990)

146 Archive of the GF, f.1, inv.1, Essential contents of the telephone conversation between M. S. Gorbachev and President Mitterrand of france (6 September 1990)

147 Ibid

148 Ibid

149 Chernyaev's diary, entry of September 13, 1990

150 Ibid

151 As Gorbachev told to a Politburo member Vadim Medvedev. Medvedev's diary, entry of September 9, 1990.

152 Archive of the GF, f.1, inv.1, Transcript of the meeting between M. S. Gorbachev and G. Bush, President of the USA, in Helsinki (September 9, 1990)

153 Bush and Scowcroft, p. 364

154 Archive of the GF, f.1, inv.1, Transcript of the meeting between M. S. Gorbachev and G. Bush, President of the USA, in Helsinki (September 9, 1990)

155 Ibid

156 *Belonogov, p.p. 142-143*

157 Ibid, p.174

158 Ibid, p.p. 174-177

159 As Gorbachev told to a Politburo member Vadim Medvedev. Medvedev's diary, entry of September 9, 1990.

160 Ibid

161 Baker, p.p. 292-293

162 Ibid

163 Bush and Scowcroft, p.368

164 UN document S/21436

165 GF Archive, f. 1, op. 1, Transcript of the meeting between M.S. Gorbachev and F. Mitterrand, 28 October 1990

166 GF Archive, f. 1, op. 1, Transcript of the meeting between M.S. Gorbachev and F. Mitterrand, 29 October 1990

167 Archive of the GF, f.1, inv.1, Transcript of the meeting between M. S. Gorbachev and G. Bush, President of the USA, in Helsinki (September 9, 1990)

168 Ibid

169 Ibid

170 Archive of the GF, f.1, inv. 1, Transcript of the meeting between M. S. Gorbachev, US state secretary J. Baker, trade secretary R. Mosbacher and a group of leading American businessmen (September 13, 1990)

171 Ibid

172 Chernyaev's diary, entry of September 14, 1990

173 Archive of the GF, f.1, inv.1, transcript of the meeting between M. S. Gorbachev and J. Baker (September 13, 1990)

174 Chernyaev's diary, entry of September 14, 1990. Exclamation point is Chernyaev's

175 Ibid

176 Archive of the GF, f.1, inv.1, Transcript of the meeting between M. S. Gorbachev and Douglas Hurd, foreign minister of Great Britain (September 14, 1990)

177 Archive of the GF, f.1, inv.1. M. S. Gorbachev's reception of Y. Moda'i, finance minister of Israel, and Y. Ne'eman, minister of energy, science and technology of Israel (September 14, 1990)

178 Ibid

179 Ibid

180 Ibid

181 Ibid

182 Archive of the GF, f.1, inv.1, Transcript of the meeting between M. S. Gorbachev and Saud al-Feisal, Foreign Minister of Saudi Arabia (September 17, 1990)

183 Archive of the GF, f.1, inv.1, Transcript of the meeting between M. S.

Gorbachev and G. de Michelis, Foreign Minister of Italy (September 15, 1990)

184 Ibid

185 Yevgeny Primakov. *Voina, kotoroi moglo ne byt'*. Pravda, February 28, 1991

186 Ibid

187 Archive of the GF, f.1, inv.1, Transcript of the meeting between M. S. Gorbachev and Saud al-Feisal, Foreign Minister of Saudi Arabia (September 17, 1990)

188 Baker, p.397

189 Bush and Scowcroft, p.377

190 Yevgeny Primakov. *Voina, kotoroi moglo ne byt'*. Pravda, February 27, 1991

191 Belonogov, p.171

192 Ibid, p.172

193 Ibid, p.p. 172-173

194 Chernyaev's Diary, entry of October 14, 1990

195 Archive of the GF, f.2, inv.1, Memo by A. S. Chernyaev about Primakov's mission in the settlement of the Middle East conflict (October 13, 1990)

196 Chernyaev's Diary, October 14, 1990

197 Chernyaev's Diary, entry of October 14, 1990

198 Belonogov, pp. 172-177

199 Archive of the GF, f.2, inv.1. Memo by A. S. Chernyaev with considerations concerning E. A. Shevardnadze's resignation and possible candidatures for his vacant position (December 21, 1990)

200 Bush and Scowcroft, p. 378

201 Ibid

202 Ibid, p.379

203 Archive of the GF, f.2, inv.1, Memo by A. S. Chernyaev about Primakov's mission in the settlement of the Middle East conflict (October 13, 1990); Chernyaev's Diary, entries of October 14 and October 20, 1990

204 Bush and Scowcroft, p. 378

205 Chernyaev's Diary, entry of October 20, 1990

206 Ibid

207 Ibid, entry of October 21, 1990

208 quoting from Belonogov, p. 180

209 Archive of the GF, f.1, inv.1, Transcript of the meeting between M. S. Gorbachev and J. Baker (November 8, 1990)

210 Coughlin, p. 265

211 Archive of the GF, f.1, inv.1, Transcript of the meeting between M. S. Gorbachev and Mitterrand, 29 October 1990

212 Belonogov, p. 186

213 UN SC Resolution 660

214 UN Charter, Article 41

215 Archive of the GF, f.1, inv.1, Transcript of the meeting between M. S. Gorbachev and Mitterrand, 29 October 1990

216 Ibid

217 Archive of the GF, f.1, inv.1, Transcript of the meeting between M. S. Gorbachev and J. Baker, the US State Secretary (November 8, 1990)

218 Archive of the GF, f.1, inv.1, Transcript of the meeting between M. S. Gorbachev and G. Bush, Paris, 19 November 1990

219 Belonogov, p. 203

220 Archive of the GF, f.1, inv.1, Transcript of the meeting between M. S. Gorbachev and G. Bush, Paris, 19 November 1990

221 Archive of the GF, f.1, inv.1, Transcript of the meeting between M. S. Gorbachev and President of France F. Mitterrand, Paris, 19 November 1990

222 Ibid

223 Archive of the GF, f.1, inv.1, Transcript of the meeting between M. S. Gorbachev and G. Bush, Paris, 19 November 1990

224 Bush and Scowcroft, p. 409

225 GF Archive, F. 1, op. 1, Transcript of the meeting between M.S. Gorbachev and R. Lubbers, Prime Minister of the Netherlands (Paris, 20 November 1990, mistakenly dated 20 December)

226 See, for example: *Ted Kennedy was a 'Collaborationist'* by Herbert Romerstein. *Human Events*, December 8, 2003

227 Vasiliy Mitrokhin. *The KGB in Afghanistan.* Woodrow Wilson International Center for Scholars, 2002

228 GF Archive, F. 3, op. 1, V. Zagladin's notes from his meetings with Sen. E. Kennedy, 5 February 1986, 6 February 1986

229 Ibid

230 GF Archive, F. 3, op. 1, Summary of a meeting with L. Horowitz, 11 December 1989

231 GF Archive, f.3, op. 1, Note by V. V. Zagladin on Larry Horovitz's considerations regarding the situation in the USA on the eve of the visit of M. S. Gorbachev, 24 May 1990

232 F. 3, op.1, Memo by V. V. Zagladin on a conversation with L. Horowitz, 27 November 1990

233 Archive of the GF, f.1, inv.1, Transcript of the meeting between M. S. Gorbachev and J. Baker, the US State Secretary (November 8, 1990)

234 GF Archive, f.2, op.1, Memo by A.S. Chernyaev about the possible meeting between M. S. Gorbachev and Chung Yu-yung (South Korea) and the record of negotiations with him (2 November 1990)

235 Medvedev's diary, 24 November 1990

236 Archive of the GF, f.1, inv.1, Transcript of the meeting between M. S. Gorbachev and R. Dumas (12 February 1991)

237 See Bush and Scowcroft, p.431

238 Ibid

239 Shakhnazarov's notes from the meeting of the Soviet of the Federation (12 June 1990); Medvedev's note from the joint session of the Presidential Soviet and the Soviet of the Federation (20 July 1990)

240 GF Archive, f.1, op.1

241 Transcript of the telephone conversation between M. S. Gorbachev and President of France F. Mitterrand (18 January 1991); Transcript of the telephone conversation between M. S. Gorbachev and Chancellor H. Kohl (18 January 1991). Gorbachev claimed that US Ambassador Matlock 'recently' enquired about this, but there had been no reply from Saddam.

242 *Baker, P. 379*

243 Chernyaev's diary, 15 January 1991

244 Chernyaev's diary, 16 January 1991

245 Belonogov, p. 268

246 Transcript of the telephone conversation between M. S. Gorbachev and F. Mitterrand (18 January 1991)

247 Transcript of the telephone conversation between M. S. Gorbachev and F. Mitterrand (18 January 1991) On the same day, Gorbachev also informed German chancellor Helmut Kohl of this message to Saddam. 18.01.1991

248 Chernyaev's diary, entry of January 18, 1991

249 Transcript of the meeting between M. S. Gorbachev and R. Dumas (12 February 1991)

250 Transcript of the meeting between M. S. Gorbachev and A. A. Velayati, the foreign minister of the Islamic Republic of Iran (15 February 1991)

251 Chernyaev's diary, 29 January 1991

252 Belonogov, p.p. 307-308

253 Quoting from: *The Guardian,* 16 February 1991

254 F. 1, op.1, Transcript of the telephone conversation between M.S. Gorbachev and H. Kohl, 20 February 1991

255 F.1, op.1, Transcript of the meeting between M.S. Gorbachev and Tariq Aziz, deputy Prime Minister and Foreign Minister of Iraq. 18 February 1991

256 Chernyaev's diary, 18 February 1991

257 Bush and Scowcroft, p.p.473-474

258 P.473

259 Transcript of the meeting between M. S. Gorbachev and T. Aziz, 22 February 991 (mistakenly dated 23 February)

260 Quoting from: Transcript of the telephone conversation between M.S. Gorbachev, G. Bush and J. Baker (22 February 1991)

261 F.1, op.1, transcript of the telephone conversation between M. S. Gorbachev and J. Major, 23 February 1991, 12.45-13.25

262 F.1, op.1, transcript of the telephone conversation between M. S. Gorbachev and J. Andreotti, 23 February 1991, 13.25-13.55

263 F.1, op.1, transcript of the telephone conversation between M. S. Gorbachev and F. Mitterrand, 23 February 1991, 15.20-15.50

264 F.1, op.1, transcript of the telephone conversation between M. S. Gorbachev and H. Mubarak, 23 February 1991, 14.35-15.05

265 Belonogov, p.p. 338-341

266 Ibid, 341-342

267 Quoting from Belionogov, p. 342

268 Ibid., p.343

269 Transcript of the meeting between M. S. Gorbachev and J. Andreotti, 22 May 1991

270 Chernyaev's diary, 2 March 1991

271 Transcript of the telephone conversation between M.S. Gorbachev and H. Kohl, 5 March 1991, 19.47-19.59

272 Transcript of the meeting between M.S. Gorbachev and Turgut Ozal, President of Turkey (11 March 1991)

273 Transcript of the meeting between M.S. Gorbachev and J. Baker, 15 March 1991

274 F.1, op.1, Transcript of the meeting between M.S. Gorbachev and J. Andreotti, 22 May 1991

275 F.1, op.1, Transcript of the meeting between M.S. Gorbachev and F. Mitterrand, 6 May 1991

276 F.1, op.1, Transcript of the meeting between M.S. Gorbachev and J. Andreotti, 22 May 1991

Epilogue

The century-long drama is now coming to its end. Indeed, its final act has begun as this book is about to go to the printing press. The world of Red Arabs has reached its own Year 1989. The Arab Gorbachev, Comrade Mubarak, has fallen. One day, we saw him making a defiant speech to the rebellious crowd, boasting he was a heroic veteran of four wars with Israel and pledging to defend the Socialist regime to a bitter end. Next day, the great statesman's heath suddenly failed him, he fell into coma, resigned and disappeared without a trace. The aforesaid three events occurred at exactly the same moment. Careful investigations of that moment are not encouraged.

As I am writing, Libya has fallen into a terrible civil war, with Comrade Gaddafi desperately fighting for survival; and the waves of protest are rising higher and higher in about a dozen other regimes in the region. By the time you read this, no doubt, more and more Red Arab dictators will be fighting for survival - or will have already lost.

So, are we now to see a free Middle East which I dreamt about in the last chapter - a few lines above, one historical era ago?

I fear this is far from certain. And what should worry us most is the position taken by the West.

◆ ◆ ◆

It is astonishing that while so much depends on the Middle East today, we know so little about it; and the experts, of course, know less than anybody else. The place where the future of the planet now hangs on the balance is a mystery world covered in twilight.

Nevertheless, there are two patently obvious facts about it, which are crying out to be noticed, yet are most carefully ignored.

Firstly, this will not necessarily be a Democratic revolution. This will not necessarily be an Islamist revolution. But whatever it will be, it most certainly won't be both. After the downfall of Arab Socialism, the succession will be contested by its two major historic adversaries in the Middle East; and it is no good pretending there is just one. The ensuing battle between Arab Democrats and Islamists will be one of the most important battles in this century. And may I be bold enough to contradict the consensus of experts: it does matter which side shall win. We have to take sides.

Secondly, the Red Arab regimes are in agony; but they are not yet dead. There is no doubt that they will collapse soon; but in what way? As history shows, this can make all the difference in the world. Future years and decades shall depend on what the dying regime will have done in its final months and weeks.

Then, of course, there is the interconnection between these two obvious problems, and that is where it becomes complicated. It is not just that, in more senses than one, the Arab Democratic movement is infantile, Islamism is ageing, and Socialism is dying. It is not just that there are three actors on the stage - the good, the bad and the ugly. There is also a long and complex history of relations between them: alliances, double-crossings, infiltration, manipulation, betrayals. That history will largely determine what will happen in the critical years ahead.

It has, indeed, become fashionable to call it the Arab 1989 with an air of absurd optimism. Yet, nobody seems to be thinking of how to avoid the mistakes of 1989. The history of 1989 in East Europe is a history of fake opposition movements, bogus revolutions, and cynical power-sharing deals behind the scenes. That was a year when East Europe lost its chance to establish genuine democracy and free market, and was doomed to decades of 'post-communist' nonsense. The downfall of Communist regimes had been inevitable form the moment of their genesis - because every socialist regime eventually exhausts its economy and the patience of its people. But the 1989 scenario was one of the worst. It corrupted the new democracies from the very start, and undermined the recovery enormously.

Still, few exceptions aside, it is still democracy and a recovery in East Europe. In the Middle East, it can be much worse.

Like the 1989, the 2011 had been inevitable all along. The tragedy is that the Red Arabs and the Islamists have been preparing for this moment for many years; but the West is, as usual, caught by surprise. All we can think of is supporting El Baradei, best known for his covering up of Iraqi and Iranian nuclear programmes, because he is one Arab name we've already memorised. The 'experts', barely concealing their bewilderment, offer us a choice between the hopeless course of supporting the doomed regimes and the suicidal course of going along with the future Islamic Republics.

On close examination, these two options are exactly the same.

It is no coincidence that the Muslim Brotherhood is the only organised opposition in Egypt. Mubarak's KGB (or whatever is Arabic for Gestapo) had been working to achieve this for years, ruthlessly stifling any alternative, any embryonic democratic movement, but sparing the Islamist opposition. It is, no doubt, densely infiltrated by secret police agents and informers. And now the events are moving towards the worst-case scenario from 1989: some 'roundtable' negotiations between the regime and the selected opposition groups, leading to some 'transitional' power-sharing deal, giving the Islamists a bridgehead in the government. All the democrats, all those brave boys fighting on the streets, whose only organisation is Twitter, will go by the board. By the time of 'elections', the only choice will be between the Red Arabs and Muslim Brotherhood.

It is too late now to prevent all this? We must at least try - but we are not even trying. What is our policy? What forces are out there on the 'Arab street' - that very street our experts are supposed to have researched for years? Which of them we want to win?

It may be too much a strain on the experts' intellectual equipment to work this out. But there is one obvious, fool-proof thing to do: stand up for one oppressed minority which is immune to both Socialism and Islamism - Christians. As I am writing this, daily reports are coming from Egypt: the regime's army has destroyed the wall of an ancient Coptic monastery in the desert; the revolutionary mob has burnt a Christian church near Cairo; the Islamist paramilitaries attack a Christian demonstration; Christians are still denied fundamental rights... The West stays silent. Why not make one obviously sensible political step - which is, incidentally, also a moral and legal duty: stand up for human rights? That would not be very much; but at least, we could have made some friends in Egypt. At least, we would have supported one decent force on the ground, ensure it is not overwhelmed by one or the other of the totalitarian movements. Why is not the West doing this?

I am not asking much. I am not expecting as much as any degree of wisdom from the State Department. I am not even asking the experts to draw lessons from history. But can they at least try and avoid the mistakes made within living memory - in 1989, the date which they themselves mention so often in connection with the present events?

For instance, 'stability' is a word we'd better forget - there is no such thing in a revolution. 'Stability' will be the motto of the Islamo-Socialist roundtable, whereas our only potential allies are young street-fighters who demand freedom, not stability.

Another word to forget is 'moderate'. Revolutions are never won by moderates; they are won by radicals. The Islamists must not be allowed to 'sell' themselves as the most radical force. Indeed, they are not - they are too closely interlinked with the regime. We should support those who demand a complete dismantling of the regime, putting it on trial, opening all its secret archives, revealing the names of all secret police informers. I bet we would find many Muslim Brothers' names there. This is radical; this is also something the Islamists would not like. Indeed, this is about the only trump card I can see in the hands of democrats.

Perhaps my view is prejudiced by my own experience, but I seriously think it is almost a golden rule for all revolutions: *follow the secret archives*. They can work miracles. The Iranian revolution of 1979 was hijacked by Islamists because they captured the Kuzichkin records. The East European revolution of 1989 was hijacked by opportunists because the communist archives were not opened. It is important to know who started the 2011 revolution; it is more important to know who will hijack it. The archives are the key to that. If made public, they will work for democracy and against the Islamists and Socialists. If either or both of the enemies get there first, God help us.

It is not for nothing that there are already reports of violence over the secret archives of the Egyptian secret police - now captured by Islamists in some locality, now taken into the Army custody. One can tell the battle has begun. Unfortunately, the Western media hardly appreciates the significance of secret archives in revolutions; so it is difficult to follow this key line of developments. On the whole, I suspect it is not going too well. There have certainly been no great revelations yet - with the exception of very selective prosecutions of Mubarak's ministers - which suggests that all the archives are in the hands of those who have an interest in a cover up.

There are undoubtedly genuine pro-democracy forces present on the ground; but they need to be identified and supported. Of course, Red Arabs and Islamists will smear all democrats as Western agents - whether the West really supports them or not. Somewhat paradoxically, they are most likely to be hanged as Western agents precisely if the West does nothing to help them, both morally and financially. Their only protection against hanging would be winning; and winning a revolution is very money-intensive. This is awfully prosaic but, alas, true; and undoubtedly Iran and others are already showering their friends on the ground with money. The Western support to the democrats must match this support to their rivals. Moral support, too, would be no less important - in a revolutionary turmoil, the foreign opinion is usually seen as something of an impartial arbiter.

Finally, perhaps most importantly, we must not take a narrow view of these revolutions, so that our attention is fixed on Egypt and we have no idea what happens in Tunisia, then our attention is fixed on Libya and we have no idea what now happens in Egypt, etc. We should not only keep an eye on all the ongoing revolutions, but also on the next one, and the one after the next. It is one matter if the revolution spreads to Saudi Arabia, and quite another if it spreads to Iran. This is a regional mass movement and must be understood as such. It started, as we now can see, a couple of years ago in Iran; now, fortunately, it seems to be returning to Iran. And if any place is crucial to the future of the whole region, it is Iran.

Indeed, a downfall of the Ayatollahs would change everything in the region. But even the very fact that 'the other Iran' (to adapt a phrase from Russian politics) is seen to be alive and kicking has a huge significance. If there is a major confrontation between the Iranian regime and the Iranian people, regimes and peoples across the region will have to take sides. And it would be very difficult now to manipulate, say, Egyptians to support a regime against the people, contrary to their own recent experience. A crisis in Iran inevitably means a crisis of Islamism across the region: the Islamists will face a painful dilemma where they cannot defend Iran and cannot condemn it. Remember what happened to communists in the West whenever there was a crisis in the Soviet empire? So the future of the Middle East - nay, the world - is being decided now on the streets of Tehran.

◆ ◆ ◆

Right now, the war in Libya has practically obscured the general picture of the wider battle for the Middle East. In Libya, the events have taken an unexpected turn: Comrade Gaddafi has determined to drown the revolt in blood - he has chosen a Tiananmen scenario, so to speak. A terrible civil war erupted.

On the face of it, the Western response - a military intervention on the side of the rebels - seems entirely adequate. As we remember, the West did nothing in a similar situation in 1991 in Iraq, and suffered disastrous consequences. Now, it seems, we have learned some lessons from the bloody history of the 20th century. We have finally realised that socialist massacres cannot be a purely internal affair; that an evil regime which threatens us all may not claim sovereign rights; and that it may be in our interest to fight for 'instability' against 'stability'. All this sounds too good to be true - and indeed, this is not true.

To begin with, who are the rebel leaders? Who controls this National Transitional Council which has been so readily recognised by the West? Obviously, this question is crucial; and yet, it is given very little attention. Now and then, one or another name is mentioned. More often then not, we discover that the given revolutionary leader had been, until recently, a high-ranking minister in the Gaddafi regime. Further henchmen are defecting Gaddafi one by one, and are enthusiastically embraced by the rebels - and by the West - without asking too many questions about their past. Clearly, a popular uprising is one thing, and some kind of an internal squabble within the Libyan Politburo is quite a different matter. Do we really know what we are dealing with here? Have we secured ourselves against the 'enemy of my enemy is my friend' trap?

Undoubtedly, a lot of genuine democrats in Libya support the rebels.

They would support anyone or anything that could rid them of Gaddafi - like their predecessors in Europe used to support Hitler against Stalin and Stalin against Hitler. In all probability, however, the rebels also include a considerable Islamist element; and a number of former Gaddafi Socialists for leaders.

At this stage, on the battlefield, all this does not matter. However, this will matter a lot after the rebels win. Will Libya get rid of Gaddafi but remain an Islamic Socialist 'Jamahiriya' for all other intents and purposes? Will it, perhaps, become a bit more Socialist or a bit more Islamic? Clearly, this scenario is not worth fighting for. Clearly, the West will need to differentiate among the rebels and support genuine democrats. Do we, at least, know who they are?

The way it goes, however, we may never see a victory and what happens afterwards. The West is fighting this war not on the basis of a military strategy or a realistic political strategy. This is another 'new world order' war. The intervention was initiated by the French government - and, apparently, the 'Eurabia' doctrine had some influence on their thinking. Then we had the farce of coalition-building all over again. The most important thing, politicians told us, was to have a UN resolution authorising *'all necessary means'* to give effect to the witty scholastic doctrine of *'responsibility to protect'* (codenamed R2P). Secondly, the turkeys in the Arab League must be persuaded to vote for the Christmas, in one, separately taken, country.

Of course, all those resolutions were spoiled not only with the 'new world order' newspeak, but also with the new world order substance. The camel, it is said, is a horse designed by a committee; here we are going to war in the land of camels, waving resolutions drafted by committees. When Gaddafi forces are advancing, we may bomb them. When they begin to retreat, we must stop. Then, of course, they no longer have a reason to retreat, so they advance again - and we bomb them. This is a stalemate - and the whole arrangement had been a recipe for stalemate all along.

Meanwhile, the lawyers of the world are debating whether it would be legal, under the UN resolution, to kill Gaddafi. The predominant view is that it will be legal if, and only if, it happens by accident. Military orders were issued accordingly: kill Gaddafi without ever targeting him. A fine scholastic formula which the military commanders, and most other sane people in the world, will find it difficult to understand it.

All in all, the prospects are hardly inspiring. If we had really learned the lessons of history and become serious about supporting democracy in the Middle East, this would have been a very different war.

All the above follows quite inevitably from mere common sense. This is why it is so much a variance with the official version, which is being told to us in 24-hours-a-day TV coverage. Their so-called analysis does not go beyond drawing a simple black and white picture of the people versus tyrants, and then speculating upon the most childish question: who is winning?

This is, of course, a question for bookmakers; this is not a question for experts. Especially because each and every one of them is prudent enough to offer two alternative answers; and then conclude: 'we'll have to wait and see'.

I don't mind nonsensical platitudes - that is what experts are for. But this is worse than nonsensical platitudes. This is a manipulation. Any sensible and honest discussion should have begun not from 'who is winning?', but from 'who is fighting?' 'People' and 'tyrants' are fine labels - for poems, but not for analysis. Any analysis of a revolution begins from discussing the nature of the regime, and continues with discussing the nature of the opposition. 24-hour TV reporting is now going on from Libya, as it went on from Egypt before. But (if, like me, you foolish enough to watch that) how many times have you heard the phrase ***Islamic Socialism*** mentioned? Yet, that is the official name of Comrade Gaddafi's regime and ideology. That is what it is all about, and not only in Libya.

We are being told subtle lies, and it takes quite a time and quite an effort to see through it. On Egypt, we were repeatedly told that Mubarak was a dictator , that he had been in power for 30 years, and that he was backed by the West. Each of these statements is factually correct. Taken together, repeated a hundred times without any further elaboration, they tell a grossly misleading story. By leaving out the rise and fall of Arab Socialism, they turn the causes and significance of the current events inside out, and picture Mubarak as someone like a local Pinochet, or a local Batista, or a local Shah of Iran. They make him almost a reincarnation of King Farouk, while in fact he was almost a reincarnation of Nasser.

In today's television coverage of the Middle East drama, we can see the whole machinery of making 'official versions'. Just a few gentle touches - an omission here, a small lies there; then repeat it a few hundred times, and the overall picture is the very opposite of the truth. Only Egyptians interviewed on the ground ever refer to the sixty years of the socialist regime - an occasional bit of truth is the inevitable price of live reporting. That is balanced by all Western commentators' perpetual cliché about 'thirty years of Mubarak's dictatorship'. So we are left with the entirely false impression that the problem is called Mubarak and that his departure, by definition, is the happy ending of the whole story.

Or take this repeated lies that Egypt (and most other countries in the region) have never yet known democracy. This may be quite correct ideologically, but this is simply not true factually. Immediately before the present regime emerged, the Kingdom of Egypt was a British-style parliamentary system with free elections, free press, and a very corrupt political class. It may have been a weak democracy, but it was a democracy - whatever you may think of King Farouk or of the British Empire. Both, no doubt, deserved much criticism on a number of points. But it was against the faults of democracy, not of tyranny, that Nasser and comrades rebelled.

It is equally false to draw parallels between the coups of Nasser and his followers in other Arab countries and what is happening there now. Nasser's was not a popular revolution - it was a Lenin-style coup by a small, conspiratorial, professional group, overthrowing a weak democracy to establish a totalitarian regime. What is happening today is the opposite of that - indeed, a counter-revolution to that.

All this misleads us to pay more attention to things which matter to experts as opposed to things which matter to street fighters - and which will determine the future of the region; oil and stability as opposed to bread and freedom. Oil and stability are certainly important, but putting them first right now means putting a cart before a horse. Do the experts fail to understand this - or are they telling us lies?

Are they simply telling us, in this soft manipulative manner, that it is too dangerous to let such nations as Iran or Egypt go too fast and too far; that democracy cannot work in that part of the world; and that therefore the best we should hope for is an Islamo-Socialist roundtable which would restore stability? Are they telling us it is all right to throw one hated dictator to the crowd to let them satisfy their wild passions, but it is too dangerous to dismantle the whole regime and let these wild people govern themselves? Are they, in effect, telling us that they prefer Islamists or Socialists or Fascists, with whom they at least can make secret deals, to a crowd of free people with whom they cannot make secret deals?

Alarmingly, such hints are becoming more and more transparent in the statements of Western governments nowadays. Those statements sound awfully familiar; and whenever we heard such things in the past, that was a smokescreen for a treachery. If that is their policy, it will bring no stability - after all, it never did in the past. But the generation of rebels who lost their friends on the streets of Tehran and Cairo will never forgive this betrayal.

If there is any hope for stability and freedom in the Middle East, all of it lies in the mood of people who have gone bare-handed to defy tanks and suddenly won.

This miracle is what creates great democracies. Nothing else ever does.

This mood of freedom is now the greatest headache of surviving Red Arabs and conspiring Islamists in the Middle East. However cunning they may be, it is not within their power to extinguish this spark. But the dullest Western leaders can do that - as Bush and Baker did that in Iraq and in Russia. Because the only thing that kills that mood is treachery. Only a great betrayal can make people cynical enough to accept a new tyranny in place of the old, to accept a Stalin as a replacement of a Hitler.

The West, I fear, is about to commit this crime again. If we do that, that will be a death warrant to any hope of freedom and stability in the Middle East within the lifetime of the present generation. This would be incredibly mean. This would be incredibly mad. This would be, indeed, a typical foreign policy devised by politicians and experts.

Before it is too late, we must try and stop them.